Prehistoric Archeology and Ecology
A Series Edited by Karl W. Butzer and Leslie G. Freeman

Prehistoric Life on the Mississippi Floodplain

Stone Tool Use, Settlement Organization, and Subsistence Practices at the Labras Lake Site, Illinois

Richard W. Yerkes

The University of Chicago Press

Chicago and London

Richard W. Yerkes is assistant professor of
anthropology at Ohio State University

The University of Chicago Press, Chicago 60637
The University of Chicago Press, Ltd., London
c 1987 by The University of Chicago
All rights reserved. Published 1987
Printed in the United States of America

96 95 94 93 92 91 90 89 88 87   54321

Library of Congress Cataloging-in-Publication Data

Yerkes, Richard W.
        Prehistoric life on the Mississippi floodplain.
        Bibliography: p. 251.
        Includes index.
        1. Labras Lake Site (Ill.) 2. Man, Prehistoric--
Illinois. 3. Illinois--Antiquities. 4. Excavations
(Archaeology)--Illinois. I. Title. II. Series.
E78.I3Y47 1987   977.3'89   86-19137
ISBN 0-226-95150-2
ISBN 0-226-95151-0 (pbk.)

To my father, David M. Yerkes (1929-1985)

Contents

Figures

Tables

Series Editors' Foreword

One of the major concerns in contemporary archeology is to develop and refine models of the relationships between environment and culture. A sophisticated understanding of the environmental matrix, and its interactions with past lifeways, is critical to such models. This can be achieved through flexible geoarcheological research, on the one hand, and seasonality and subsistence studies, on the other. But in default of substantial architectural remains, the identification and interpretation of activity areas is exceedingly difficult. Sites with excellent bone preservation have often proven amenable to detailed archeo-taphonomic analysis, but where lithic artifacts constitute the best surviving record, archeological efforts to use morphological typologies as surrogates for function have reached an impasse.

The American Bottom refers to the broad alluvial plain below the confluence of the Missouri, Mississippi, and Illinois rivers. In this heartland of the Midwest, a century of research has been devoted to an unusually dense and complete archaeological record, the most conspicuous part of which belongs to the Mississippian culture complex. The present study fortuitously derives from a salvage project at Labras Lake that brought together investigators with diverse and complementary talents: James Phillips, Bruce Gladfelter, Robert Hall, and the author. Detailed reports have already resulted from this project, but Richard Yerkes has taken up the task of synthesizing the mass of diverse data. In this process, he attacks the central issue of activity areas by a systematic analysis of lithic micro-wear, using Lawrence Keeley's methodology, coupled with lithic refitting.

After reviewing previous research on the American Bottom, Yerkes discusses the geo-archeological context of habitation and cultural change with the goal of integrating the hydrological and paleoenvironmental data with the archeological evidence. He then summarizes the various settlement models that have been proposed for the three time periods in question before turning to the Labras Lake material itself. The bio-archeological data are processed next to answer questions about seasonal occupation, differential activities, and the composition and functions of household units. Yerkes' microwear results follow, after which he addresses the whole spectrum of issues related to site utilization and subsistence change over the past four millenia.

Among Yerkes' substantive findings is that new types of tools were manufactured and utilized at Labras Lake as each society expanded its subsistence base. Plant knives were not present in Late Archaic samples but were found in Late Woodland and Mississippian assemblages. This reflects the importance of starchy plants in the later diets; similar differences are found with the introduction of maize. The diversity of exploited resources increased over time, but evidence for "specialized" food production is lacking. New techniques allowed successive populations to add to their diets, but they always retained the old staples. Nuts were not replaced but supplemented by seeds; seeds in turn were not replaced by maize. In short, a "focal" subsistence system, exploiting a limited number of plant and animal species, cannot be verified for this site complex.

Such results were possible because meticulous recording and analysis allowed detailed resolution of site components and, consequently, more precise identification of season of occupation and the dominant uses of lithic artifacts. Such refined information is not possible from the conventional practices of earlier researchers in the Bottom who have been content with more broadly defined components, activity patterns deduced from artifact morphology, and settlement type analysis that is largely guesswork.

One of the consequences of Yerkes' work is that he can establish what others think are large "sedentary encampments" to be in reality just sequences of small residential occupations for a narrow range of activities during shorter, seasonal periods. Yerkes' contribution to the study of the development of sedentism is potentially far-reaching. He has placed before us the means for achieving an objective assessment of the duration and size of a contemporaneous occupation, thus enabling us to determine the place and timing of the appearance of true permanent settlements through objective measurement of differences in the duration of occupation.

By virtue of its sophisticated methodology and the well-integrated and interdisciplinary conclusions, Prehistoric Life on the Mississippi Floodplain has the potential of becoming a benchmark study in North American archaeology. We belive that it could and should serve as a model for a "site report" in the late 1980s.

Karl W. Butzer

Leslie G. Freeman

Preface

In this study, data obtained during the University of Illinois at Chicago FAI-270 Archeological Mitigation Project investigations have been summarized and reanalyzed. My involvement in the UIC FAI-270 project began in 1979 when I became the field director for the Labras Lake excavations and continued while I was employed as a research associate in the Department of Anthropology at UIC. I was involved in the initial analysis of the FAI-270 data and in the preparation of the final contract report (Phillips et al. 1980).

In the present study, activities and subsistence practices at the Labras Lake site (11-S-299) during the Late Archaic, Late Woodland, and Mississippian periods were investigated to learn how the site's residents organized their settlements and interacted with their physical surroundings. Was each prehistoric group's procurement system designed to cope with a specific set of environmental and cultural conditions, or was there a basic subsistence pattern that persisted for some 3,000 years?

Environmental change on the American Bottom was documented, microwear analysis was undertaken to determine what activities were performed during each habitation period, and floral and faunal remains were examined to obtain information about past diets and seasonality. It was believed that only by applying these methods of analysis to the Labras Lake data could a clear understanding of adaptive strategies be obtained.

The time-scales used in the study are shown in figure 1. These include the substages of the Wisconsin Glacial Period (A, after Willman and Frye 1970; B, C, after Evenson et al. 1976), Holocene climatic episodes for the North American Mid-Continent (D, after Bryson and Wendland 1967), Stoltman's (1978) temporal model for eastern North American prehistory (E), and the proposed cultural periods (F) and phases (G) for the archaeology of the American Bottom (Porter 1983). This chart should allow the reader to put the events at Labras Lake into a general temporal, climatic, and cultural context.

While data gathered during the University of Illinois at Chicago FAI-270 Archaeological Mitigation Project was used in this study, the results reflect the views of the author, who is solely responsible for the accuracy of the presentation.

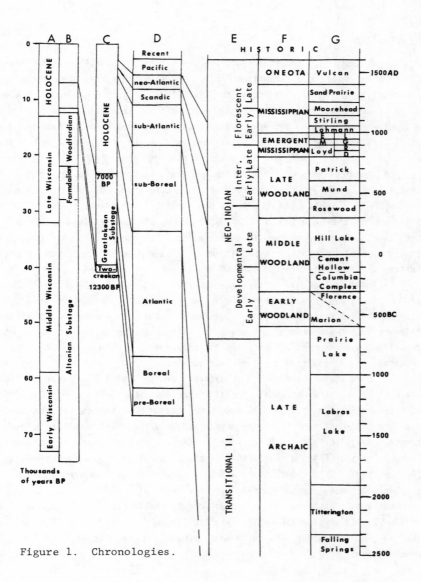

Figure 1. Chronologies.

Acknowledgments

This work is a revision of my doctoral dissertation. I would like to thank my advisors, Professors David A. Baerreis, James C. Knox, and James B. Stoltman, and the members of my dissertation committee, Henry T. Bunn, Gary M. Feinman, and T. Douglas Price, for their advice and assistance.

I had the opportunity to collaborate with Bruce G. Gladfelter, Robert L. Hall, and James L. Phillips during the FAI-270 project. Jim Phillips also served on my dissertation committee. These individuals (and the entire UIC Labras Lake crew) provided invaluable assistance, including access to the artifacts examined here.

Dr. John Walthal, Earl Bowman, and George Lammers of the Illinois Department of Transportation provided advice and assistance throughout the course of the FAI-270 project. I would like to offer my sincere thanks to them.

I would like to acknowledge the support of my wife, Bonnie Miller Yerkes, my children, and my parents. The friendship and counsel of Lawrence H. Keeley are also deeply appreciated.

Numerous individuals in Beloit, Chicago, Columbus, Madison, and Milwaukee have commented on this study, but I am particularly indebted to Elizabeth Benchley, James Brown, William Dancey, Thomas Emerson, Melvin Fowler, Peter Gendel, Ronald Lippi, George Milner, John Penman, Rodney Riggs, Robert Salzer, William Sumner, and Nicole Symens.

Anita Durbin, Deborah Crooks, Lisa Fusco, Lucia Ivanovici and the OSU Department of Anthropology office staff prepared the drafts and final version of the manuscript.

1 Introduction

Archeologists have been studying subsistence change in the midwestern United States for over a century, and a copious amount of data on prehistoric plant and animal exploitation has been compiled. While there is considerable debate about the causes and consequences of subsistence change, some general trends have been outlined. Procurement strategies have been categorized as either focal or diffuse depending on the diversity of resources exploited by prehistoric populations and on the relative intensity of different subsistence practices (Christenson 1980; Cleland 1976; Ford 1977; Stoltman and Baerreis 1983; Styles 1981).

Changes in midwestern subsistence patterns have been summarized in this fashion: low human population densities were characteristic of Paleo-Indian and Early Archaic cultures, and these groups exploited a limited number of animal and plant species. This "focal" economy may have been an adjustment to the low fertility of midwestern environments during the early Holocene (Parmalee 1968). Middle Archaic populations broadened and diversified their subsistence base in response to population growth and the "maturation" of the environment (Christenson 1980:52). This diffuse economy persisted among Late Archaic and Woodland groups who began to cultivate cucurbits (Kay et at. 1980) and native starchy seed plants (Johannessen 1982), but who still exploited a variety of wild plants and animals. When productive varieties of maize became available around A.D. 900, Mississippian populations became fully agricultural and developed a focal economy based on the intensive cultivation of maize and other exotic domesticates (Cleland 1976; Ford 1977; Stoltman and Baerreis 1983).

Past environmental conditions are poorly documented for many periods of midwestern prehistory, but it has become standard practice to assume that there has been no significant change in the composition of the local flora and fauna since 4000 B.C. (cf. Asch et al. 1972; Zawaki and Hausfater 1969). For example, many believe that prior to Anglo-European contact, all of the cultural groups who inhabited the American Bottom had access to the same wild food resources. It has been argued that the Archaic, Woodland, and Mississippian populations who occupied this section of the Mississippi River floodplain were surrounded by plant and animal communities that were nearly identical to those described by the United States federal land (GLO) surveyors who visited the region in the nineteenth century (Gregg 1975; Johannessen 1981; Kelly et al. 1979).

Projecting the nineteenth century "pre-settlement" biotic communities back into prehistory and using them as a static environmental background for the study of cultural processes could lead to what King and Graham (1981) have called Error Type I in paleoenvironmental models that are used in archeological research. If stability (or change) is assumed in environments where it did not exist, the effects of environmental change on human ecology may be misunderstood.

Recent studies have shown that adaptive processes in living systems do not involve adjustments to changes in average environmental conditions. Instead, "well-adapted" systems require effective responses to risks arising from environmental unpredictability (Alland 1975; Kirch 1980; Lewontin 1970, 1978; Slobodkin and Rapoport 1974; Winterhalder 1980). The paleoenvironmental data that are used to reconstruct prehistoric biotic communities (e.g. pollen, phytoliths, macrobotanical material, and faunal remains) reflect generalized ("average") environmental conditions (Butzer 1982:181-82). Reconstructions may show that there was no significant change in the composition of the "generalized" biotic communities of the Midwest during the last 6,000 years, but this apparent stability may mask the unpredictability of the available resources in specific prehistoric environments from one year to the next.

The dynamic nature of hydrological and biotic conditions on the American Bottom floodplain (e.g., flood cycles, channel shifts, the expansion and construction of wetland habitats) must be investigated before the context of subsistence change and social evolution can be understood.

Many recent studies of prehistoric subsistence change have drawn their models from economics and animal ecology. These "least-cost" schemes assume that population density was the key variable that shaped prehistoric procurement systems (Earle and Christenson 1980; Keene 1979; Reidhead 1979; Winterhalder and Smith 1981). The approach used in this study explores the relationships between site activities and subsistence strategies in specific cultural and environmental contexts. Technological, sociocultural, and environmental variables are considered as well as population growth (cf. Green 1980a, 1980b).

This study was undertaken to learn how the Late Archaic, Late Woodland, and Mississippian groups that resided at Labras Lake organized their settlements, and to understand the environmental dynamics of the region during each prehistoric occupation. Did each group develop a distinctive subsistence strategy to cope with particular environmental, technological, and cultural conditions, or did a single pattern persist at Labras Lake (with slight modifications) for 3,000 years?

To answer these questions, the methods of geoarcheology, microwear analysis, and seasonality and subsistence studies were applied to the Labras Lake data. The sedimentary context of the archeological remains at Labras Lake was considered, and changes in the configuration of the Mississippi River channel, associated floodplain features, and biotic zones were investigated. The nature of the activities that went on at the Labras Lake site during each habitation period were deduced from the functional information provided by microwear analysis of a sample of chipped stone artifacts from each component. Analysis of the recovered floral and faunal remains provided information about subsistence activities and the duration and seasonal pattern of each occupation.

Most functional interpretations of chipped stone artifacts are based on the formal attributes of the implements and on ethnographic analogy. In this study, wear traces on the edges of the artifacts were microscopically examined and compared with the wear patterns found on experimental stone tools that had been used for specific tasks (e.g., scraping dry hide, cutting meat, engraving antler). The microwear evidence was used to determine the functions of the prehistoric implements (cf. Keeley 1980).

Results

The archeological and paleoenvironmental record at Labras Lake is not complete. Prehistoric human habitation at the site occurred several times between 1859 and 800 B.C., around A.D. 920, and around A.D. 1235 (Hall 1986). Geomorphic evidence suggests that the Late Archaic occupations at Labras Lake were contemporary with a highly sinuous meandering Mississippi River that covered much of the American Bottom, while the Late Woodland and Mississippian occupations occurred after the Mississippi River had shifted its course to the western valley margin, leaving a broad floodplain with numerous backwater lakes and sloughs.

The earliest settlements at Labras Lake date to between 1700 and 1450 B.C. (northwestern Lake Archaic area) and to between 1850 and 1400 B.C. (south central Late Archaic area). The inhabitants of these settlements used projectile points that show some stylistic affinity with the Late Archaic Riverton Culture (Winters 1969), which flourished in the Wabash Valley in eastern Illinois between 1700 and 1450 B.C. (Hall 1986). The early Late Archaic settlements at Labras Lake contained few deep pits or domestic areas (shelters) and seem to have functioned as temporary camps. The northwestern area consisted of three large artifact concentrations, nine small hearths (burned areas), twenty-one pits, six small artifact scatters, and fourteen postholes. These features contained virtually nothing but lithic artifacts and chipping debris, and 75% of the chipped stone pieces were thermally altered. It is believed that lithic manufacturing and repair were the primary activities that were performed in the northwestern Late Archaic area.

Most of the Late Archaic features in the south central area of the Labras Lake site were shallow pits, but three hearths and five deep pits were present as well. The south central area seems to have been a temporary settlement, but some 8,222 bone fragments were recovered from this area, and these accounted for 79% of the bone recovered from Late Archaic contexts at Labras Lake. The 8,222 bone fragments were distributed among twenty-two of the fifty-one features in the south central area, but 61% of the faunal remains came from three features. The main activities performed by the Late Archaic inhabitants of the south central area seem to have been the butchering of large mammals (white-tailed deer and elk) and the processing of their hides.

This reconstruction of the activities that were performed in the northwestern and south central areas of the Labras Lake site has been corroborated by microwear analysis. Hide-working, butchering, wood-working, and bone- or antler-working tools were identified in samples of chipped stone artifacts from all four Late Archaic components at Labras Lake, but the implements in the sample from the northwestern area were used for only six different tasks (cutting meat, scraping hide, reaming hide, scraping wood, engraving wood, and scraping bone or antler). Six (40%) of the fifteen utilized artifacts in this sample could have been hafted. These hafted tools may not have been used in the northwestern area but could have been discarded there after they were replaced in their hafts by newly made tools. This would be expected if this component served as an activity area devoted to lithic manufacture and repair (cf. Keeley 1982).

Only five different tasks were performed with the utilized artifacts in the microwear sample from the south central area (cutting meat, scraping hide, reaming hide, scraping wood, and scraping bone or antler). Twenty of the twenty-seven utilized artifacts (74%) were used in butchering or hide-working activities. It is clear that the south central area served as a meat- and hide-processing station, but it is possible that it was part of a larger Late Archaic settlement that included other areas of the Labras Lake site.

The other two Late Archaic components at Labras Lake date to between 1450 and 1150 B.C. (southwestern area), and between 1300 and 800 B.C. (north central area). These two occupations span the Labras Lake phase and the "terminal" Late Archaic Prairie Lake phase of the new American Bottom chronology (Emerson 1984; McElrath and Fortier 1983). The "younger" Late

Archaic components in the southwestern and north central areas of the Labras Lake site contained more features than the "older" Late Archaic components in the northwestern and south central areas. More domestic areas and storage/ refuse pits were found in the southwestern and north central areas, and roasting pits were present there as well, although these deep pits with baked clay bases were not found in the northwestern or south central areas of the Labras Lake site.

Flotation samples from the pits, hearths, and structures in the southwestern and north central areas contained a greater variety of floral materials than samples from features assigned to the older Late Archaic components. More faunal elements were present in the flotation samples taken from features in the south central area, but the density of biotic material and the diversity of identified plant and animal species in the flotation samples from features in the southwestern and north central areas suggest that these settlements were occupied for a longer period of time than the northwestern and south central areas.

Microwear analysis showed that the tools in the samples from these terminal Late Archaic components were used to perform many different tasks, and there were more refits and matches between the lithic artifacts from these components. This suggests that the Late Archaic settlements in these areas were long term and that the lithic refuse that was produced during the manufacture and repair of stone tools was discarded in several dump areas across the site (see Hayden and Cannon 1983 for a discussion of the significance of dispersed dump areas).

A broad spectrum of plant and animal resources were exploited by these terminal Late Archaic groups, and food seems to have been stored in deep pits after it was collected and processed. Some have suggested that the distribution of excavated Late Archaic period sites on the American Bottom indicates that bluff-base settings were preferred locations for base camps. It has been argued that these sites at the margin of the floodplain were selected so that both upland and floodplain resources could be utilized (Emerson 1984; McElrath and Fortier 1983). However, active channels of the Mississippi River that moved across the central portion of the American Bottom may have destroyed Late Archaic sites that were located within the meander belt.

Recent work at the Cahokia Interpretive Center Tract (Lopinot 1983) showed that Late Archaic populations who occupied the point bars near the meandering channel of the Mississippi River exploited a wider variety of flora and fauna than groups who inhabited the bluff-base settlements. The density

and diversity of floral and faunal material found in a small sample of
features from this site in the center of the American Bottom indicate that
floodplain localities may have been more desirable to Late Archaic populations
than bluff-base settings. The concentration of Late Archaic sites along the
eastern margin of the American Bottom floodplain is probably the result of
differential site preservation rather than cultural preference.

The Late Woodland Occupation

The Late Woodland (Early Bluff) settlement at Labras Lake dates to around
A.D. 920 and follows an 1,800 year hiatus in the occupational record. Early
Woodland and Middle Woodland groups apparently did not settle this portion of
the American Bottom, since there are only Late Archaic, Late Woodland, or
Mississippian components at other excavated sites in the Labras Lake-Falling
Springs vicinity. This occupational hiatus occurred when the Mississippi
River channel shifted from the central meander belt to a straighter course
along the western margin of the American Bottom floodplain (sometime between
450 B.C. and A.D. 850, according to Gladfelter 1980b).

The Late Woodland settlement at Labras Lake was located between a
spring-fed stream and several oxbow lakes and sloughs. The Late Woodland
population subsisted on both cultivated and wild plants, but most of the
identified macrofloral remains from Late Woodland features were native
domesticates. Carbonized maize was found in only one of the fifteen Late
Woodland features at Labras Lake. Both terrestrial and aquatic animals were
being hunted and processed at the site, but there were more fish, turtle,
mussel, and muskrat remains in the Late Woodland faunal samples than there
were in the Late Archaic faunal assemblages.

Cross (1982) has shown that fish and other aquatic species are quite
common in faunal collections from Early Bluff (Late Woodland) sites located on
the American Bottom and the adjacent uplands. Her data suggest that there is
an expansion of population into new areas of the American Bottom that were not
previously occupied during the Early and Middle Woodland periods (also see
Braun and Plog 1982). At Labras Lake, we see the resettlement of a site that
had been unoccupied since the Late Archaic period.

This settlement pattern fits Hall's (1973) model of Late Woodland
expansion into uplands after the introduction of the bow and arrow and the
beginning of slash-and-burn cultivation. However, most of the cultivated
plants were native starchy or oily seed varieties (e.g., marsh elder, goosefoot, knotweed, and maygrass), while maize was a minor part of the Late
Woodland diet.

The microwear sample from the Late Woodland component at Labras Lake included nineteen artifacts that had been used to perform seven different tasks (cutting meat, scraping hide, scraping wood, cutting plant material, sawing bone or antler, and engraving bone or antler). Plant-processing tools were not found in any of the Late Archaic microwear samples, but the rest of the tools in the Late Woodland assemblage resemble the collections associated with the short-term Late Archaic settlements at Labras Lake. There were no dwellings among the Late Woodland features at Labras Lake, and this component may represent a semisedentary settlement.

The Mississippian Occupation

The final prehistoric occupation at Labras Lake dated to around A.D. 1235 and involved a Mississippian population with Stirling phase (Fowler and Hall 1975) affinities. The Mississippian procurement system included maize cultivation, nut collecting, wild plant harvesting, fishing, and hunting or collecting a variety of terrestrial and aquatic animal species. The Mississippian economy on the southern American Bottom does not conform to the model of a "focal" agricultural system where outlying farmsteads such as the Labras Lake site produced surpluses of maize for consumption by the inhabitants of larger Mississippian temple towns (Fowler 1974; Porter 1974; Williams 1979). Instead, Labras Lake seems to have functioned as a self-sufficient hamlet, where a variety of wild and domesticated foods were exploited.

The evidence for the diversification of the Mississippian procurement system is significant, since it is often assumed that prehistoric societies who cultivated domesticated plants had less variety in their diets than groups who subsisted by hunting, gathering, fishing, and plant tending.

Microwear analysis of lithic samples from Mississippian features revealed a diversity in tool function. The eighty-two utilized implements that were associated with six Mississippian household units were used to perform thirteen different tasks (cutting meat, cutting hide, scraping hide, reaming hide, drilling shell, sawing wood, scraping wood, boring wood, cutting plant material, sawing bone or antler, and engraving bone or antler).

A comparison of the microwear assemblages from the Late Archaic, Late Woodland, and Mississippian components at Labras Lake reveals that new types of tools were being manufactured and utilized as the subsistence base was expanded and certain kinds of resources were more intensively exploited. Plant knives were not present in the Late Archaic microwear samples, but they were found in the Late Woodland Mississippian assemblages. This may reflect the increased importance of plants with starchy and oily seeds in the Woodland and Mississippian diet. Agricultural tools such as chipped stone "hoes" (and the "hoe chips" produced when these tools were resharpened), ground stone celts (adzes?), and grinding stones were almost exclusively found in the Mississippian lithic assemblages.

This study shows that the inhabitants of the Labras Lake site developed subsistence systems that allowed them to adjust to the dynamic conditions of life on the American Bottom. A trend toward more sedentary settlement patterns can be documented, beginning with the terminal Late Archaic settlements, and continuing with the Late Woodland and Mississippian communities. The variety of plant and animal species exploited by the inhabitants of the Labras Lake site increased over time, but evidence for specialized food production was not found in the functional and bioarcheological data. New techniques of cultivation, hunting (with the bow and arrow), and food processing (including the use of ceramic vessels) may have allowed successive prehistoric populations to add new food items to their diets, but they retained most of their old staples. Food complexes were not abandoned and replaced by new types of diets as each cultural group modified its subsistence practices. Nuts were not replaced by seeds, and seeds were not superseded by maize. At Labras Lake wild nuts were harvested in quantity by agriculturual Mississippians around A.D. 1235, and a variety of native wild (and domesticated) seed plants were also included in the Mississippian diet.

Population growth need not have been the primary cause of subsistence change on the American Bottom. While the data from Labras Lake support the notion that the number of procurement strategies expands as a prelude to food production (Earle 1980:21), once it was established, agriculture was not emphasized at the expense of other subsistence practices. A focal economy does not seem to have developed in response to population growth. Instead, new production strategies were added by each successive group who occupied the Labras Lake site. Resource diversity (the number of different species of plants and animals consumed by a human group) and niche width (the proportions in which different resources are consumed) actually increase through time (contrary to the expectations of Christenson [1980]), and a focal economy never seems to have existed.

Summary

This study of site activities and subsistence at the Labras Lake site
begins with a review of previous research on the American Bottom (chapter 2).
Most of the archeological work in the region has focused on the Cahokia site
and Mississippian culture. However, most investigations of the evolution of
Mississippian society have failed to consider the environmental context of the
political and economic developments that led to the emergence of this complex
cultural system.

In the contextual approach used here, the biophysical environment is a
dynamic factor, not a body of descriptive background data (Butzer 1980).
Archeological sites are viewed as parts of human ecosystems, and cultural
change is not simply the result of a cause-and-effect relationship between
environment and culture but develops from systematic interactions between
cultural, biological, and physical factors and processes (Butzer 1982; Ford
1977; Stoltman and Baerreis 1983).

In chapter 3 of this study, the geoarcheology of the American Bottom is
discussed in effort to (1) understand both the natural and cultural context of
the archeological materials at the Labras Lake site and at related sites in
the vicinity of Labras Lake, (2) establish the time and duration of human
occupation at these sites, and (3) reconstruct the past environmental
conditions that were contemporary with each human habitation episode.

The present hydrology of the American Bottom is a poor analog for the
prehistoric situation. Modern landform and vegetation patterns have been
altered by natural and human agencies. Entire archeological sites may have
been destroyed by shifts in the channel of the ancient Mississippi River, as
well as by modern construction activities. Any observable patterns in
prehistoric site distribution on the American Bottom may not reflect the
aboriginal preference for certain types of settlement locations, but may be
the result of past geomorphic processes and archeological excavation strategies that were adopted to cope with the impact of recent urban expansion.

Chapter 3 is more than just a summary of the recent geomorphological
investigations that were carried out in conjunction with the FAI-270
Archeological Mitigation Project (Gladfelter 1980a, 1981). It is an attempt
to integrate the hydrological and paleoenvironmental data with the
archeological evidence and to reconstruct the Late Archaic, Late Woodland, and
Mississippian subsistence systems.

The artifacts and biological materials that were studied to obtain functional, economic, and seasonal information were almost always taken from "sealed" depositional contexts such as the fill of pits or house basins to that the effects of postdepositional processes (Gifford 1981; Wood and Johnson 1978) on artifact associations could be controlled.

Chapter 4 summarizes some of the settlement models that have been developed for the Late Archaic, Late Woodland, and Mississippian populations that inhabited the American Bottom. In addition, the prehistoric components at Labras Lake are described, and the stage is set for the analysis of activity patterns and procurement systems at the site.

Labras Lake contains one of only ten excavated Late Archaic settlements on the American Bottom and adjacent bluffs. There is a small Late Woodland settlement at the site as well, and it is typical of the Early Bluff gardening communities described by Johannessen (1983). The Mississippian occupation at Labras Lake has been described as a fourth-line farming hamlet (Phillips 1980), and as a "nodal point" community in a dispersed settlement system. Emerson and Milner (1982) hypothesized that a minor leader may have resided at Labras Lake, and this leader could have had some jurisdiction over the surrounding Mississippian settlements.

In chapter 5, the floral and faunal data from the Labras Lake site are summarized and evaluated. All of the plant and animal remains that were recovered in the field or found in the 1,386 flotation samples that were processed during the University of Illinois-Chicago excavations at Labras Lake were sent to the Illinois State Museum, where the floral material was identified by Frances B. King, and the faunal remains were analyzed by Bonnie W. Styles and James R. Purdue (King 1980; Purdue and Styles 1980). A small sample of fish scales from the UIC excavations were examined by the author (Yerkes 1981a). All of the bioarcheological data have been rechecked, retabulated, and integrated into the present study.

Direct and indirect methods of seasonal analysis have been used to determine if each component at the Labras Lake site represents a year-round occupation, or if habitation was restricted to certain seasons of the year. The direct methods of seasonality estimation (Monks 1981) include (1) noting the presence or absence of species of plants that are assumed to be available only during certain seasons of the year, (2) examining the incremental growth structures on fish scales found in faunal samples (Yerkes 1977, 1980), and (3) recording the relative abundance of wood charcoal in the fill of refuse pits associated with different household units. A recent study of bioarcheological material from the Aztalan site in Wisconsin (Yerkes 1981b) produced a correlation between the volume and weight of charcoal in the fill of a feature and the season of the year that the pit was filled (based on fish scale growth rings and other seasonal indicators). The highest concentrations of charcoal were found in the refuse pits that were filled during the winter months (October to February), while lesser amounts of charcoal were present in the pits filled during the warmer months of the year.

The indirect methods that were used to estimate seasonality include studying the contents of the features and structures associated with each household unit (e.g., the lithics and ceramics as well as the bioarcheological material) and determining if the functions of the artifacts seems to be "seasonally specific" (Cleland 1976; Monks 1981:22).

The functional analyses of the lithic samples from each household unit and component at Labras Lake are described in chapter 6. This work was undertaken to determine if the site was used for different purposes during each habitation phase. This microwear study was not overly concerned with lithic technology or with discovering the processes involved in the formation of different types of use-wear traces on the edges of stone tools. The goal of this research was the recognition and identification of microscopic features on the implements that could be used to determine their functions.

In order to understand the settlement and subsistence strategies that were in operation during each occupational episode at Labras Lake, the activities associated with each component must be defined. The best way to reconstruct these activities is by determining how the artifacts in each assemblage were used. In this study, more than 1,000 chipped stone artifacts were examined for microscopic wear traces. These artifacts were selected from "household units" (Flannery 1982) that included eight Late Archaic domestic areas and associated pits, hearths, and artifact concentrations, a single cluster of Late Woodland features, and six Mississippian wall-trench houses and their surrounding features. Lithic refits and ceramic cross-mends were used to link up the features in each household unit. This procedure allows comparison on the household level as well as the settlement level when the temporally distinct occupational episodes at Labras Lake are described and analyzed.

A comparison of the results of functional analyses of chipped stone tools based on microwear traces and Carr's (1982) morphological system is presented in chapter 6 as well. The results of this comparison should help archaeologists evaluate the functional interpretations of stone tools that are found in the literature on midwestern prehistory, but the microwear study presented here has gone beyond formal/functional considerations. Unretouched flakes as well as formal tools were included in the microwear samples so that more information about site activities could be obtained, and a large number of implements were examined (1,009) to enhance the reliability of the results.

Chapter 7 contains a summary of the research and discusses the changes in site utilization and subsistence practices at Labras Lake during the past four millennia. It is argued that functional studies of artifact assemblages associated with the different cultural groups that inhabited the American Bottom are necessary in order to understand the adaptive patterns of the groups and the internal organization of their settlements, and to document any changes in these patterns through time. Site classification schemes must be based on a knowledge of the activities that occurred at each type of site within a settlement system. Contextual archeology is the organizational framework that was used to examine the prehistory of the American Bottom, and the Labras Lake site provided useful, if incomplete, data that were used to evaluate some of the current models that attempt to explain the changes in site activities and subsistence in the region.

2 Previous Research

The American Bottom is a broad alluvial plain located south of the confluence of the Illinois, Missouri, and Mississippi rivers (figure 2). There are approximately four archeological sites per square kilometer on this stretch of the floodplain, and research has been conducted there for over a century, yet there are still gaps in the prehistoric record. Most of the prior work has focused on the Cahokia site, a large temple town that was the center of the most complex social and political organization ever known in the prehistoric United States.

Archeological description and classification of the Mississippian populations who had attained this high degree of cultural complexity began in the 1880s when William McAdams, Dr. John F. Snyder, and Dr. A.J.R. Patrick mapped and excavated portions of the Cahokia site and several smaller Mississippian sites. Their work was followed by more systematic investigations carried out by David I. Bushnell, Jr., Warren King Moorehead, Fay-Cooper Cole, A.R. Kelly, and Dr. Paul F. Titterington. Unfortunately, prehistoric sites that were inhabited by other cultural groups were virtually ignored in these early studies (Fowler 1978).

In the 1950s, the University of Michigan began a research program that was designed to widen the scope of archeological investigation on the American Bottom. However, after a small area was surveyed, and limited excavations were conducted at Cahokia and at the Lundsford-Pulcher site, the Michigan project was discontinued for lack of funds (Fowler 1974; Griffin and Spaulding 1951; Griffing and Jones 1977).

A cooperative salvage operation on the American bottom was instigated ten years after the Michigan work by the Illinois Archeological Survey (IAS) and the Illinois Department of Transportation (IDOT). Salvage excavations were conducted at several locations within the Cahokia site limits, at the Mitchell site, and at a number of smaller sites on the American Bottom and adjacent bluffs during the construction of Interstate Highways 55 and 70 (Fowler 1962, 1963, 1964). Volunteers from the IAS crews rapidly excavated several sites that were not included in the highway contracts but were threatened by borrow pit earth-moving operations that went on while the highways were under construction. The IAS also began a program of intensive archeological survey on the American Bottom in conjunction with the cooperative highway salvage program (Harn 1971; Munson 1971).

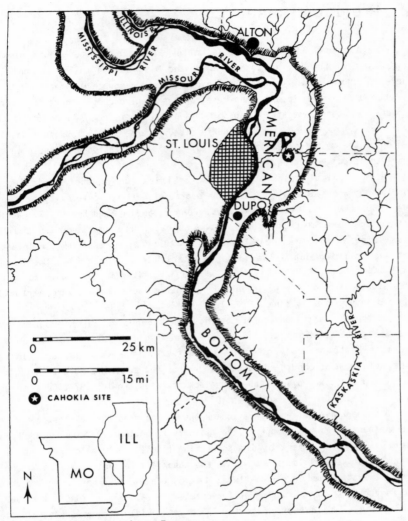

Figure 2. The American Bottom.

At the close of the highway salvage program in the 1960s, American Bottom archeologists tried to develop integrated, regional research programs for their area similar to what Struever (1969) had proposed for the Lower Illinois Valley. However, urban expansion made it difficult to implement these plans. Numerous archeological sites had already been destroyed by private and public construction, and it was only after protective legislation such as the National Historic Preservation Act, the National Environmental Policy Act, and the Archeological and Historical Preservation Act had been approved that regional research programs could be developed.

Melvin L. Fowler designed the first regional archeological research plan for the American Bottom. He set out to study the processes that led to the formation of a complex society and the evolution of an urban community at Cahokia, by defining the limits of the Cahokia site proper, refining the chronological framework for the rise of Mississippian Culture in the region, and reconstructing the Cahokia settlement system from survey data compiled by Harn (1971), Munson (1971), and Brandt (1972).

James Porter began another regional research program that involved several Historical Sites Survey projects for the Illinois Department of Conservation (IDOC). Jean Linder, Paul Dickenson, Glen Freimuth, Andrew Fortier, John Kelly, George Milner, and Richard Yerkes conducted intensive surveys and limited test excavations along the eastern side of the American Bottom from the mouth of the Kaskaskia River north to the Lundsford-Pulcher site. Porter used the site distribution data obtained during these surveys and test excavations to construct a chain settlement model for the Late Woodland/Mississippian villages that were located along the water courses of the American Bottom (Porter 1974:24-29).

Porter believes the linear settlement pattern that characterized Late Woodland and emergent Mississippian sites was replaced by a hexagonal "central place" pattern of settlement distribution when the merchant class gained ascendancy at Cahokia. He suggests that several "capitals" emerged in response to the new political system, with lesser supporting communities spaced at equal distances from the centers (Porter 1974:29-38).

Late Woodland and Mississippian settlement patterns were also emphasized in the archeological research conducted on the American Bottom in the 1970s (Bareis 1976; Benchley 1974; Norris 1978; Salzer 1975; Szuter 1978), and the data provided by these investigations have been used to develop two antithetical explanations for the emergence of the Cahokia Mississippian cultural system. One plan traces the evolution of stratified Mississippian social organization from within the indigenous Late Woodland cultures. It is argued that increases in population coupled with improved maize horticulture and widening of the subsistence base placed a strain on the available land and led to disputes over territory that could only be resolved by centralized authority (Williams 1979). In the other model, cultural groups located farther south in the Lower Mississippi Valley are responsible for a short-lived cultural climax at Cahokia through trade connections and cultural diffusion (Kelly 1980; Porter 1974, 1980).

A more comprehensive explanation for the emergence of Cahokia Mississippian Culture was presented by Robert L. Hall (1973, 1975), who considered the effects that environmental change, population dynamics, the development of effective maize agriculture, and the use of the bow and arrow had on Late Woodland and Mississippian subsistence and settlement patterns between A.D. 400 and A.D. 1200. Hall believes that after the Hopewellian cultural climax in Illinois, there was a period of reorganization rather than decline. Archeological evidence indicates that the aboriginal population did not decrease during this time period, but that there was a redistribution of people over the landscape (Farnsworth 1973). Late Woodland groups settled in upland forests and prairie-edge areas that had not been occupied by the Hopewellians, who had concentrated their settlements in the lowlands along major water courses. Prior to A.D. 400, subsistence in these bottomland settings was based on aquatic resources such as fish, waterfowl, and wetland plants (Asch et al. 1978). However, after A.D. 400, the base was laid for effective agriculture, although maize farming did not become widespread in Illinois until after A.D. 900 (Bender et al. 1981).

The bow and arrow replaced the atlatl and dart as the principal weapon some time between A.D. 400 and 700 (Fowler and Hall 1978; Hall 1973). By practicing slash-and-burn cultivation of native and introduced plants, and by ambush hunting with the bow and arrow, dispersed groups of Late Woodland farmer-hunters could exploit the upland forests and prairies adjacent to the alluvial valleys.

Opening the forest through slash-and-burn cultivation of native and tropical domesticates would have had additional benefits for Late Woodland groups: wild plants that are normally found at the forest-prairie edge would colonize the openings in the climax forests, and white-tailed deer populations could have increased when these forest-edge habitats were at a maximum.

Population increases among Hopewellian groups prior to A.D. 400 may have been the initial impetus for some of them to leave the riverine resources of the floodplain behind and move into the uplands, but by opening the forests for cultivation, they could have triggered a positive feedback mechanism that reinforced the direction of this adaptive change (Farnsworth 1973; Hall 1973, 1980).

From A.D. 800 to 1000, the Late Bluff variant of Late Woodland Culture was characterized by small, sedentary farming villages located on the American Bottom and adjacent uplands. The emergence of Mississippian Culture was marked by an increase in the number of sites on the bottom and by formal changes in local ceramic styles. After A.D. 900, large, centrally located temple towns were constructed at Cahokia and Lundsford-Pulcher. External contacts between these temple towns and cultural groups in the Caddoan area, the Lower Mississippian Valley, and the Upper Great Lakes increased; and Cahokia continued to grow until a population of 10,000 or more may have been present at the site (Fowler and Hall 1978). Many smaller single-mound sites may have been adandoned at this time, but the populations of the larger sites such as Cahokia, the Mitchell site, the East St. Louis (Metro) site, and the St. Louis Mound groups seem to have reached maximum size (Harn 1973).

Cahokia's influence waned between A.D. 1250 and 1500, and it was no longer the center of Mississippian culture. Hall suggests that the increased use of Northern Flint corn, or Eastern Eight Row (see Cutler and Blake 1979), with its superior adaptability to the colder conditions of the Neo-Boreal climatic episode (Baerreis et al. 1976), and the availability of bison as a source of protein both contributed to the decline of Cahokia as an administrative center.

The Mississippian hierarchy at Cahokia had been able to mitigate environmental stress during the dry Pacific climatic episode through a network of redistribution across the American Bottom (Chmurney 1973), but sometime between A.D. 1250 and 1500 they seem to have lost their control over the surrounding settlements. Outlying Mississippian populations could have dispersed and become more autonomous when Eastern Eight Row corn and bison were adopted as their dietary staples (Hall 1973, 1975). Hall believes that when climatic stress waned at the close of the Pacific episode, Mississippian populations who were exploiting bison and Eastern Eight Row corn would no longer be dependent on bottomland resources or need a strong central authority to ensure that each community received enough food (Hall 1973).

The causality could be reversed, however, with population dispersal leading to changes in exchange patterns and in the varieties of maize that were cultivated. Better data on past environmental conditions are needed to evaluate Hall's interpretation of late prehistoric developments on the American Bottom.

The FAI-270 Archeological Mitigation Project

The FAI-270 Archeological Mitigation Project was designed to mitigate the impact of the construction of a 91 meter wide and 34 kilometer long stretch of the Greater St. Louis Beltline Highway on the cultural resources of the American Bottom. The IAS conducted a three-year intensive survey of the FAI-270 right-of-way, and a long-term excavation program that involved over 100 sites located in the path of the highway and on bluff tops where fill would be obtained for the construction of highway ramps and other right-of-way features (Bareis 1979; Kelly et al. 1979).

The FAI-270 project provided archeologists and other earth scientists with an opportunity to investigate a series of sites located within a north-south transect across the American Bottom and on the adjacent bluff tops. Geomorphic and paleoenvironmental data that were gathered during these investigations can be used to reconstruct the different ecosystems that were functioning during each phase of the 4,000-year-long sequence of human evolution on the American Bottom. These data can also be used to examine the effects of environmental and cultural change on the prehistory of the region.

The University of Illinois at Chicago participated in the FAI-270 project by conducting a program of sediment sampling, controlled surface collection, and excavation at three sites within the highway right-of-way. Bruce G. Gladfelter carried out the geomorphological investigations, while the archeological work was directed by James L. Phillips and Robert L. Hall (Gladfelter et al. 1977). The testing program at these three sites indicated that no further excavations would be necessary at two of them since no significant cultural resources were found within the right-of-way limits, but the third, Labras Lake, required mitigation. Consequently, UIC conducted a two-year joint archeological and geomorphological program at the Labras Lake site (11-S-299). The author served as field director during the second year of this project (1979).

The Labras Lake Site

Labras Lake is a multicomponent site located near the town of Dupo, in St. Clair County, Illinois (UTM coordinates: E745900 N4269400, zone 15). It is situated about 300 meters south of the Goose Lake meander scar, and about 500 meters west of the base of the Illinois bluffs. The excavation of over 10,000 square meters of this site by UIC crews revealed occupations by Late Archaic, Late Woodland, and Mississippian cultural groups. The Late Archaic occupations consisted of four spatially separate components that have been dated to between 3,460 and 2,830 radiocarbon years before the present (B.P.).

A single radiocarbon date from wood charcoal in a Late Woodland feature was 1040+/-100 B.P., MASCA corrected to A.D. 920+/-100 (RL-1234), but the ceramics associated with the Early Bluff component are similar to types assigned to the Patrick phase (A.D. 600-800) of the new American Bottom chronology (Porter 1983).

The ceramics found in Mississippian features at Labras Lake have affinities with types from Cahokia that have been assigned to the Stirling phase (A.D. 1050-1150), but eight radiocarbon dates from this component range between 1030 B.P. and 630 B.P. (A.D. 940-1320).

The results of the UIC investigations have been submitted to IDOT and published (Gladfelter 1980a; Phillips et al. 1980), but further analysis of the materials from Labras Lake have been undertaken here so that changes in activities and subsistence patterns at the site can be studied from an ecosystems perspective.

3 Geoarcheology

Landscape Context: The American Bottom

The broad section of the Mississippi floodplain that stretches from the Piasa Hills south to the mouth of the Kaskaskia River (figure 2) is known as the American Bottom (Brackenridge 1814:186; Hus 1908:155). Here the modern Mississippi River flows for some 128 kilometers beneath cliffs of St. Louis dolomitic limestone that line the western valley wall. The bottomland on the Missouri side of the river is usually less than two kilometers wide, but on the Illinois side it is more than three times that width, averaging nearly 6.5 kilometers from the east bank of the Mississippi to the eastern bluffs (Hus 1908).

In the archeological literature, the term "American Bottom(s)" has been used to refer to the northern portion of the floodplain where the valley expands from a width of five kilometers at Alton, Illinois, to a maximum span of 18 kilometers due east of St. Louis, and then narrows to a width of 6 kilometers near Dupo, Illinois (Benchley 1975; Gregg 1975; Fowler 1978; Kelly 1980; Munson 1971). The wider valley opposite St. Louis resulted from greater erosion of the softer Pennsylvanian coal and shale deposits in that area during early Pleistocene meandering and downcutting by the ancient Mississippi River.

Steep bluffs were carved in the more resistant Mississippian limestone located to the north and south (Chmurney 1973; Fenneman 1909; Yarbrough 1974), and a 12-meter-deep and 3-kilometer-wide inner channel was cut in the bedrock when the ancient river flowed at the level of the valley floor (Schumm 1977:186).

Aggradation during the Wisconsin glacial age may have raised the Mississippi floodplain as much as 18 meters above its present level, while up to 30 meters of loess accumulated on the limestone bluffs. Degradation by the ancient Mississippi River during interglacial periods removed the outwash deposits that had covered the valley floor, and upland creeks cut deep trenches through the loess deposits as they flowed down to the lowered floodplain (Chmurney 1973:78).

Up to 50 meters of alluvial sediment has been deposited over the bedrock floor of the American Bottom, including Wisconsin-age medium to coarse sands and gravels of the Henry Formation (Willman and Frye 1970:70-71). This valley train material was deposited by glacial meltwaters and underlies the Wood

River (Roxanna) terraces at the northeastern end of the American Bottom. The sands and gravels of the Henry Formation are buried by silt, clay, and clayey fine sands of the Cahokia Alluvium, which is Late Wisconsin and Holocene in age (Willman and Frye 1970:75-77). All of the surface features on the American Bottom between Alton and Dupo, Illinois are formed on Cahokia Alluvium, except for the Wood River and Poag terraces (figure 3). Munson (1974) believes these terrace remnants are part of the Festus terrace system defined by Robertson (1938), and that they correlate with the Deer Plain outwash terrace in the Lower Illinois Valley (Rubey 1952).

The shape of the American Bottom suggests that the Mississippi River should be flowing along the eastern side of its floodplain where the alluvium is more than 50 meters thick (figure 4). Instead, it flows over bedrock at the Chain-of-Rocks on the western margin of the valley (Schumm 1977:184-86). Some have speculated that uplift due to rebound from glacial loading over the Great Lakes provided sufficient lateral slope to keep the river on the western side of the floodplain for the last few centuries (Simons et al. 1974:14), but the evidence for this is not conclusive. The modern Mississippi River is relatively straight between the Jefferson Barracks Bridge (river mile 169) and the Missouri confluence (river mile 198), with a sinuosity ratio (P, channel length/valley length) of 1.1. The floodplain here has a gentle southward slope of less than 1% over 50 kilometers, or a grade of about 7 centimeters per kilometer (Chmurney 1973; Gladfelter 1979a).

Archeologists cannot agree on how the Mississippi River has behaved since the last glacial period. Kelly (1980) maintains that the Middle Mississippi River has been downcutting for the past 4,000 to 6,000 years, with channel migrations limited to a 1.5- to 2.5-kilometer-wide corridor along the western valley wall. He believes the river's stable position followed a period of meandering that ended some 6,000 years ago (Kelly 1980; Kelly et al. 1979).

Chmurney (1973) has argued that the most noteworthy changes on the floodplain of the American Bottom over the past 4,000 years have been lateral, through meandering, rather than vertical, through degradation or aggradation. He believes that since the end of the Wisconsin glacial age the Middle Mississippi River has slowly shifted from a centrally located meander belt to a straighter course along the western edge of its floodplain (Chmurney 1973).

Chmurney, following Jordan (1965), has argued that the abrasive action of the suspended sediments that are concentrated along the west bank of the Middle Mississippi River (where the flow velocity is also greater) caused the river channel to migrate across the American Bottom. The concentration of

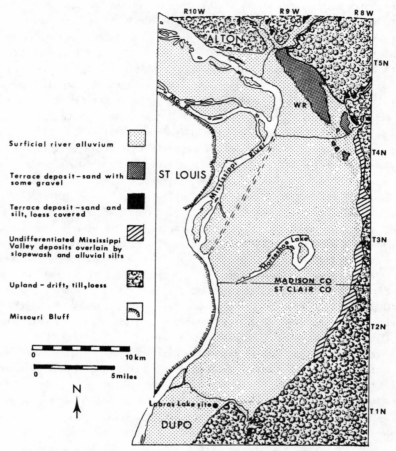

Figure 3. Surface geology of the American Bottom. The
Illinois bluff line approximates the boundry of the upland
loess. After Bergstrom and Walker (1956), Gladfelter (1980a).
WR = Wood River Terrace, P = Poag Terrace.

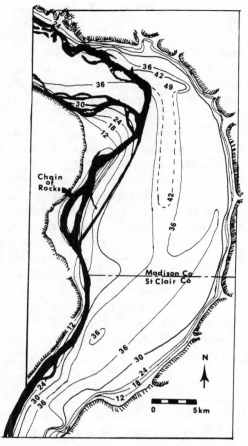

Figure 4. Thickness of alluvium on the American Bottom
(after Bergstrom and Walker 1956). Alluvium is thin or
absent at the Chain of Rocks. Isopatch interval is 6 m.

suspended load along the western bank of the Mississippi at St. Louis is
nearly 2,400 parts per million higher than the concentration along the eastern
bank (Jordan 1965). The Missouri River (which drains an area that is three
times the size of the Upper Mississippi watershed) contributes the greater
concentration of suspended sediments to the Middle Mississippi channel even

though significant amounts of sediment are stored in upstream reservoirs (Stevens et al. 1975).

Gladfelter (1980b:2-9) has analyzed eight radiocarbon dates from four paleochannels on the American Bottom and fifteen radiocarbon dates from four nearby archeological sites. He concluded that the Mississippi River was meandering between 4400 and 2800 B.P., while the straighter channel along the base of the Missouri bluffs was established some time between 2,400 and 1,100 years ago.

Kelly's idea that the morphology of the Middle Mississippi River has not changed in the past 6,000 years may be based on Asch, Ford, and Asch's (1972) assumption that the vegetation of the Lower Illinois Valley has been stable for the last 7,000 years; or he may have misread Saucier (1974), who said that the present meander belt of the Lower Mississippi Valley was established some 2,800 years ago in the south, but may be 6,000 years old in the north. Later in his geologic history of the Lower Mississippi Valley, Saucier noted that when meander belts are placed in chronological order, if continuous occupation or reoccupation of a valley segment has occurred, only the youngest meander belt can be identified. Between Memphis, Tennessee, and Cairo, Illinois, the modern Mississippi River occupies the same area as two previous channels. It is not known if any of the surviving paleochannels or other floodplain features in this reach are associated with the older meander belts or the modern channel. Landforms in this part of the valley may be anywhere between 0 and 6,000 years old (Saucier 1974:22).

Farther north on the American Bottom, the onset (not the end) of meandering activity by the Middle Mississippi River may date to 6000 B.P. Braided stream surfaces in the St. Francis basin of northeastern Arkansas and southeastern Missouri date to between 18,000 and 9,000 B.P. These braided stream surfaces formed during the waning of the Late Wisconsin glacial period when the Mississippi River carried sediment-laden outwash south from the retreating ice front. Saucier (1981) believes the change from a braided to a meandering channel occurred first in the southernmost portion of the Mississippi Valley and proceeded upstream. However, the braided course in the northern valley was in the same location as the younger meander belts. Consequently, it was buried or removed by erosion, rather than exposed like the older braided stream surfaces in the Lower Mississippi Valley.

It is not unreasonable to assume that the Middle Mississippi River was still braided when it traversed the American Bottom 9,000 years ago, and that it did not begin to meander until several millennia after that time, even though the ancient braided channel and oldest meander loops have no expression on the modern floodplain.

In the Lower Illinois Valley, the transition from a braided river with a flat floodplain to a "convex" floodbasin with point bars, levees, and backwaters occurred between 4,000 and 5,000 years ago (Butzer 1977; Hajic and Styles 1982). On the American Bottom, the Middle Mississippi River may have undergone a similar transition at roughly the same time. The onset of meandering by the Middle Mississippi River may have resulted from the increase in precipitation that occurred in the northern Midwest between 6000 and 5000 B.P. (Bartlein and Webb 1982). The increase in forest cover that followed this climatic change may have reduced the sediment yield in the Upper Mississippi watershed (McDowell 1983:111). Discharge may have been reduced as well, since Saucier (1981:12) has noted anomalously small paleochannels and river courses in the Lower Mississippi Valley that date to between 5000 and 4000 B.P.

If the amount of sediment and the volume of water flowing through a braided stream are reduced, the channel may begin to meander. However, a decrease in the slope of the valley may have the same effect (Leopold and Wolman 1957; Schumm 1977). Fisk (1944) concluded that changes in stream regime (braided or meandering) and aggradation or degradation of the Mississippi Valley were the result of changes in the slope of the overall valley. He believed that base level (sea level) changes controlled the valley slope, and that a rise in sea level would lead to alluviation as a response to decreased valley slope, while a drop in sea level would increase the overall slope and cause entrenchment by the river.

Saucier (1981) argued that the Mississippi River responded to sea level fluctuations no farther north than Baton Rouge, Louisiana. He suggested that aggradation and degradation in the northern valley were a direct response to changes in the volume of water and the volume and type of sediments carried by the river as it adjusted to glacial advance and retreat in its headwaters. The Mississippi Valley would never have been swept clean of sediments during maximum low sea levels but would have always contained a sequence of coarse alluvium that originated as outwash.

A radiocarbon date on material found within the coarse alluvium of the Henry Formation at a depth 26 meters below the surface of the American Bottom was 25,000+/-800 B.P. (Rubin and Alexander 1958). If this date is not on re-entrained material, it suggests that coarse alluvium covered the valley floor throughout most of the Late Wisconsin glacial period.

Saucier (1981) believes the Mississippi Valley filled slowly between 7,000 and 12,000 years ago. Floodplain surfaces may have been stable for several hundred years during this period of aggradation, and the 12,000 B.P. surface may be buried by only 1.5 to 3.0 meters of Holocene deposits at localities north of Memphis. This surface is within the depth of scour of the modern Mississippi River, and Paleo-Indian sites that were located on it may have been destroyed by subsequent channel migration and erosion.

Fisk (1944) argued that there were no great changes in the discharge of the Mississippi River during the aggradation of the alluvial valley. However, Saucier (1981) cited some evidence for a decline in discharge between 12,000 and 11,000 B.P. that coincides with the formation of a northeastern outlet for the Great Lakes Basin via the St. Lawrence lowland, and the diversion of some of the glacial meltwater away from the Mississippi drainage.

Saucier believes there was a second period of reduced discharge that falls at the end of the Hypsithermal climatic episode (5000-4000 B.P.). The discharge in Mississippi River paleochannels that were active at that time may have been only 40% to 60% of present levels.

Post-Pleistocene Vegetation

Post-Pleistocene vegetation changes in the midwestern United States have been reviewed by James E. King (1980, 1981). He noted that the late Pleistocene spruce forests that covered most of the area began to degenerate south of the ice front as early as 16,500 B.P. By 10,500 B.P., they were replaced by mesic oak-dominated deciduous forest. Webb and Bryson (1972) have argued that post-Pleistocene climatic warming in the Midwest had ceased by 10,500 B.P., and that climatic variation throughout the Holocene was keyed to changes in precipitation, not temperature. King has supported this theory with pollen data from the Mississippi Valley. At the Old Field site in southeastern Missouri, the vegetation has responded primarily to water table fluctuations for the past 9,000 years (King and Allen 1977).

Increased dryness (with possible increases in temperature) continued from 9000 B.P. until the maximum drought conditions of the Hypsithermal were reached about 7,000 years ago. Pollen data from a number of midwestern sites have recorded this dry period when prairies were expanding eastward across Illinois (Wright 1976). The Hypsithermal terminated gradually, with some slight amelioration about 6,500 years ago in southeastern Missouri (King and Allen 1977), and around 6300 B.P. in northern Iowa (Van Zant 1979). Dryness continued, however, until at least 5700 B.P. at Old Field, and around 4500

B.P. in northern Illinois (King 1981), while trees did not return to northern Iowa until 3200 B.P. (Van Zant 1979).

King believes that late Holocene conditions in the Midwest were more mesic than the Hypsithermal, but with less effective moisture than the early Holocene, since some of the more moisture-dependent plant species that were present in the early post-Pleistocene pollen records are absent in the late Holocene pollen assemblages. Nonetheless, climatic trends throughout the late Holocene have been in a more mesic direction, with an increase in pine pollen at 1075 B.P. shown in deep water cores from Late Michigan, and a contemporary increase in birch pollen at Volo Bog in northern Illinois, signaling the onset of Neo-Boreal cooling and forest expansion into the prairies (J.E. King 1980, 1981).

The Modern Mississippi River

The U.S. Army Corps of Engineers and private landowners have been constructing navigation improvement structures and flood protection works in and along the Middle Mississippi River since 1824. Dams, dikes, and jetties have been built to maintain a 9-foot-(2.7-meter)-deep channel for year-round navigation between St. Louis and Cairo, Illinois. Artificial levees have been erected to protect the bottomland farms and villages from floods. These developments have reduced the surface area of the Mississippi River, limited the migration of its main channel so that it cannot form new side channels and islands, and allowed existing side channels to fill with sediment. Maximum flood stages have increased since the modification of the river began, while annual minimum flood stages have decreased significantly. The depth of the water in the river is now greater than it was in the past at all discharge levels (Simons et al. 1974).

In Life on the Mississippi, Mark Twain wrote that before the river was confined, it changed its course so often that river pilots whose boats were in port at St. Louis used to travel downriver just to see where the main channel was located. Navigation in the "natural" Mississippi River was hazardous, and people living on the floodplain were subject to frequent inundations. In fact, Charles Dickens described the Middle Mississippi River as "an enormous ditch, sometimes three miles wide, running liquid mud, six miles per hour: its frothy current choked and obstructed everywhere by huge logs and whole forest trees" (Dickens 1972:216).

The riverbed area of the modern Mississippi has been reduced to 87% of what it was in 1821, and to only 67% of the 1888 riverbed area. River width (the distance between the tree lines measured normal to the direction of flow) increased at St. Louis from 945 meters in 1803 to 1,280 meters in 1849, but it was then reduced to 640 meters by dike construction (Stevens et al. 1975:124).

The average depth of the Mississippi River at St. Louis has increased from 9 meters at bankfull stage in 1837 to 14 meters in 1973. However, the cross-sectional area of the modern channel is only two-thirds of the natural channel. Narrowing the channel has increased the flow velocity and transport capability of the water in the river and has led to degradation of its bed to an average elevation 2.4 meters lower than the 1888 riverbed.

The construction of levees along the floodplain has affected the flows of the Middle Mississippi River. The floodplain serves as a storage area for floodwaters when the river rises above bankfull stage, and it provides some channel capacity. Artificial levees cause a decrease in floodplain storage and an increase in the flow discharges that are larger than bankfull (Stevens et al. 1975:126). The construction of storage reservoirs, artificial levees, dikes, and landuse changes in the Mississippi watershed do not seem to have affected the mean annual flows of the river, but very large and very small peak discharges were more common in the natural river.

The American Bottom in the Nineteenth Century

Artificial canals and ditches that were constructed during the last century have altered the natural surface drainage patterns on the American Bottom. Upland draining streams have been confined by artificial levees as they cross the floodplain enroute to the main channel of the Mississippi River, and the local groundwater table has dropped 1.5 meters since 1900 (Schicht and Jones 1962), greatly reducing the extent of wetlands on the American Bottom.

When Henry M. Brackenridge visited the American Bottom in 1811, he described it as "a tract of rich alluvial land. . . . Several handsome streams meander through it; the soil is of the richest kind, and but little subject to the effects of the Mississippi floods. A number of the lakes are interspersed through it, with fine high banks; these abound in fish, and in autumn are visited by millions of wild fowl." Brackenridge remarked that there was "no spot in the western country capable of being more highly cultivated, or of giving support to a numerous population, than this valley" (quoted in McAdams 1887:102-3).

In 1828, Timothy Flint described the American Bottom as a "beautiful tract of country,(a) plain of exhaustless fertility," where maize had been cultivated for over a century without the slightest depletion of the soil (Flint 1828, vol. 2, 117-18). Flint noted that the bottom was equally divided between timbered lands near the Mississippi channel and alluvial prairies that extended out from the base of the bluffs. He observed many small ponds and bayous in the alluvial prairies that "fill from the rivers, and from rains, and are only carried off, during the intense heat of summer, by evaporation". These backwaters were filled with fish from the Mississippi River during high flood stages; "As the waters subside, and their connecting courses with the river became dry, the fish are taken by the cart loads among the tall grass" (Flint 1828,1: 41). Flint noted the herds of deer that scoured the floodplain and the large flocks of waterfowl that visited the prairie ponds and bottom-land lakes during the spring and autumn. However, he also remarked that these wetlands were unhealthy, and that the stagnant water had to be drained to prevent sickness.

Charles Dickens had a much less favorable impression of the American Bottom. In 1842, Dickens referred to it as "an ill-favoured Black Hollow," and remarked that "though the soil is very rich. . . , few people can exist in such a deadly atmosphere. . . , and everywhere was stagnant, slimy, rotten, filthy water" (Dickens 1972:221-22).

A more neutral description of the vegetation and physiography of the American Bottom can be found in the field notes of the United States General Land Office (GLO) surveyors, who compiled "witness tree" data between 1805 and 1815, when the township grids were surveyed in Madison and St. Clair Counties, Illinois. Several archeologists have used the GLO survey data to reconstruct the nineteenth-century, or "pre-settlement," vegetation of the American Bottom (Gregg 1975; Johannessen 1981; Welch 1975). Modern ecological studies were used to supplement the GLO data, but it must be remembered that vegetation recorded in the witness tree notes may have been influenced by the colder and moister conditions of the Neo-Boreal climatic period (King 1978; Wood 1976).

The Neo-Boreal period of A.D. 1550-1850 (Baerreis and Bryson 1965; Bryson and Wendland 1967) was marked by an expansion of the circumpolar vortex with a far south jet stream in winter and reduced summer penetration by tropical air northward across the United States into Canada. The boreal forest extended about five degrees of latitude farther south in the Great Lakes region, and summers in the eastern United States were cool, while autumns were cold (about four degrees below normal).

On the American Bottom, summers would have been cool and cloudy, with more effective precipitation. Winters were very cold (about four degrees below the present average winter temperature), and the Mississippi River was said to freeze so solid that it was possible for people to walk across it for a period that lasted up to eight weeks (Flint 1828, 1: 52). In recent times, it is remarkable if the river freezes over for a single day (Chmurney 1973: 108-9).

The colder winters of the Neo-Boreal seem to have eliminated some southern species of plants and animals that once inhabited the American Bottom (Chmurney 1973 : 109). Timothy Flint saw bald cypress trees (Taxodium distichum), sweet gum trees (Liquidambar stryraciflua), and giant canes (Arundaria gigantea) no farther north than the mouth of the Ohio River in 1828, and these plants are not found on the American Bottom today (Steyermark 1963). The modern range of the rice rat (Oryzomys palustris) is also south of the Ohio confluence (Vickery et al. 1981). Yet the remains of bald cypress, sweet gum, giant cane, and rice rat have all been found beneath Mound 51 at Cahokia in Mississippian contexts that have been radiocarbon dated to between A.D. 1000 and 1300 (Chmurney 1973:147,166).

Rice rat remains have been found at Late Woodland or Mississippian sites such as Mound 34 and Powell-Zurklen at Cahokia (Parmalee 1975), and at the Range, Julien, Dohack, and Lohmann sites on the American Bottom (Kelly 1981:96-104). The base of a bald cypress log and a number of wood fragments identified as T. distichum were in several post pits at the Mississippian Mitchell site as well (Porter 1969, 1974).

Johannessen (1981) argues that the vegetation patterns contemporary with Archaic, Woodland, and Mississippian occupations on the American Bottom did not differ significantly from the patterns noted in the nineteenth-century GLO surveys, because all of the wood charcoal she identified from the five archeological sites that she studied were present in the "pre-settlement" forest.

Johannessen maintains that for the last 3,000 years, changes in the vegetation patterns on the American Bottom were the result of human disturbances, not climatic variation. She speculates that as early as 1000 B.C., sedentary groups inhabiting the American Bottom were probably using fire to clear garden plots (since domesticated gourds and squash date to at least 2300 B.C. at other midwestern Archaic sites). Fire may have also been used to improve the yield of wild plants and the habitat of game animals. Late Archaic groups may have overexploited the local forest resources for fuel and building materials as well. These activities would have altered the natural ecological succession and created an unstable subclimax ecosystem.

Johannessen claims that in order to maintain adequate levels of food production, Late Archaic populations and their successors would have had to intensify their subsistence practices.

Man's role in changing prehistoric ecosystems on the American Bottom should not be overlooked or underestimated, but it seems unlikely that Late Archaic populations on the American Bottom were dense enough to overtax the forest resources. Even if their actions did lead to a "subclimax ecosystem, these disturbed habitats usually support a higher biomass than climax forests (Lopinot 1983; Odum 1969), and this condition would not necessarily lead to intensification of procurement systems. Before the changes in wood use patterns documented by Johannessen can be explained, climatic and hydrological variables must be considered as well.

The vegetation that was contemporary with the wide meander belt that covered most of the American Bottom between 2450 and 450 B.C. differed in proportion, if not in kind, from the floral mosaic associated with the meander scars, point bars, levees, and backwaters that covered the floodplain after A.D. 850, when the Mississippi channel shifted to the western valley margin (Phillips and Gladfelter 1983).

The Central Meander Belt

The surface features preserved in the abandoned meander belt on the American Bottom have been examined by several archeologists who attempted to date the sequence of meander loops and relate the changing channel configurations to prehistoric settlement patterns (Bareis 1964; Chmurney 1973; Munson 1974). The locations of "dated" archeological sites near abandoned meander features have been used to estimate the "minimum" cutoff dates for the meander loops. It was assumed that sites found immediately inside the convex bank of a meander scar had been occupied after (or possibly a few years before) the time of meander cutoff, since any sites that were inhabited prior to the migration of the meander would have been destroyed (Munson 1974). Any sites found immediately outside the concave bank of a meander scar had to have been occupied after cuttoff, because active meanders would have destroyed the site by lateral migration, or would have buried it beneath the alluvium of a natural levee.

Unfortunately, if archeological sites are used to estimate the time meander loops were cut off, there is no way of knowing how much time had passed between the cutoff event and the first occupation of the site. Most of the sites used by Munson to establish his meander chronology were "dated" with diagnostic surface finds. If buried components were present at these sites, the "cultural date" would be too young, and if redeposited older artifacts were present in the surface assemblages, the date would be too old.

A time frame for the origin, development, and abandonment of the meander loops on the American Bottom can only be established after their channel fill has been interpreted and accurately dated, and these dates must be corroborated by alluvial chronologies and excavated and dated archeological material. The investigations of Bareis, Chmurney, and Munson have provided valuable data on past hydrological conditions, but stratigraphic information obtained from boreholes, backhoe trenches, and excavated archeological sites provides a clearer picture of the paleohydrology of the meander belt.

Various authors have identified a total of eighteen different meander segments on the American Bottom (Gladfelter 1979a, 1979b, 1980b; Kelly et al. 1979; Munson 1974; Phillips and Gladfelter 1983). These paleochannels can be grouped into five meander systems: the Horseshoe Lake, Pittsburg Lake, Goose Lake, Prairie Lake, and Hill Lake systems (figure 5). From their names it is obvious that most of these scars were oxbow lakes prior to artificial drainage alterations that lowered the groundwater table during the last century.

The Horseshoe Lake Meander System

Munson (1974) believes the oldest meanders in the Horseshoe Lake system are the McDonough Lake meander and the Spring Lake-Jones Park meander loops. He thinks both of these meanders were cut off by the Edelhart Lake meander sometime prior to 2800 B.P., since the Late Archaic McDonough Lake site (11-Ms-46) was found on the concave bank of that meander, and another Late Archaic site, Bullfrog Station (11-S-65), is located on the outside bank of Spring Lake. Munson argues that the Edelhardt Lake meander was truncated by the Horseshoe Lake meander prior to 2200 B.P., because the Early Woodland Miller Lake site (11-M2-34) is located on a point bar remnant adjacent to the convex bank of Edelhardt Lake. Bareis (1964) argued that the lateral movement of the Horseshoe Lake meander had ceased prior to 900 B.P., since the Late Woodland-Early Mississippian Powell-Zurklen (11-Ms-2/2) and Horseshoe Lake (11-Ms-37) sites lie outside the concave bank of that paleochannel. Gladfelter (1979a) maintains that the initial phase of expansion by the elongate Horseshoe Lake meander created the Edelhardt Lake point bars. Rotation of the upstream limb of this loop formed the McDonough Lake simple asymmetrical meander loop, which is now partly occupied by Cahokia Creek. After this channel was abandoned by a neck cutoff, expansion of a new simple symmetrical

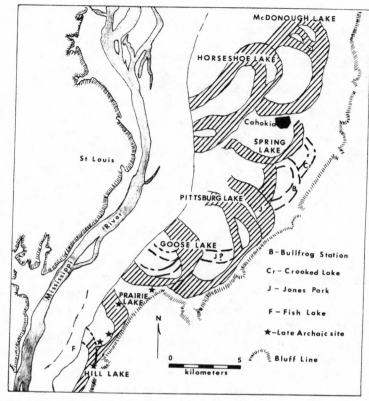

Figure 5. Meander scars and excavated Late Archaic sites on the American Bottom.

meander loop marked the first stage in the development of Horseshoe Lake. Expansion and rotation of the upstream limb of this meander created the present configuration of the lake, and subsequent cutoffs formed Walker's Island and Canteen Island.

A radiocarbon date on material found 9 meters below the surface of Horseshoe Lake at the base of lacustrine deposits filling in the meander scar was 3270+/-80 B.P. (ISGS-563). This date would place the cutoff of Horseshoe Lake some 2,400 years before the "minimum date" Bareis had estimated using the positions of archeological sites on the outside bank of the meander scar.

The 3270 B.P. date marks the end of active meandering by the Mississippi River between Canteen Island and the Illinois bluffs, since the Horseshoe Lake loop is the youngest meander in this system. Unless this date is on re-entrained material, the point bars associated with the Horseshoe Lake meander system would have been available for human settlement since 3300 B.P. Although Late Archaic cultural material has been found on the surface of several sites in this area, subsurface Late Archaic features have only been found at the Cahokia Interpretive Center Tract. Eighty Late Archaic features were located between 60 and 120 centimeters below the present surface within a point bar sequence associated with the Spring Lake meander (Benchley and DePuydt 1982). Three radiocarbon dates from features in a "sealed" context between 60 and 80 centimeters below the surface place the occupation at around 3200 B.P., or 1200 B.C. (Nassaney et al. 1983).

The Pittsburg Lake Meander

South of the Horseshoe Lake system, where the floodplain narrows from 18 kilometers to about 12 kilometers, the Pittsburg Lake (or Grand Marais) meander complex can be found. Munson believes this meander was cut off prior to 1600 B.P., since Middle Woodland ceramics were found on the surface of the Lalumier (11-S-54) and Lohmann (11-S-49) sites, which are located adjacent to the convex bank of the Pittsburg Lake loop. Kelly, Linder, and Cartmell (1979) reported Early or Middle Woodland artifacts from seven additional sites within the Pittsburg Lake point bar system, but none of the excavated features at any of the sites located on the Pittsburg Lake point bars are more than 500 years old.

Wood found 17 meters below the surface of the Pittsburg Lake meander in unoxidized channel sand and gravel provided a radiocarbon date of 3090+/-140 B.P. (RL-1064). The wood was 9 meters below the contact with the overlying fine sand, silt, and clay that was deposited while the Pittsburg Lake channel was expanding to the northeast. This sample was obtained from an IDOT borehole taken at the Turner site (11-S-50), a Mississippian settlement on the Cahokia Downs point bar complex between the Alorton Chute and the Pittsburg Lake meander scar (Gladfelter 1981).

The coarser sediments that contained the radiocarbon sample were aggraded in the channel before Cahokia Downs became a point bar setting. This indicates that the Pittsburg Lake channel was active around 3,100 years ago, unless the wood had been re-entrained by more recent fluvial activity (Gladfelter 1981: 6).

At Frank Holten State Park, 1,500 meters northeast of the borehole at the Turner site, Gladfelter investigated the northern reach of the Pittsburg Lake meander. Ten IDOT borehole logs, two backhoe trenches, and seven Giddings cores were used to reconstruct the cross-section of the Pittsburg Lake channel (figure 6).

This channel was cut into the coarse sands and gravels of the Henry Formation. It has the asymmetrical profile of the sinuous reach of a meander

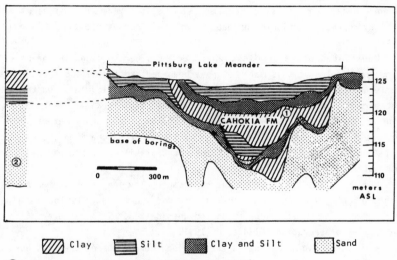

Figure 6. Geologic cross-section of the Pittsburg Lake meander at Frank Holten State Park. Reconstruction from IDOT boreholes (after Gladfelter 1981).

bend. The maximum width of this meander is 850 meters, while it extends as much as 14 meters below the present surface, with a cross-sectional area of 12,000 square meters. The cross-sectional area of the natural Mississippi River at St. Louis in 1837 was 10,800 square meters at bankfull stage, with a maximum width of 1,110 meters and a maximum depth of 9 meters (Simons et al.

1974). The Mississippi River was wide and shallow in 1837, with a width to depth ratio (b/d) of 123. It is possible that the 1837 channel was transporting more sand, and less silt and clay, than the Pittsburg Lake channel, which had a narrower and deeper profile (b/d=61), since high width/depth ratios have been correlated with greater amounts of bed load and lesser amounts of suspended load (Schumm 1977).

The fill sequence in the Pittsburg Lake meander begins with up to 5 meters of sand, silt, clay, and clayey silt that probably were aggraded when the main trunk of the Mississippi flowed through this meander. These deposits are covered by up to 6.7 meters of organic clay that accumulated after the channel became inactive. There are some silt layers within this clay plug that may represent periodic inundations of the floodplain by the Mississippi River.

Many botanical and Coleoptera specimens were present in the dark clay plug, and samples of this material have been sent to the Illinois State Museum for future study. Pollen was not abundant in the organic clay, and the grains that were recovered are oxidized and abraided. Francis King identified some wood fragments that were encountered between 4.8 and 5.2 meters below the surface in this clay plug as silver maple (Acer saccharinum), oak (Quercus sp.), and ash (Franxinus sp.). A large chunk of silver sample was radiocarbon dated at 2470+/-120 B.P. (RL-1229).

Mottling and concretions in the organic clay levels above and below the radiocarbon sample indicate that there was rapid aggradation within the meander with periodic inundation and dessication. This may account for the poor pollen preservation (Gladfelter 1981: 5).

The two radiocarbon dates from the northern reach of the Pittsburg Lake channel show that it was active at 3100 B.P. and was expanding to the north-east when it deposited the overbank flows that buried the dated material at the Turner site. The radiocarbon date on the fragment of silver maple in the clay plug deposits that fill the channel at Frank Holten State Park shows that the Pittsburg Lake meander was cut off by 2500 B.P. Unfortunately, these two dates do not establish the exact time that the meander was isolated from the main channel of the Mississippi River.

Gladfelter speculates that the Alorton Chute (a linear depression 10 meters wide and 3 meters lower than the Pittsburg Lake point bar complex) was formed by overbank discharge stages during the final development of the Pittsburg Lake loop. Calcite concretions located 2.1 and 2.7 meters below the surface in top stratum and swale fill deposits exposed by two backhow trenches through the Alorton Chute have been radiocarbon dated to 3280+/-1520 B.P. (RL-1060).

The precise conditions that promoted the precipitation of these concretions are unknown. However, a somewhat drier floodplain setting may have existed around 3280 B.P., when they formed in the Alorton Chute. At Labras Lake, the same type of biogenic concretions were found in a similar sedimentary context and have been radiocarbon dated to 3150+/-140 B.P. (RL-1063). These drier conditions would have been contemporary with the earliest Late Archaic occupations at the Labras Lake site.

Meander development at Pittsburg Lake began sometime before 3300 B.P. when a simple symmetrical loop with a north-south axis was formed. The Centerville point bar complex was created by expansion of this initial meander loop. When the Illinois bluffs obstructed its outer bank, rotation of the upstream limb formed the compound asymmetrical meander that is presently occupied by Pittsburg Lake. This channel was active at 3100 B.P., but it was cut off sometime prior to 2500 B.P. The Centerville and Cahokia Downs point bars would have been available for habitation since that time, but a Late Woodland pit at the DeMange site (11-S-447) is the oldest excavated feature in the area (Milner 1983:21-23).

The Goose Lake Meander

The Goose Lake meander scar marks the southern limit of the paleomeander belt that covers the widest part of the American Bottom. In the narrower floodplain farther downstream, relic meander features are not clearly described on the surface (Gladfelter 1981).

In historic times, this meander scar was occupied by lakes and marshland. The upstream limb was called Goose Lake, while the downstream segment was known as Cahokia Lake. Both lakes are shown on the 1908 Mississippi River Commission (MRC) charts (Gladfelter 1980a: figure 16), but today they are drained and under cultivation. Depending on the year they were drafted, nineteenth century maps show dry, lacustrine, or marsh conditions. Changing water conditions within this oxbow may have resulted from fluctuations in the local water table, inundations by the Mississippi River, or variations in the amount of runoff from upland-draining streams that reached Goose Lake. For example, Fenneman (1909) reported that Schoenberger Creek would flow north across the floodplain to Cahokia Creek, or south to Pittsburg Lake and then on to Goose Lake, depending on how sediments diverted the creek when it reached the floodplain.

Munson (1974) suggested that the Goose Lake meander was cut off prior to 1100 B.P., since the initial Late Woodland (Early Bluff) Julien site (11-S-63) is located adjacent to its convex bank. Nine sites in this area were excavated during the FAI-270 project, and the Early Woodland component at the Florence Street site (11-S-458) was the oldest settlement in the area. Three radio-carbon dates from material found in Early Woodland features there range between 2400 B.P. and 2130 B.P., but Middle Woodland (1950-1750 B.P.), Early Bluff (1350-1150 B.P.), and Mississippian (950-450 B.P.) groups also occupied the Goose Lake point bars (Emerson et al. 1983).

Gladfelter has reconstructed the Goose Lake meander sequence as follows: initial of the meander created the Lily Lake point bars, but this expansion ceased when lateral migration was halted by the Illinois bluffs at Stolle. Even with the radius of curvature fixed, the upstream limb may have continued to expand and increase the width of the channel in its northern reach. Interchannel bars and sloughs seem to have formed within the upstream limb of the meander during this later phase of expansion. The anomalous Maplewood Park bars formed after the Lily Lake point bars had developed, but before the upstream limb of the Goose Lake meander had become entrenched. The Maplewood Park bars may have been created by a slough that carried overbank flows from the Goose Lake channel during the end of its active phase.

The Goose Lake channel widens again downstream from Stolle when it moves away from the base of the Illinois bluffs. The maximum width of the meander is 1,700 meters, three times wider than where it was entrenched at the bluff base. The maximum depth of the channel is 14 meters (revealed by IDOT boreholes and backhoe trenches in the vicinity of Labras Lake). However, over 30 meters of alluvial deposits are present in this cross section (figure 7).

The Goose Lake channel is entrenched in an older channel system and is marked by complex lateral and vertical accretion deposits. A deep, thick clay deposit was encountered beneath the Goose Lake channel within the Henry Formation 20-38 meters below the present surface. This clay unit was not recorded in the Henry Formation at any other location in the American Bottom (Gladfelter 1980b; 1981).

Two samples of detrital wood chips (each weighing 2.75 grams) recovered by a split spoon from within unoxidized medium to coarse sand 11-12 meters below the surface of the Goose Lake meander yielded radiocarbon dates of 3900+/-230 B.P. (RL-1280) and 3350+/-260 B.P. (RL-1281). The samples were in channel alluvium at the top of nearly 6 meters of fine sand and below nearly 11 meters of clay and site (Gladfelter 1980a:A33).

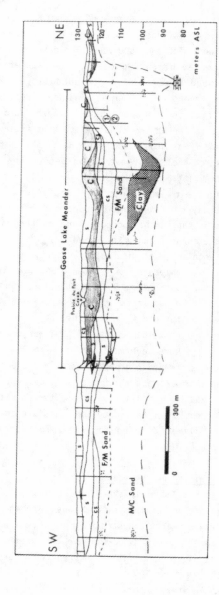

F/M: Fine to medium sand M/C: Medium to coarse sand s: Silt c: Clay cs: Clay and Silt

① Radiocarbon date 3900+/-230 BP (RL-1280)

② Radiocarbon date 3530+/-260 BP (RL-1281)

Figure 7. Goose Lake meander stratigraphy. Vertical lines show the location and depth of IDOT boreholes used to reconstruct the stratigraphic sequence (after Gladfelter 1981).

The Goose Lake channel could not have been active at 3700 B.P. (the mean age of RL-1280 and RL-1281), since it is superimposed on the Pittsburg Lake meander, which was cut off between 3000 and 2500 B.P. The dated material is either from an older channel preserved below Goose Lake that was active at 3700 B.P., or they are older wood chips that were redeposited during a cut-and-fill episode. Gladfelter favors the former explanation (1981: 30).

The finer sediments that fill in the Goose Lake meander could not be dated, but the Early Woodland occupation at the Florence Street site indicates that the convex bank of the meander was stable enough to be inhabited by 2400 B.P. Expansion of the Goose Lake channel must have begun before that time, but not before 3100 B.P., when the Pittsburg Lake meander was still active.

The oldest Late Archaic components at Labras Lake are older than the active Goose Lake meander but may have been contemporary with the channel buried beneath it. The most recent Late Archaic occupations at the site may have occurred after the Goose Lake channel began to expand.

The Early Woodland, Middle Woodland, and Mississippian settlements on the Goose Lake point bars would have been located next to an oxbow lake that was cut off from the main channel of the Mississippi River, but they would have been inundated by river floods or upland stream flows that reached the lake through a web of meander scars and bottomland water courses.

Palynological research conducted by Schoenwetter (1962) suggested that conditions on the American Bottom may have been moister between 950 and 100 years ago, when Late Bluff and Mississippian groups inhabited the Goose Lake point bars. However, pollen grains extracted from a core taken near the Julien site were poorly preserved (Bardwell 1980), and wetter conditions in the Goose Lake area at that time could not be documented. If late prehistoric conditions were wetter, either climatic change or variable hydrological conditions could have been the cause.

The Prairie Lake Meander

The Prairie Lake meander lies adjacent to steep limestone bluffs east of Dupo, Illinois. Only about 4 kilometers of this paleochannel are visible on the modern floodplain, but a fragment of the upstream limb can be traced to a point just south of Falling Spring where it swings to the southeast and follows the base of the Illinois bluffs until it is apparently cut off by the Hill Lake paleochannel.

Organic debris found 16.46 meters below the surface of this meander yielded a radiocarbon date of 5450+/-75 B.P. (ISGS-638). The sediments containing this debris have been interpreted as slack water deposits that accumulated after the channel was abandoned by a neck cut off (White 1982; White and Bonnell 1981). Unless this date is on re-entrained material, the cutoff of Prairie Lake would have occurred around 5,500 years ago, but the earliest occupation at the MoPac #2 site (11-S-46) on the point bar ridge next to the meander did not occur until approximately 2,500 years after that time (McElrath and Fortier 1983).

White (1982) argues that all of the landscape surrounding the Prairie Lake point bars would have been inundated and uninhabitable until around 3000 B.P. There was an active channel of the Mississippi River west of the site between 5500 and 3000 B.P., and paludal areas existed in the east, but there were no interchannel bars or ridges within the meander scar.

Radiocarbon dates obtained from alluvium fix the age of the material dated, not necessarily the time the material was deposited (Gladfelter 1985:44). The radiocarbon dates from the fill of the Goose Lake meander were older than the active channel they were "dating," and it is possible that a similar situation occurred at Prairie Lake. The excavated archeological sites that lie next to this meander are not deeply buried. They occupy almost all of the habitable landforms near the Prairie Lake meander, and they all were first settled around 3,000 years ago.

The Prairie Lake meander was cut off from the main channel of the Mississippi River by 3000 B.P., but the cut off event many not have occurred at 5500 B.P. The floodplain position of the Prairie Lake meander suggests that it is older than the Goose Lake loop, but if the 5500 B.P. cut off date is accepted, then the Prairie Lake channel would be 3,000 years older than Goose Lake, 2,200 years older than the Horseshoe Lake meander, and 1,800 years older than the buried channel beneath Goose Lake.

If that date is correct, Prairie Lake must have been isolated for 5,500 years while all subsequent fluvial activity occurred to the west within a stretch of floodplain that was only 4 kilometers wide. At least 3,000 years of that fluvial activity would have involved meander loops the size of Pittsburg Lake and Goose Lake, and yet White suggests that large meanders such as these did not encroach upon Prairie Lake. It is more likely that the 5500 B.P. date (which comes from a depth more than 16 meters below the surface) is associated with an older, buried channel, or that the date is on re-entrained material.

A pollen diagram (Bardwell 1980) constructed from data obtained in a core taken from the middle of Prairie Lake shows a high percentage of non-aboreal pollen (NAP). This supports Schoenwetter's (1962, 1963) conclusion that much of the prehistoric American Bottom was open prairie.

The Prairie Lake pollen diagram also records a series of environmental changes beginning with drier conditions when chenopods and ambrosia dominated the pollen counts, followed by wetter conditions marked by an increase in aquatic plants, and then a return to drier conditions. The core is undated, so it is not known if this sequence represents a period of rapid or slow deposition, or if it correlates with Schoenwetter's chronology. Schoenwetter (1962) had wet conditions that began sometime before A.D. 700 followed by a dry spell that lasted from A.D. 750 to 850. An environmental disturbance occurred between A.D. 850 and 1350, and it was followed by wetter conditions that persisted until historic times.

The Hill Lake Paleochannel

South of the Prairie Lake meander, the base of the Illinois bluff line is characterized by aprons of Peyton Colluvium and a series of gently sloping alluvial fans where low-order upland streams enter the American Bottom. A paleomeander belt is not inscribed on the floodplain here, and the constricted alluvial surface is nearly devoid of relief (Phillips and Gladfelter 1983). Archeological material from seven excavated sites found within or near two of these alluvial fans postdate the last phase of meandering by the Mississippi River.

A paleochannel that parallels the bluff here has been called the Hill Lake meander (White and Bonnell 1981). Hill Creek and Hill Lake Creek presently occupy part of this old channel, and alluvial fans extend out over its surface. A core taken 300 meters west of the Carbon Monoxide site (11-Mo-593) within the Hill Lake scar, shows up to 19 meters of a fining upward sequence, with coarse sand and gravel at the base and 2.5 meters of silty clay at the top (Gladfelter 1980b; White 1982).

Wood was found within coarse sand granules in this core at a depth 15.85 meters below the surface. A radiocarbon date of 4390+/-90 B.P. (ISGS-572) was obtained from this sample (White 1982). Another core taken just 100 meters to the west, recorded a similar sedimentary sequence, and wood that was found in silty fine sand 13.4 meters below the surface in this second core has been dated to 2910+/-75 B.P. (ISGS-571).

A core taken 50 meters west of the Mund site (11-S-435) in the northern section of the Hill Lake paleochannel contained three radiocarbon samples that were collected between 9.14 and 10.66 meters below the surface. White (1981) reported that wood fragments that were found in moist, dark grey sandy silts overlying bedrock at the bottom of the eastern cutbank of the Hill Lake scar have been dated at 3130+/-75 B.P. (ISGS-700), 3240+/-80 B.P. (ISGS-701), and 3400+/-75 B.P. (ISGS-702).

The oldest excavated archeological site on the American Bottom is located on the east bank of the Hill Lake channel. Fortier (1984) reported that the Titterington complex at the Go-Kart North site (11-Mo-552N) has been radiocarbon dated to between 4130+/-75 B.P. (ISGS-697) and 4020+/-100 B.P. (ISGS-628).

Early Woodland occupations at the Carbon Monoxide and Mund sites were located within the confines of the Hill Lake channel. Carbon Monoxide covers an intrachannel sand ridge along the southeastern margin of the Hill Lake scar. This site was first occupied around 2,100 years ago. At the Mund site, alluvial fan aggradation covered a marshy area within the Hill Lake channel. This aggraded surface and the cutbank of the channel were both occupied around 2,250-2,450 years ago.

White (1982) argues that an active channel of the Mississippi River flowed in the Hill Lake scar about 4,400 years ago. He thinks a chute cut off (the Fish Lake channel) was diverting the flow through the Hill Lake reach between 3400 and 2900 B.P., but the channel must have been filled by 2450 B.P., when Early Woodland groups occupied the Mund and Carbon Monoxide sites. White noted that the alluvial fans on the Hill Lake paleochannel did not aggrade at the same time. He suggests that climatic change, human over-intensification of upland plant resources, changes in material resistance, and natural intrinsic threshold events can trigger increased sedimentation and fan building. Aggradation may follow one or more of these triggers, but there may be a period of lag time between the trigger and the response.

These fan-building episodes could have reduced the available wetlands near the Hill Lake channel by filling in the intrachannel marshes. The shrinking paludal habitat may have limited the aquatic resources in the area and forced prehistoric populations to relocate.

White suggests that the Late Archaic Titterington settlement at Go-Kart North (4150-3950 B.P.) was situated on the cut bank of an active Mississippi River channel (1982:9), but the channel did not encroach upon the site. If White's interpretation of the 4400 B.P. and 2900 B.P. dates from the Hill Lake channel is to be believed, it must be assumed that only 2.5 meters of sediment accumulated in the channel between 4400 and 2900 B.P., but that 13 meters of alluvium were deposited between 2900 B.P. and 2400 B.P. Two millennia of aggradation are represented by these dates, but the sedimentation rate for the first 1,500 years is only 0.17 centimeters per year, while it was 2.6 centimeters per year during the last 500 years, a fifteenfold increase in the rate of sedimentation.

It is more likely that an active channel of the Mississippi River occupied the Hill Lake scar about 3,500 years ago, and that the Titterington component at Go-Kart North predates this fluvial activity. By 2400 B.P., this channel was filled, and Early Woodland groups settled on its surface. Alluvial fans extended out into the channel scar and filled in some of the intrachannel swales in a series of aggradations that lasted until the historic period (Gladfelter 1981).

West of the Carbon Dioxide site, the modern floodplain is devoid of even subtle depositional landforms until the break in slope at the edge of Fish Lake. West of the slope break, an alluvial surface is marked by linear ridges and swales that parallel the modern Mississippi channel. At Schmids Lake, a gravel pit located within the interchannel zone of the modern Mississippi River, Gladfelter examined a large maple log that had been dragged from the bottom of the quarry. Calcareous silt surrounded the base of the log at a dept 6 meters below the surface. The quarry walls show 3 meters of brown, well-sorted, and cross-bedded sand above the modern water table. Bedding structures indicate a southernly paleocurrent direction.

The exterior wood fiber of this buried maple log has been radiocarbon dated to 1120+/-110 B.P. (RL-1279). This date shows that by 1100 B.P., the Mississippi River had assumed its present course along the western margin of the floodplain.

All of the dated archeological sites that are located along the slope break overlooking the interchannel zone of the Mississippi River are younger than the maple log at Schmids Lake. The 2-kilometer-wide interchannel zone between the slope break and the confined bank of the modern Mississippi River has been the active floodplain of the natural river for at least 1,100 years. Channel shifts and scouring have erased the archaeological record on this part of the American Bottom, and no surface or subsurface sites have been reported (Benchley 1975).

Paleosols and Buried States

No deeply buried paleosols were encountered in the IDOT boreholes taken on the American Bottom during the FAI-270 project, or during earlier boring activities (Gladfelter 1980b; Willman and Frye 1970). Shallow paleosols were recognized in a few 2-3-meter-deep backhoe trenches, but a paleosol associated with a cultural horizon was only present at the Mund site (White 1981). The absence of paleosols that were associated with Late Archaic or Early Woodland cultural materials suggests that changes in floodplain morphology were too rapid for surfaces near the meanders to remain stable enough for pedogenesis. The absence of paleosols makes it difficult to accept White's interpretations of the Prairie Lake and Hill Lake paleochannels. He believes the meander activity had ceased 5,500 years ago and 3,300 years ago in those channels; but apparently, there was no soil formation on those "stable" surfaces.

Except for the sites covered by alluvial fans, all of the subsurface features at excavated archaeological sites on the American Bottom have been found within 1.5 meters of the surface. Very little aggradation has occurred since the oldest dated sites were occupied. At multicomponent sites, the cultural materials are not stratified (with the exception of the sites found within alluvial fans), and most of the alluviation that has taken place at these sites took place in the last 700 years (Gladfelter 1980b).

Schumm (1963,1977) has noted that sediment yields per unit area decrease with basin size, but sediment storage increases. Historic disturbances have increased sediment yields in upland areas, but small-and-intermediate sized drainage basins in these areas have stored these sediments, so lesser amounts of sediment have found their way onto the floodplains of higher order streams. Archeological sites in the small drainages would be buried deeper than contemporary sites on large floodplains such as the American Bottom (Gladfelter 1985). Still, the oldest archeological sites on large flood plains should be buried the deepest and would be the most likely to survive (Wiant et al. 1983), except for the fact that channels migrate over broad areas on large floodplains and have the potential to destroy sites.

The distribution of excavated Late Archaic sites on the American Bottom shows a concentration near the base of the Illinois bluffs south of the paleomeander belt. The surface of this southern portion of the American Bottom seems to have been stable for the last 4,000 years, with little aggradation by the Mississippi River even though the Hill Lake channel was active some time between 3500 and 3000 B.P. Late Archaic sites that were located in this stable area would be more likely to escape erosion by meandering channels than sites that occupied the point bars in the central meander belt.

Meandering channels have been absent from the rest of the American Bottom since at least 1100 B.P., and possibly since 2400 B.P. Late Woodland and Mississippian sites would not have been destroyed by any river activity east of the 2-kilometer-wide interchannel zone of the Mississippi River, and Early Woodland and Middle Woodland sites may have been spared as well.

Landscape Context: The Labras Lake Site

The Labras Lake site is located 300 meters south of the Goose Lake meander scar and 500 meters west of the base of the Illinois bluffs. An interior stream once flowed between the site and the talus slope at the bluff base. This stream may have been fed by Falling Spring, which lies 1,200 meters south of Labras Lake, but a search of the nineteenth-century literature revealed that another spring had flowed out of a round hole in the bluff face half a mile (800 meters) north of Falling Spring (figure 8). Wild (184-1:85-86) noted that this northern spring "ripples over moss-grown rock until it reaches the bed of a rivulet which it forms." The rivulet fed by the northern spring probably flowed northwest past the Labras Lake site until it joined the Goose Lake channel. The artificial pond called Labras Lake now occupies this former stream course.

A small backhoe trench (the Reese Trench) was cut across this channel and exposed 4.2 meters of a stratified fill sequence that began with 1.2 meters of laminated silts and mottled clay with concretions separated by abrupt, smooth boundaries (figure 9). At 123 meters above sea level (ASL), this unit is overlain by 65 centimeters of silty clay with a zone of concretions at the top. A layer of disarticulated mollusk shell was also present near the top of the silty clay unit, and the laminar bedding structures around the shells indicated they were buried by natural alluviation (Gladfelter 1980a:D156). A radiocarbon date on the shell was 3780+/-140 B.P. (RL-1278).

Above the concretions, sediments fine upward from clayey silt to silty clay with slickenside development and massive structure. At 124.5 meters ASL, or about 1 meter above the dated shell, a lense of "oxidized" sediments was encountered. The author's analysis of materials from this lense showed that it contained burned shell, burned fish and mammal bone, chert chips, carbonized seed and nut fragments, daub, and extremely small (5.0 millimeters in diameter) ceramic fragments that may have been tempered with grit.

This lense is capped by another meter of the fining upward sequence before the base of the A Horizon is encountered at 125.7 meters ASL, or 30 centimeters below the surface of the paleochannel. A 10-centimeters-thick

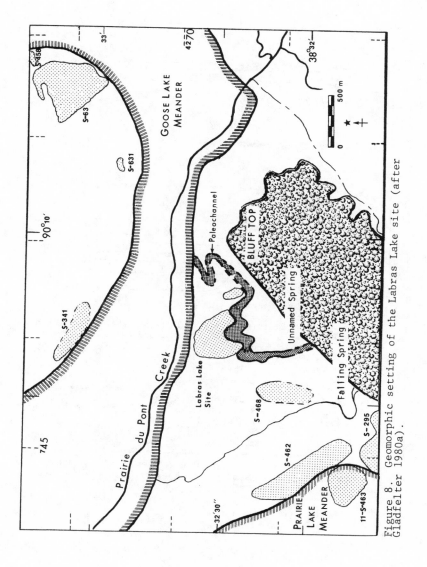

Figure 8. Geomorphic setting of the Labras Lake site (after Gladfelter 1980a).

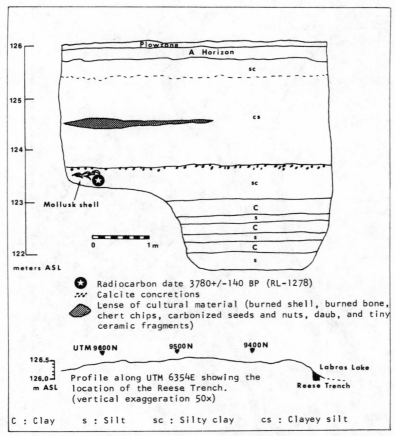

Figure 9. Cross-section of the Reese Trench at the edge
of the interior stream (Labras Creek) now occupied by Labras
Lake.

plowzone truncates the A Horizon and extends to the surface.

The sediments in the bottom of the Reese Trench aggraded while the ancient channel that lies below the Goose Lake meander was active. This interior low-energy channel (Labras Creek) was active then and probably was flowing throughout the Late Archaic occupation sequence at Labras Lake, since the 3,870 year-old-shells were not found at the top of the channel fill, but lie buried beneath two meters of sediment. The cultural materials in the lense 1 meter above the dated shell show that Labras Creek was still active when Early Bluff people inhabited the Labras Lake site around 1040 B.P.; and if Wild's account is accurate, then the spring-fed Labras Creek would still have been flowing past the site in 1841.

The Labras Lake site is situated on a wedge-shaped parcel of land between the Prairie Lake and Goose Lake meander scars and is bounded on the southeast by the Labras Creek paleochannel (figure 8). The relief at the site is only 70 centimeters, with a gentle southwest slope and some barely perceptible ridges and swales that rise a total of 2 meters above the dry floors of the meander scars (Gladfelter 1980a).

The earliest Late Archaic occupation at Labras Lake occurred in the south central area and has been dated to between 3350 and 3800 B.P. It may have been contemporary with the active phase of the channel that is buried beneath the Goose Lake meander (3700 B.P.). More recent Late Archaic occupations at Labras Lake occurred in the northwestern area (3600-3350 B.P.) and the southwestern area (3400-3100 B.P.). These settlements would have been inhabited during the end of the Horseshoe Lake meander sequence, but it is not known if an active channel of the Mississippi River flowed near the Labras Lake site at that time. The last Late Archaic occupation of the site was in the north central area (3250-2800 B.P.), and it may have occurred when the Pittsburg Lake meander was in the last phase of expansion (3000-2500 B.P.), or at the beginning of the Goose Lake meander sequence.

By the time the Early Bluff and Mississippian populations inhabited the Labras Lake site, the surrounding meanders were inactive and occupied by oxbow lakes or marshes. The main channel of the Mississippi River was located 2 kilometers to the west, but Labras Creek still flowed past the southeastern edge of the site, and Prairie duPont Creek may have discharged into Goose Lake.

Summary

The wide Mississippi floodplain opposite St. Louis was created by Pleistocene fluvial processes, but the surface features of the American Bottom are the result of more recent river activities. The widest portion of the floodplain is marked by a broad paleomeander belt that may have erased most of the prehistoric record prior to the Late Archaic period. While channel shifts were common and rapid during meandering phases of the Mississippi River that lasted from at least 4400 B.P. until 2400 B.P., aggradation across the floodplain was minimal.

The Mississippi River shifted from a centrally located sinuous course to a western channel with very little meandering sometime between 2400 and 1100 B.P. The river has remained within a broad and shallow channel that is marked by many interchannel islands and side channels, and it has not wandered more than 2 kilometers east of the base of the Missouri bluffs since that time.

The Late Archaic populations who settled near the eastern margin of the floodplain exploited riverine and lacustrine resources, but they were faced with an ever-shifting river channel and wetlands that were sometimes flooded, sometimes dry. Spring-fed streams flowing out of the bluffs in the southern portion of the American Bottom were probably the most reliable source of the water and may have drawn the hunter-gatherers to these localities where they established base camps intermittently between 4,100 and 2,500 years ago.

Early Woodland populations continued to exploit acquatic resources in backwater areas. These sites date to between 2500 and 2100 B.P. They were often buried by alluvial deposits that covered the point bar and intrachannel ridges and formed the surfaces where Middle Woodland and Late Woodland settlements were established. This period of aggradation is broadly contemporary with the major shift in the Mississippi River channel.

The Early Bluff, Late Bluff, and Mississippian populations who inhabited the floodplain extended from the edge of the interchannel zone to the base of the Illinois bluffs. Wetlands near some of these sites were encroached upon by alluvial fan building on the southern American Bottom, but acquatic resources such as fish and mollusks continued to be exploited and made up the bulk of the faunal remains in samples from both bottomland and upland sites (Cross 1982).

At Labras Lake, the environmental setting changed from riverine to lacustrine, but an interior spring-fed stream remained constant. The available plant and animal resources probably changed more in degree than in kind, with no significant change in average species composition until the Neo-Boreal. However, shifting channels and differential flooding may have caused significant variation in the amount of wild food that was available from one year to the next.

4 Settlement Systems

Current Models

In most of the prehistoric subsistence and settlement models that have been developed for the central Mississippi Valley, it is assumed that the local environment has not changed significantly in the past 6,000 years, and that site function and season of occupation can be deduced from feature and tool morphology, or from site locations within "pre-settlement" biotic zones.

Environmental conditions at the Labras Lake site have not been static for the last six millennia, and the biotic communities that were exploited by Late Archaic, Late Woodland, and Mississippian populations were not identical; nor were they the same as those that have been described by nineteenth-century surveyors and travelers. The channels, backwaters, and interior streams that cross the American Bottom have changed their configurations and flow regimes several times during this period, and animal and plant communities associated with those fluvial systems have responded to the changes.

Chmurney (1973) has shown that several different species of plants and animals that were found in Mississippian contexts at Cahokia were not present on the American Bottom when GLO surveyors visited the area in the early part of the nineteenth century. He attributed their absence to the onset of colder climatic conditions during the Neo-Boreal period, but climatic variation was not the sole cause of environmental change on the American Bottom. Human modification of the landscape (Johannessen 1981) and paleohydrological developments may have also played a role.

Archeological sites that were occupied by Late Archaic and older prehistoric groups may have been destroyed by the shifting channel of the Mississippi River, so settlement distribution data for these prehistoric populations are incomplete. If functional and seasonal aspects of prehistoric settlement systems on the American bottom are to be derived from site location and catchment analysis, rather than, "meager subsistence data" (Emerson 1984), it is necessary that the information on site distribution and available resources is complete and accurate for each occupational phase.

The classification of sites within settlement systems should be based on functional analyses of the features and artifacts present at each type of site, not on subjective evaluations of feature form and tool morphology (cf. Carr 1982; Emerson and McElrath 1983). The classification of archeological features is usually subjective, based on ethnographic analogy and interpretation of the cultural materials that are associated with different types of features. Yet nearly all of the features described in site reports are given functional designations (e.g., hearth, storage/refuse pit, smudge pit, earth oven, etc.)

These feature designations are really morphological, not functional, but the presence or absence of certain types of features is considered diagnostic of certain "kinds" of archeological sites in many settlement models. For example Winters (1969:137) believes that permanent houses, numerous storage pits, and many burials are characteristic of Riverton Culture settlements (which were occupied in the winter), while sites with many clay platforms, but no houses, and few storage pits and burials are classified as summer base camps.

Functional classification of sites within a settlement system should be based on more than the size of each site and the number of features that are present. Classification can be improved if the kinds of activities that went on at each site are determined, and studies of artifact functions are an important step in this process.

The FAI-270 excavations have exposed a nearly unbroken sequence of settlements occupied by Late Archaic hunter-gatherers, plant-tending Woodland groups, and complex Mississippian societies. However, the data obtained during the excavation of these sites have not yet been used to build new models of changing site utilization and cultural evolution on the American Bottom.

The complete cultural sequence for this area is not preserved at Labras Lake, but a functional and ecological analysis of the artifacts, biotic materials, and features in the Late Archaic, Late Woodland, and Mississippian components at the site is presented here in an effort to understand some aspects of the changing settlement and subsistence patterns on the American Bottom during the past 4,000 years.

Late Archaic on the American Bottom

The Late Archaic component at Labras Lake is one of only ten excavated Late Archaic settlements in the American Bottom region (figure 10). Nine of these Late Archaic sites were excavated during the FAI-270 project. They include the Labras Lake, Dyroff, Levin, MoPac #2, Range, Tep, Go-Kart North, McLean, and George Reeves sites. The other Late Arachaic settlement was on the Interpretive Center Trace (ICT), or Museum Tract, of the Cahokia site

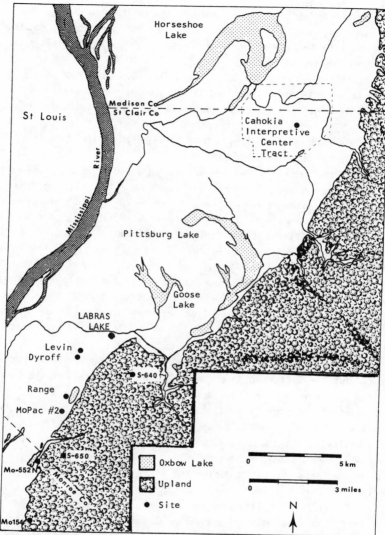

Figure 10. Excavated Late Archaic sites on the American Bottom and adjacent uplands.

(Benchley and DePuydt 1982; Nassaney et al. 1983). The FAI-270 sites have yielded cultural materials and radiocarbon dates that were used to construct a four-phase Late Archaic chronology for the American Bottom that spans the period from 3000 to 600 B.C.

The Falling Springs phase (around 3500 B.C. until 2300 B.C.) is the earliest phase in the chronology, and it is based on a side-notched projectile point complex that was found on the surface of the Falling Springs site (11-S-295). The type site for this phase lies at the base of the Illinois bluffs where a spring still flows out of the limestone cliff face (figure 8), but this site has not been excavated.

Radiocarbon dates from the McLean site (11-S-640), which is located in a bluff-top borrow pit overlooking the American Bottom, and stratigraphic and radiocarbon-dated contexts for similar side-notched points such as the Helton, Matanzas, Godar Side-notched, and Raddatz types found outside of the American Bottom (Brown and Vierra 1983; Cook 1976; Perino 1973; Wiant et al. 1983; Wittry 1959) have been used to establish the time range for the Falling Springs phase.

Shallow side-notched points associated with the Middle Archaic Helton (Cook 1976) and Carrier Mills (Jeffries and Buttler 1982) complexes are usually dated at 3000 B.C. or earlier. However, the dates from the McLean site are 2650 b.c. and 2410 b.c. (table 1), and the Falling Springs phase has been classifed as early Late Archaic (Emerson 1984).

The Titterington focus (Montet-White 1968) is recognized as a mortuary complex, but the Titterington phase (2300-1900 B.C.) refers to the cultural materials that were found without associated burials in radiocarbon-dated contexts at the Go-Kart North side and in undated features at the upland George Reeves site (11-S-650). Large lanceolate and stemmed bifaces of the Etley, Wadlow, and Sedalia types are diagnostic of this phase (Brown and Vierra 1983; Fortier 1984; Perino 1968).

The artifacts recovered during the UIC excavations at the Labras Lake site (Phillips et al. 1980) were used to define the Labras Lake phase (1900-1000 B.C.). The late Archaic assemblage at Labras Lake has been characterized as a variant of the Riverton Culture (Emerson 1984), with small stemmed projectile points similar to the Merom, Trimble Side-notched, and Riverton types defined by Winters (1969).

Springly, Table Rock Stemmed, Smith Basal Notched, and Durst projectile points (Chapman 1975; Harn 1971; Wittry 1959) are characteristic of the Prairie Lake phase on the American Bottom, along with the newly defined Dyroff

TABLE 1. Radiocarbon dates from Late Archaic sites on the American Bottom.

SITE NAME	IAS NUMBER	RCY BP+/-		CALENDAR AGE	LAB. NO.
Tep	(11-Mo-154)	5150	100	3200 b.c.	ISGS-983
McLean	(11-S-640)	4360	120	2410 b.c.	ISGS-730
McLean		4600	75	2650 b.c.	ISGS-736
Go-Kart North	(11-Mo-552N)	4130	75	2150 b.c.	ISGS-697
Go-Kart North		4110	100	2160 b.c.	ISGS-630
Go-Kart North		4100	130	2150 b.c.	ISGS-693
Go-Kart North		4100	75	2150 b.c.	ISGS-698
Go-Kart North		4060	100	2110 b.c.	ISGS-629
Go-Kart North		4060	80	2110 b.c.	ISGS-695
Go-Kart North		4020	100	2070 b.c.	ISGS-628
Cahokia ICT		4570	210	2620 b.c.	Beta-5311
Cahokia ICT		3210	60	1260 b.c.	Beta-5309
Cahokia ICT		3140	100	1190 b.c.	Beta-5307
Cahokia ICT		3110	80	1160 b.c.	Beta-5310
Cahokia ICT		2150	90	200 b.c.*	Beta-5308
Labras Lake	**(11-S-299)**				
South Central Area		3460	140	1510 b.c.	RL-1233
South Central Area		3220	130	1270 b.c.	RL-1294
South Central Area		3120	140	1170 b.c.	RL-1283
Northwestern Area		3220	130	1270 b.c.	RL-1231
Northwestern Area		3180	140	1230 b.c.	RL-1061
Southwestern Area		3020	130	1070 b.c.	RL-1285
Southwestern Area		2910	140	960 b.c.	RL-1357
North Central Area		2900	160	950 b.c.	RL-1292
North Central Area		2880	140	930 b.c.	RL-1291
North Central Area		2670	130	920 b.c.	RL-1287
North Central Area		1510	210	A.D. 440*	RL-1230
Missouri Pacific *2	(11-S-46)	2860	75	910 b.c.	ISGS-601
Missouri Pacific *2		2800	75	850 b.c.	ISGS-588
Missouri Pacific *2		2755	75	805 b.c.	ISGS-605
Missouri Pacific *2		2540	75	590 b.c.	ISGS-599
Range	(11-S-47)	2870	200	920 b.c.	ISGS-1101
Range		1960	70	10 b.c.*	ISGS-913

* Anomalous Date.

SOURCES: Nassaney *et al.* (1983); Phillips *et al.* (1980); Porter (1982, 1983).

point (Emerson 1984), which really may be a resharpened Springly point (Nassaney et al. 1983). Late Archaic features at the MoPac #2, Dyroff, Levin, Range, and Cahokia ICT sites have been assigned to this phase.

Not much can be said about settlement patterns on the American Bottom during Late Archaic times, since only ten sites have been confirmed by excavations, and they fall within four phases that span a total of 2900 years.

The only well-dated sites that fall within the time range of the Falling Springs phase are small bluff-top campsites with clusters of shallow pits. The Tep site (11-Mo-154) has been characterized as a specialized nut-procurement station (Esarey and Moffat 1981); and although a radiocarbon date of 3200 b.c. has been reported from one of the pits at that site, the only projectile points that were found there were Kramer points, a type that is usually associated with Early Woodland cultures (Munson 1971).

The McLean site lies on the bluff top overlooking Labras Lake, and it too has been interpreted as a nut-processing station (McElrath et al. 1980: 113). Only expanding-based projectile points have been found at the McLean site, although the radiocarbon dates from the site fall within the Falling Springs phase (McElrath and Bentz 1981: 63).

Only one Labras Lake phase site and two Titterington phase sites have been excavated; and while five sites have been assigned to the Prairie Lake phase, radiocarbon dates have been reported from only three: MoPac #2, Range, and the Cahokia Interpretive Center Tract (table 1). The seven radiocarbon dates from Go-Kart North are tightly clustered and are not contemporary with any dates from any other Late Archaic site on the American Bottom (figure 11). The lone radiocarbon date from the Late Archaic component at the Range site does not match any other dates either. The temporal span of the dates from Labras Lake, MoPac #2, and the Cahokia Interpretive Center Tract is wider, and several dates do overlap.

Some of the dates from Labras Lake fall within the Prairie Lake phase, and the dates from the Cahokia ICT span the Falling Springs and Labras Lake phases. These dates probably are associated with several occupation episodes at each site, but most of the radiocarbon dates from the Cahokia Museum Tract, Labras Lake, and MoPac #2 fall between 1300 and 600 B.C.

Except for the Cahokia Interpretive Center Tract, all of the excavated Late Archaic sites on the American Bottom are found on the interior margin of the southern portion of the floodplain. These sites are not deeply buried, and it is possible that many contemporary Late Archaic sites that were located adjacent to the meandering Mississippi in the central portion of the floodplain were destroyed by channel shifts that occurred between 4400 and

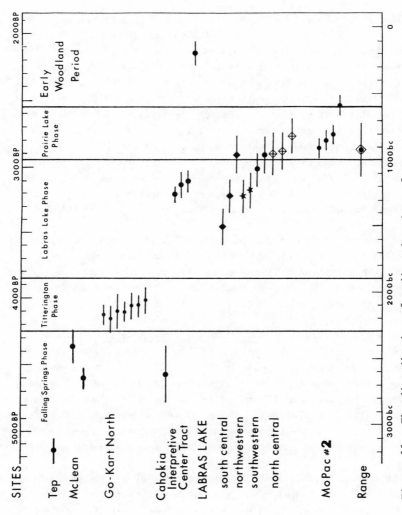

Figure 11. The distribution of radiocarbon dates from Late Archaic sites on the American Bottom and adjacent uplands.

2400 B.P. Consequently, studies of Lake Archaic settlement and subsistence
have been based on data from only a part of the potential settlement system.

Some have suggested that bluff-base sites wre preferred locations for
late Archaic base camps that were established to exploit both upland and
floodplain resources (Emerson 1980; Emerson and McElrath 1983; Fortier 1984).
However, bottomland settings in the paleomeander belt may have been more
productive at that time, since a greater diversity of exploitable species
would have been available there (Lopinot 1983). The analysis of floral
remains from a 400-square-meter area at the Cahokia ICT revealed an
"unusually diverse and very dense" complex of carbonized seeds (Lopinot 1983:
106). The density of seeds per liter of flotation-processed soil at this
floodplain site was 136 and 189 times greater than the seed densities at the
bluff-base MoPac #2 and Dyroff-Levin sites (McElrath and Fortier 1983; Emerson
1984).

The shifting channel of the Mississippi River could have kept vegetation
communities within the meander belt in a constant state of successional
change. The disturbed habitats would have supported more species of
seed-bearing plants with a higher biomass than the "climax" communities found
along the bluff base (Lopinot 1983).

Late Archaic Occupations at the Labras Lake Site

Surface surveys located five Late Archaic "base camps" within a
20.8 hectare area at Labras Lake (Kelly et al. 1979). Two of these habitation
areas were found within the FAI-270 right-of-way, and they were excavated by
crews from the University of Illinois at Chicago during the highway mitigation
program (Phillips et al. 1980). The excavated Late Archaic components at
Labras Lake included a 900-square-meter southwestern area where 94 features
were found, and a 5,800-square-meter central area that contained 185 features
(figure 12).

Late Archaic occupation in the southwestern area extended beyond the
limits of the UIC excavations (budget constraints would not allow the complete
excavation of this component); but a large domestic area (or shelter) was
uncovered, and it was surrounded by two hearths, forty-eight pits, five
artifact concentrations, two smaller domestic areas, and thirty-four postholes
(figure 13). Although Archaic structures are associated with the Middle
Archaic phase (7300-6850 B.P.) at Koster (Brown and Vierra 1983: 184), the
domestic areas in the southwestern component of the Labras Lake site are the
oldest excavated structures on the American Bottom.

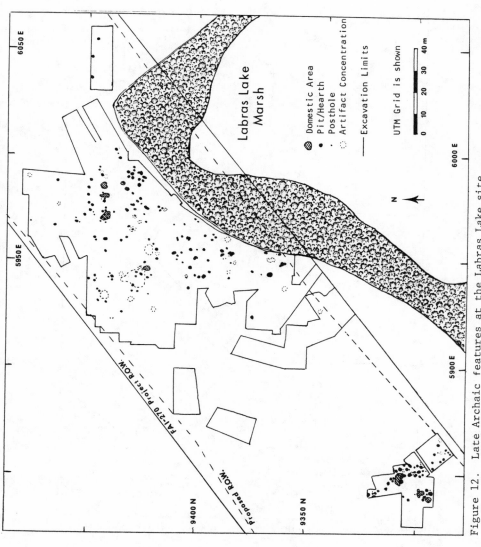

Figure 12. Late Archaic features at the Labras Lake site.

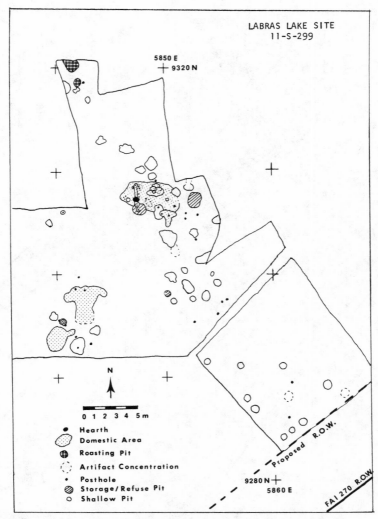

LABRAS LAKE SITE
11-S-299

5850 E
+ 9320 N

N

0 1 2 3 4 5m

● Hearth
Domestic Area
⊕ Roasting Pit
Artifact Concentration
● Posthole
Storage/Refuse Pit
○ Shallow Pit

Proposed R.O.W.

9280 N +
5860 E

FAI 270 R.O.W.

Figure 13.   The southwestern Late Archaic component.

Both of the hearths in this component were found in the southwestern corner of the large domestic area (Feature 1172). The larger hearth (Feature 941) overlies the smaller hearth (Feature 946), and both are superimposed on a trench that runs north-south through the structure (figure 14). Radiocarbon samples were taken from the 53 grams of charred hickory nutshells that were found in the fill of these hearths. A date of 3020+/-130 B.P. (RL-1285) was obtained for the upper hearth, while the lower hearth was dated to 2910+/-140 B.P. (RL-1357). Hall (1986) used the Suess and Clark tree-ring/radiocarbon calibration curves to estimate that the calendar age of the structure in the southwestern area would fall between 1450 and 1150 B.C.

These two radiocarbon dates would place the southwestern area occupation in the last half of the Labras Lake phase. It would postdate the Titterington phase occupation at Go-Kart North by 400 years, and precede the Prairie Lake phase settlements at MoPac #2, Range, and Dyroff-Levin, but it would be contemporary with the Late Archaic settlement at Cahokia, which has been dated to around 1200 B.C. (Nassaney et al. 1983: 109)

Ten projectile points were found in the southwestern area, including a Kramer point (Munson 1971) and a number of stright- or expanding-stemmed forms that resemble Springly points or the assymetrically barbed Dyroff points (Emerson 1984). Straight-stemmed, traingular-bladed points like these have been reported from the MoPac #2, Dyroff-Levin, and Cahokia ICT sites on the American Bottom, and they are commonly found at southern and midwestern sites that were occupied during the end of the Late Archaic period (Emerson 1984).

Floral remains from the southwestern area included 69 grams of burned nutshell, of which 67.2 grams (97%) have been identified as hickory nut (King 1980). Less than 1 gram each of carbonized hazelnut, acorn, and black walnut shell were recovered. It would appear that intensive hickory nut processing was going on at this part of the Labras Lake site. However, several archeologists have suggested that prehistoric groups may have used hickory nuts for fuel as well as a food (Hilliard 1980; McCollough and Faulkner 1976: 236; Wetterstrom 1978: 107).

Lopinot (1982: 729-43) has used experimental carbonization mass reduction data and nutmeat/nutshell ratios to show that a single gram of carbonized acorn shell from an archeological context may represent the "dietary equivalent" in usable nutmeat of anywhere between 5 and 200 grams of carbonized hickory nutshell. Consequently, hickory nutshell is usually overrepresented in archeological floral samples, and the abundance of hickory nut remains in the flotation samples from the southwestern area may not

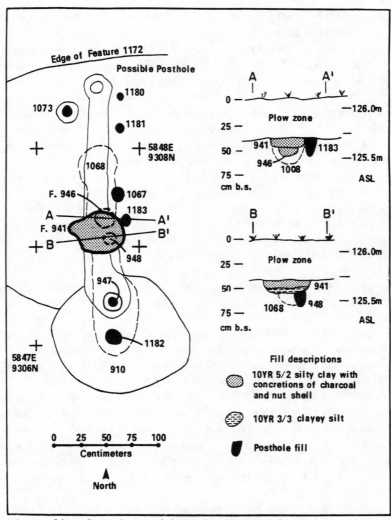

Figure 14.   Superimposed hearths inside of Feature 1172.

indicate a specialized procurement strategy where hickory nuts were selected over other thin-shelled nut species.

Only one nutting stone and a single mano were found in the excavated portion of the southwestern Late Archaic component at Labras Lake, and one might think that more of these artifacts should be present at intensive nut-processing areas. However, at the Cahokia Interpretive Center Tract, where 30.42 grams of carbonized nutshell were found in 18 small pits, no grinding stones, slabs, or manos were recovered (Nassaney et al. 1983:111). The absence of nut-processing tools at Cahokia and their low numbers at the southwestern area of the Labras Lake site may reflect the incomplete excavation of those Late Archaic components rather than the minimal use of such tools by the inhabitants of each settlement. Although hickory nutshell dominated the floral samples at both of these sites, several different species of nuts were represented by carbonized shell fragments, and it is clear that they all contributed to the Late Archaic diet.

Over 10,000 bone fragments were present in flotation samples taken from Late Archaic features at Labras Lake, but only 254 (2%) were found in the southwestern area. The faunal elements were poorly preserved and do not provide much insight into Late Archaic subsistence practices (the only identified element was a sesamoid from a white-tailed deer).

Several different types of features were encountered during the excavation of the southwestern area of the Labras Lake site (figure 13). These included two large, deep "roasting pits" that had oxidized clay along their bases and walls. These roasting pits were oval in plan, with an average length of 85 centimeters and a mean width of 69 centimeters. They were the deepest Late Archaic features at Labras Lake, usually extending 40 centimeters below the base of the plowzone. Their fill was very dark and contained fragments and flecks of ash and hickory charcoal and charred hickory and black walnut husks. Phillips (1986) has suggested that the roasting pits were used to boil nuts for oil, but he noted that no fire-cracked rock was found in or near these pits. It is not clear if stone boiling was actually going on, or if the pits were used as earth ovens where other foods were roasted, and the nutshells served as fuel in the process.

Five deep pits were encountered in the southwestern area. These were round, with a mean diameter of 73 centimeters. They were slightly shallower than the roasting pits, with a mean depth of 26 centimeters. The size of these features, their depth, and the variety and density of cultural materials found in their fill set them apart from the other Late Archaic features at

Labras Lake. These deep pits have been labeled storage/refuse pits, since they contain garbage that was probably burned after deposition. However, the storage function is conjectural (Phillips 1980: 53). Similar features found at other Late Archaic sites on the American Bottom have been called "deep pits" (Emerson 1984: 232) or "flat-bottomed pits" (McElrath and Fortier 1983; Nassaney et. al. 1983).

Forty-one shallow pits were found in this area of the site. These were the most common type of Late Archaic feature at Labras Lake, MoPac #2, Dyroff-Levin, the Cahokia Interpretive Center Tract, and Range. They had a mean diameter of 68 centimeters, although they often were amorphous in plan, and their average depth was 20 centimeters. It is difficult to interpret the functions of these features, since they do not contain many artifacts. There is no evidence that they were used as garbage pits, and there are no apparent correlations between the size and shape of these pits and their material contents (Emerson 1984; Nasasney et al. 1983; Phillips 1986).

Five artifact concentrations were present in the southwest area. They are large scatters of cultural debris with no evidence of prehistoric subsurface excavation. The two hearths in the southwestern area contained the nutshell used in the radiocarbon dating of this components. These features were not stone-or clay-lined "prepared" hearths, but shallow depressions containing charcoal, burned nutshell, or seeds. No burned faunal remains were present in the two hearths.

Most of these features were found within or near the four domestic areas in the southwestern area. Domestic areas may have been open-air or roofed-over structures that were occupied by extended families of hunter-gatherers (Phillips 1986). The largest domestic area (Feature 1172) is 562 centimeters long and 288 centimeters wide. It extends nearly 50 centimeters below the plowzone in places. The other domestic areas are much smaller (figure 13), and Phillips (1986) has argued that this pattern of large and small domestic areas in the same feature cluster is reminiscent of extended family base camps where smaller structures were occupied by adolescents who were separated from the main family dwelling (Gould 1980). Or the small domestic areas may have been inhabited by other group members who were present at the site for shorter periods of time.

Lithic artifacts were found in all types of features, but most of the tools and unretouched blanks were recoved from the fill of roasting pits, storage/refuse pits, or domestic areas, where the lithic debris was concentrated in hearths and artifact scatters (table 2). Stone tool

TABLE 2. The distribution of lithic artifacts among different types of features in the southwestern Late Archaic area at the Labras Lake site.

FEATURE TYPE (n)	TOOLS NO.	%	BLANKS NO.	%	DEBRIS NO.	%	TOTAL LITHICS NO.	%	MEAN NO.PER FEA.
Hearth (2)	0	–	7	1%	112	4%	119	4%	60
Pits:									
Storage/Refuse (5)	6	8%	27	5%	87	4%	120	4%	24
Roasting (2)	11	15%	87	17%	141	6%	239	8%	120
Shallow (41)	39	52%	257	51%	1268	52%	1582	51%	38
Domestic Area (4)	11	15%	61	12%	176	7%	248	8%	62
Artifact Concentration (5)	7	9%	63	13%	660	26%	730	24%	146
Posthole (34)	1	1%	2	1%	23	1%	26	1%	<1
TOTALS: (94*)	75	100%	504	100%	2485	100%	3064	100%	32

FEATURE TYPE	TOOLS	%	BLANKS	%	DEBRIS	%	TOTAL LITHICS	
Hearths	0	–	7	6%	112	94%	119	100%
Storage/Refuse Pits	6	5%	27	23%	87	72%	120	100%
Roasting Pits	11	5%	87	36%	141	59%	141	100%
Shallow Pits	39	3%	257	16%	1286	81%	1582	100%
Domestic Areas	11	4%	61	25%	176	71%	248	100%
Artifact Concentrations	7	1%	63	9%	660	90%	730	100%
Postholes	1	4%	2	8%	23	88%	26	100%

* The feature total (94) includes a trench found inside Feature 1172 that did not contain any lithic artifacts.

manufacturing and resharpening seem to have occured around the hearths and outside of the domestic areas, where the chips and chunks accumulated, while the larger retouched and unretouched implements were discarded in the deeper pits and inside of the domestic areas.

The roasting pits were both located northwest of Feature 1172, while the storage/refuse pits were all found near the domestic areas. The artifact concentrations were either inside of Feature 1172, or to the southeast (figure 13).

An artifact concentration and a shallow pit located southeast of Feature 1172 each contained over 200 lithic items, and one other artifact concentration in this area contained over 100 chipped stone artifacts. Both of the artifact scatters were about 1 meter in diameter.

These features probably are associated with lithic manufacturing and retooling. Several cores, broken cores, hammerstones, and anvil stones were found there, along with the highest concentration of lithic debris in the southwestern Late Archaic component.

Half of the projectile points found in the southwestern area came from this area. A complete Kramer point was found in the fill of a shallow pit (Feature 283), and four projectile point bases were discarded there, suggesting that darts were being rearmed in this lithic retooling area (cf. Keeley 1982).

Matches and refits between chipped stone artifacts found in the retooling area and the cluster of pits around Feature 1172 indicate that the two areas were occupied at the same time. Two domestic areas (Features 768 and 778) are located southwest of Feature 1172, and they are linked to the large domestic area by lithic refits and matches (figure 15). There were no refits or matches between the lithics in features that lie north of the large domestic area and any of the other features in the southwestern area. While it is possible that the northern features are temporally as well as spatially separate from other features in the southwestern area, further excavation will be needed to demonstrate this.

The southwestern Late Archaic component has been described as a base camp (Phillips 1986) or a base locale (Emerson 1984), where a band of hunter-gatherers resided for many months of the year and exploited the wild food resources of the floodplain and adjacent uplands. When this base camp was occupied, a spring-fed stream flowed past its southern margin, and an abandoned channel of the Mississippi River (the Prairie Lake meander scar) was located nearby (to the west). An active river channel (the Pittsburg Lake meander) was located about 1.5 kilometers to the northeast at that time.

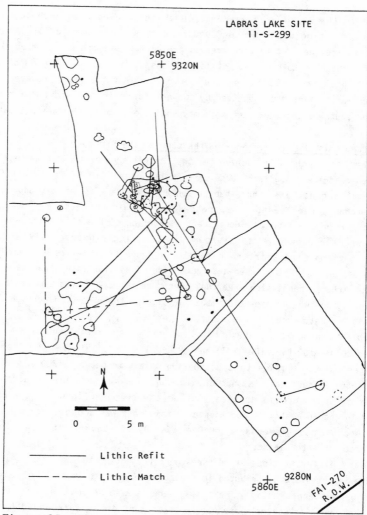

Figure 15. Matches and refits between lithic artifacts
in the southwestern Late Archaic component.

The southwestern area was only inhabited during Late Archaic times, possibly at a time when the surrounding area was somewhat drier than the present (since the southwestern area is presently lower and wetter than the rest of the Labras Lake site). It is also possible that Late Archaic bands only occupied the site during the drier months of the year. However, many different activities are suggested by the artifacts in the microwear sample from the southwestern area, and this may indicate a more sedentary occupation.

Late Archaic in the Central Area of the Labras Lake Site

The Late Archaic component in the central area of the Labras Lake site has been described as a large base camp (Kelly et al. 1979; Phillips 1980), but there are at least three habitation areas there (figure 16), and each of these probably represents a separate Late Archaic occupation (Yerkes and Philips in press). In the north central portion of the site, three domestic areas are surrounded by fifty-four pits, a single hearth, six artifact concentrations, and thirteen postholes (figure 17). Refits between lithic artifacts, and matches between artifacts made of similar lithic raw materials, link together a habitation area that covers nearly 2,400 square meters, or an area more than two-and-one-half times the size of the excavated portion of the southwestern Late Archaic component.

Three radiocarbon dates from features in the north central area range between 2670+/-130 B.P. (RL-1287) and 2900+/-160 B.P. (RL-1292). Tree-ring calibration would place this occupation at a time between 1300 and 850 B.C. (Hall 1986). These dates span the late Labras Lake and early Prairie Lake phases of the proposed American Bottom chronology (figure 11), and would placed the north central occupation at a time that was contemporary with the Late Archaic settlements at MoPac #2, Dyroff-Levin, and the Cahokia Interpretive Center Tract.

Many different types of features were present in the north central area, and the features are distributed in a pattern similar to what was observed in the southwestern area (figure 17). There is a large domestic area (Feature 171) that contains several internal features, and it is surrounded by pits, artifact concentrations, and two smaller domestic areas.

Several roasting pits lie to the north of the central household cluster, while shallow pits, storage/refuse pits, and some more roasting pits are clustered to the south. The only hearth in the north central area is located inside of the largest domestic area, Feature 171; just as the only hearths in the southwestern area were found inside Feature 1172, the largest domestic area in that component.

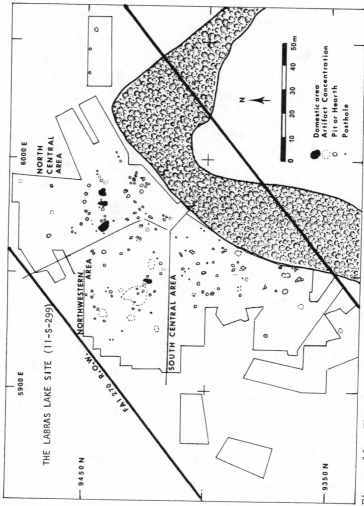

Figure 16. The three Late Archaic components in the central excavation block.

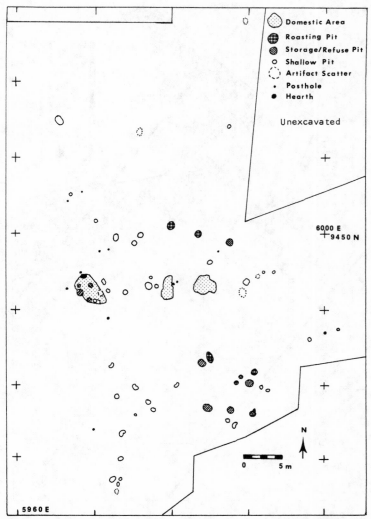

Figure 17. Late Archaic features in the north central area.

The north central Late Archaic component probably represents another base camp, similar to the one in the southwestern area. The same sorts of floral and faunal remains were present in both areas: hickory nuts were very common, but black walnuts, hazelnuts, and acorns were also present. Carbonzied seeds were found only in two superimposed storage/refuse pits located south of the three domestic areas. The circular pit, feature 879, contained two knotweed seeds (Polygonum erectum), while the oblong pit that was superimposed on it (feature 889) contained three seeds identified as marshelder (Iva annua). No manos or metates were found in the north central area, and only a few anvil/nutting stones were recovered.

While 1,840 bone fragments were unearthed in the north central area (18% of the total number of Late Archaic faunal remains), only white-tailed deer and turtle elements could be identified from the poorly preserved remains (Purdue and Styles 1980).

The Northwestern Late Archaic Component

A single domestic area is located in the northwestern portion of the central excavation block at the Labras Lake site, and three very large artifact concentrations lie near this structure, along with nine hearths, twenty-one pits, six small artifact scatters, and fourteen postholes (figure 18). There were more hearths (burned areas) and artifact concentrations in the northwestern area than there were in the southwestern and north central areas of the Labras Lake site. The distribution of the features in this cluster does not resemble the patterns that were observed in the other Late Archaic habitation areas.

The northwestern lithic assemblage contains more bifacial tools than the stone tool collections from other Late Archaic components, and plant-processing tools such as manos, metates, and nutting stones are absent. Floral and faunal remains were especially scarce, with less than 10 grams of recovered floral material. Only forty-four faunal elements (0.4% of the Late Archaic total) were found in the northwestern area.

This component may have served as a functionally distinct activity area where the inhabitants of the north central households went to manufacture and repair chipped stone tools. However, radiocarbon dates of 3180+/-140 B.P. (RL-1061) and 3220+/-130 B.P. (RL-1231) were obtained from features in the northwestern area, and when these dates are calibrated, they place the occupation at a time between 1650 and 1400 B.C., at least a century before the north central Late Archaic was inhabited.

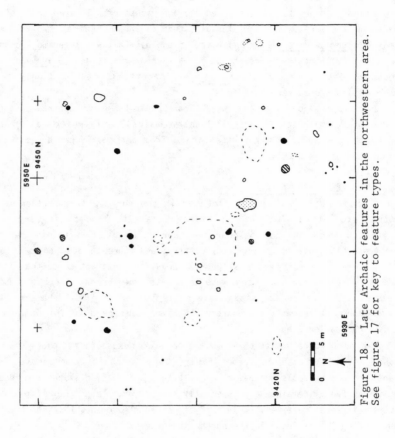

Figure 18. Late Archaic features in the northwestern area.
See figure 17 for key to feature types.

The occupation of the northwestern component would be contemporary with the Riverton Culture, which flourished in the Wabash Valley between 1700 and 1450 B.C. (Hall 1986; Winters 1969). While there is little variation between the point types found in each of the Late Archaic occupation areas at Labras Lake, variants of the Trimble side-notched and Merom expanding-stemmed projectile points associated with the Riverton Culture are the most common point types in the northwestern assemblage. This area seems to be temporarlly and spatially distinct from the other Late Archaic habitations at the site, and it shows some stylisitic affinity with the Riverton Culture.

The nine hearths in the northwestern area do not seem to have been used for food preparation. It is more likely that they were used to heat-treat chert artifacts. More than three-quarters of the implements in the northwestern microwear sample showed evidence of thermal alteration (76%), while only 56% of the southwestern artifacts, 60% of the north central sample, and 58% of the south central lithics seem to have been heat-treated. The high incidence of thermally altered lithics, the feature morphology and distribution, the few tasks represented in the microwear sample, and the scarcity of floral and faunal remains all suggest that the northwestern area of the Labras Lake site was mainly used as a lithic workshop during the later part of the Labras Lake phase.

The South Central Late Archaic Habitation Area

The third Late Archaic component in the central excavation block at Labras Lake covers about 2,200 square meters, but there are no domestic areas or structures present (figure 19). However, some twenty-eight pits, three hearths, four artifact concentrations, and fifteen postholes were excavated in this area. Radiocarbon dates from features in the south central area bracket the occupation at some time between 1850 and 1400 B.C. (Hall 1986), broadly contemporary with the northwestern Late Archaic component at Labras Lake and the Riverton Culture dates, and the nine projectile points and point fragments that were found in the area are similar to the Riverton types.

Most of the features in the south central area were shallow pits, with few hearths or deep storage/refuse pits present. Roasting pits were not found in the area. The features were dispersed, but circular arrangements of pits can be seen in plans of this area (figure 19). Carbonized hickory, hazelnut, acorn, and black walnut husks were present in these features, but few seeds or seed-processing implements such as manos and metates were present. The high density of bone fragments in flotation samples taken from the features in the

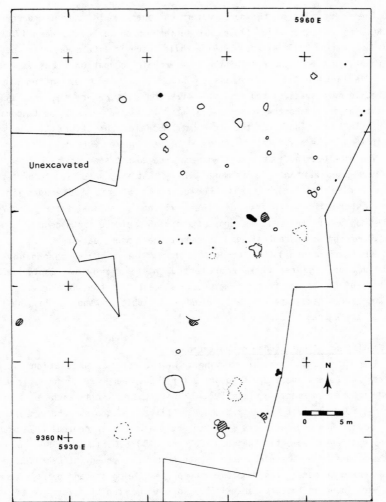

Figure 19. Late Archaic features in the south central area. See figure 17 for key to feature types.

south central component suggests that hunting and meat processing were the primary activities conducted in this area.

The Late Woodland Occupation at Labras Lake

There is a hiatus of some 1,650 years betwen the last Late Archaic occupation at Labras Lake and the Late Woodland habitation episode. Early Woodland settlements were located near Labras Lake on the point bars of the Goose Lake meander and on the bank of the Hill Lake paleochannel; and Middle Woodland groups also inhabited the interchannel ridges of the Hill Lake scar and nearby bluff tops (figure 20); but the only evidence for human habitation in the Labras Lake and Prairie Lake areas are some possible Early Woodland features at the Range site.

The Late Woodland occupation at Labras Lake consisted of ten pits, a single hearth, one artifact scatter, and three postholes that were found on the fine sandy silt ridge that rises slightly above the modern Labras Lake marsh (figures 21,22). While these features covered an area of only 40 square meters, they contained a variety of cultural and biological materials.

The 19 rim sherds and 277 body sherds in the Late Woodland ceramic assemblage have been classified as late Early Bluff (Hall 1980). Charcoal from one of the Early Bluff pits has been radiocarbon dated to 1040+/-100 B.P. (RL-1234), and this date was MASCA corrected to A.D. 920+/-100. This is compatible with two reported radiocarbon dates from the nearby Early Bluff Stolle Quarry site, which had a similar ceramic assemblage (Hall 1975). The dates from the bluff-top Stolle Quarry site were 1230+/-110 B.P. (M-1684) and 1050+/-110 B.P. (M-1683), and when they are averaged with the date from Labras Lake, the MASCA corrected mean is A.D. 870 (Hall 1986). This corrected date is too young for the Late Woodland Patrick phase, which lasts from A.D. 600 until A.D. 800 in the new American Bottom chronology, and would fall within the Emergent Mississippian Dohack phase (Porter 1983).

However, the Early Bluff ceramics from Stolle Quarry and Labras Lake are not Emergent Mississippian. They consist of cordmarked jars and bowls with inslanted or incurved rims, rounded shoulders, and round or conoidal bases (figure 23). There were no decorated Late Woodland rim sherds from Labras Lake, but 43% of the Stolle Quarry rims were stamped on the inner lip. All of the rims from both sites were cordmarked to the rim (Hall 1980). There were no shell-tempered sherds in the Late Woodland ceramic assemblage from Labras Lake, but 5% of the grit- and/or grog-tempered sherds from Stolle Quarry were slipped on the interior or exterior with a mixture of clay and crushed shell (Hall 1980:377-78)

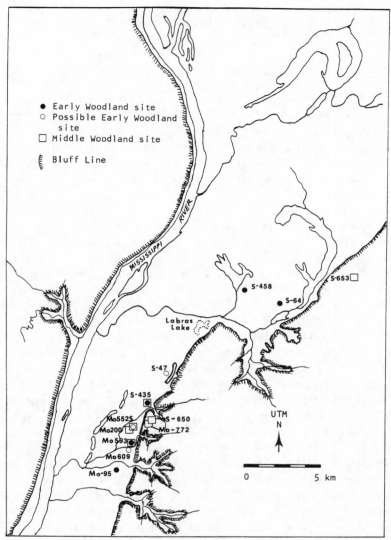

Figure 20. Excavated Early Woodland and Middle Woodland sites on the American Bottom and adjacent uplands.

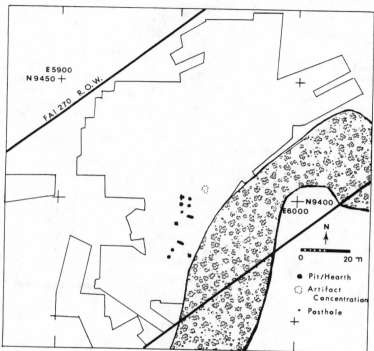

Figure 21.   The Late Woodland component at Labras Lake.

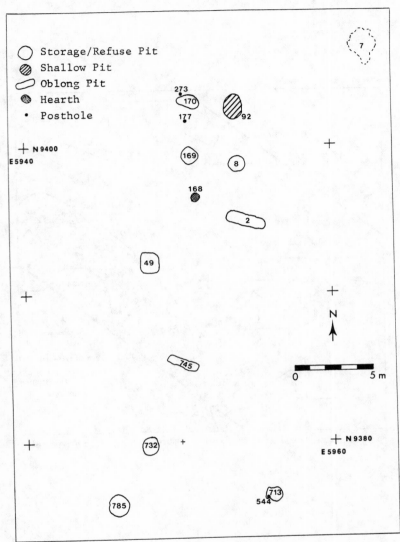

Figure 22. Late Woodland features.

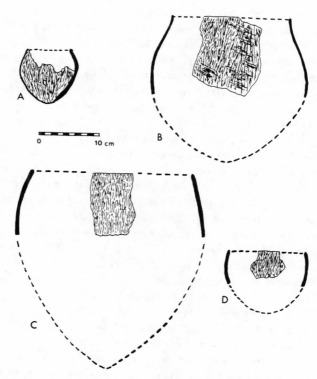

Figure 23. Examples of Late Woodland cordmarked sherds from Labras Lake. A. Grog tempered sherds found in Features 7, 8, and 169; B. Sand/grit/grog tempered sherds from Feature 732; C. Sand/grog tempered sherd from Feature 713; D. Grog tempered sherd from Feature 170.

One of the criteria that Munson (1971) used to define the Early Bluff and Late Bluff phases on the American Bottom was the shape of the cords that were passed onto the surface of cordmarked ceramics. Almost all of the cordmarked sherds in Early Bluff pottery collections showed S-twists, while Z-twists were re common in Late Bluff ceramic assemblages. The S-twist was noted on 97% of the Late Woodland cordmarked sherds from Labras Lake, and 90% of the Stolle Quarry sherds showed S-twists (Hall 1980). At the Schlemmer site (11-S-382), which lies about 4 kilometers southwest of Labras Lake on a ridge adjacent to the Prairie Lake meander scar, 91% of the Patrick phase cordmarked sherds had the S-twist (Kelly 1980; Porter and Szuter 1978).

Stumpware and Late Bluff jars with cordmarked bodies but plain necks and rims were not found at Labras Lake and Stolle Quarry. On stylistic grounds, the ceramic assemblage from the Late Woodland component at Labras Lake certainly belongs in the Patrick phase. However, the post-A.D. 800 dates from Labras Lake, Stolle Quarry site, and the Patrick phase Hilltop site, which is located on the bluffs above the confluence of the Missouri and Mississippi rivers (Kelly 1980: 20), indicate that the Early Bluff ceramic tradition lasted longer than was previously thought (Hall 1986).

The presence of hoe chips and burned limestone at small Early Bluff sites on the American Bottom has been cited as evidence for maize cultivation at these sites even though charred corn fragments are extremely rare (Kelly et al. 1979). It is believed that the hoe flakes are evidence for cultivation, and that corn was boiled in a solution that was made from the burned limestone (Katz et al. 1974; Porter 1974). The reworked hoe fragment was the only artifact in the Early Bluff assemblage from Labras Lake that had "corn gloss" on its edges, but Feature 7, an artifact concentration, contained 8.52 kilograms of limestone. This may suggest agricultural activities, but the limestone was not burned, and it may have been used for other purposes, such as dehairing hides or processing nuts (Porter 1974: 89). There were no limestone-tempered Early Bluff ceramics at Labras Lake, so carbonate rock did not seem to have been used in pottery production at that site.

Johannessen has argued that the Late Woodland (Early Bluff) Rosewood Mund, and Patrick phase floral assemblages from the American Bottom are characterized by abundant evidence for a well-established gardening complex, which included both native and non-native cultigens" (1983: 25). She included wild starchy seeds such as maygrass (Phalaris caroliniana), goosefoot (Chenopodium sp.), and knotweed (Polygonum erectum) in this complex, along with the native domesticate, marsh elder (Iva annua), and exotic cultigens like squash (Curcurbita sp.) and tobacco (Nicotiana rustica), but not maize.

The plant remains that were recovered from the fill of Early Bluff features at Labras Lake included many of the species in the Early Bluff gardening complex described by Johannessen. The identified varieties were goosefoot, marsh elder, smartweed (Polygonum persicaria), summac (Rhus sp.), some grasses (maygrass?), and several small seeds belonging to the pea family. Hickory nuts and hazelnuts were also recovered along with a total of 0.2 grams of carbonized maize (King 1980).

Two ground stone celts found in a storage/refuse pit (Feature 170) may be further evidence for Early Bluff gardening at Labras Lake. These celts may have served as the bits in adzes that were used to clear trees from garden plots in a system of slash-and-burn cultivation or wild plant tending (Kelly 1980: 47).

Some 686 bone fragments were recovered from the excavated or flotation-processed fill of the fifteen Early Bluff features at Labras Lake; and 103 of these (15%) were classified as mammal, while 25 fish bones were present (4%), and 1 turtle bone was recovered (0.15%). White-tailed deer and muskrat were the only mammalian species that could be recognized, while the identified freshwater fish were bowfin, bullheads, and sunfish species. Freshwater mussels were represented by 26 unidentifiable shell fragments, but over 77% of the bone recovered from the Late Woodland features could not even be identified to vertebrate classes.

Keyhole structures have been reported in Patrick phase components at the Range and Fish Lake (11-Mo-608) sites on the American Bottom (Fortier et al. 1984; Kelly 1982); and similar structures have been found to the east at the Hatchery West (Binford et al. 1970) and Daugherty-Monroe (Pace and Apfelstadt 1978) Late Woodland sites, and even further east in Pennsylvania (Smith 1976). These structures generally have small rectangular rooms, narrow ramps that extend eastward out from the rooms, and shallow pits at the end of the ramps. Smith (1976) thinks keyhole structures were specialized sweat lodges, where water was poured over heated limestone in the pit, producing steam that traveled down the domed ramps to the sunken rooms. Fortier believes the keyhole structures on the American Bottom functioned as winter habitation units, not sweat lodges (1984: 81).

Another type of Early Bluff structure, rectangular pithouses with single postholes, were encountered in Patrick phase settlements at Cahokia and Stolle Quarry (Fowler and Hall 1975; Hall and Vogel 1963), and in Early Bluff settlements at the Mund and MoPac #2 sites (Porter 1980). However, several excavated Early Bluff sites located on the American Bottom and adjacent bluffs contained clusters of pits, but no structures (Kelly 1980: 21). The Schlemmer, Linkeman, and Julien sites are examples of this type of Early Bluff settlement (Bareis and Munson 1973; Milner 1983; Szuter 1978); and the Early Bluff feature configuration at Labras Lake fits this pattern.

While a hearth, an artifact scatter, and three postholes were included in the Early Bluff components at Labras Lake (figure 22), most of the features were pits; and three different types of pits have been defined: oblong pits, storage/refuse pits, and shallow pits.

The two oblong pits are long and narrow, with flat bottoms and straight sides. Some human cranial fragments were found in Feature 745, and it is possible that these pits were graves. Similar features were found at the Schlemmer site, and they contained poorly preserved human skeletal remains (Szuter 1978).

The two oblong pits flanked a rectangular storage/refuse pits with straight sides and a flat bottom (Feature 49). The other six Early Bluff storage/refuse pits at Labras Lake were circular or oval in plan, with rectangular or bell-shaped cross sections. Most of the cultural material assigned to the Patrick phase component came from these storage/refuse pits, or from Feature 7, the lone artifact concentration. The only shallow pit in the cluster (Feature 92), the oblong pits, the hearth, and the postholes did not contain much refuse.

Lithic and ceramic refits tie together most of the northern features in the Early Bluff component; but refits or cross-mends are lacking between the northern and southern features (figure 24). Nonetheless, it appears that the Early bluff component represents a short-term occupation of the site around A.D. 900 by a single household. Microwear analysis indicated that a variety of domestic activities went on at the site during the period of habitation, and that hunting was as important as plant processing.

The meager faunal remains suggest that the Early Bluff inhabitants of the Labras Lake site exploited more aquatic animal species than the earlier Late Archaic occupants; while the plant remains indicate that starchy seeds were an important part of their diet (Johannessen 1983).

If the keyhole structures found at some other Patrick phase sites on the American Bottom are really winter houses, then their absence at Labras Lake, Schlemmer, and Julien could mean these sites were only occupied during the warmer months of the year.

It is also possible that Patrick phase sites without structures represent a different type of settlement that the larger communities where many keyhole features and single-post structures were present. Finney (1985: 57) characterized Early Bluff sites with pit clusters, but no dwellings, as extractive camps where the artifact assemblages should reflect an orientation toward limited numbers of resources and a seasonal occupation.

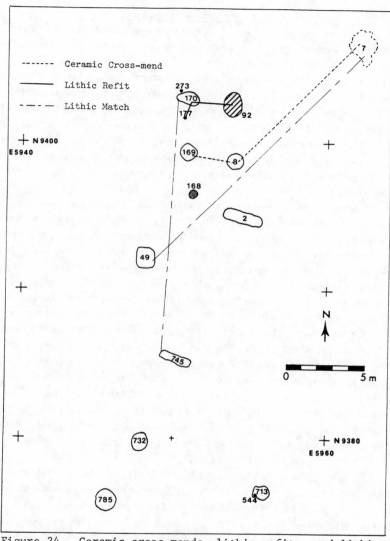

Figure 24. Ceramic cross-mends, lithic refits, and lithic matches between Late Woodland features at Labras Lake.

The Mississippian Component at the Labras Lake Site

The UIC excavations at the Labras Lake site exposed eight structures and 165 features that were assigned to the Mississippian component. There were at least six rectangular wall-trench houses and two small circular wall-trench structures at the site, along with thirty-two storage/refuse pits, fifty-two shallow pits, eleven hearths or burned areas, six artifact concentrations, and eight-five postholes (figure 25). Some special-purpose features were also discovered, including a nut-processing pit (Feature 16) and a smudge pit (Feature 140). A single wall trench was exposed near the three centrally-located wall-trench houses, and it may have been part of another structure, or the trench and surrounding postholes may represent some other type of feature (figure 26).

The ceramics that were associated with these features included plain and incised shell-tempered jars with angled or rolled rims classified as Powell Plain or Ramey Incised; shell-tempered tecomate or "seed jar" forms, effigy bowls, plain bowls, bottles, and jars of the type Cahokia Red Filmed; wide-necked shell-tempered bottles classifed as St. Clair Plain; and several shell-tempered beakers, black bowls, plain jars, and jars with handles.

Limestone-tempered wares included Pulcher Cordmarked and Pulcher Plain jars, and Monks Mound Red bowls and jars. Sherds from a grog-tempered Merrell Red Filmed bowl were also present along with a polished black grog-tempered jar. Smooth, polished, and red-filmd sherds from vessels that were engraved or finely incised and tempered with fine grog and fine shell were found in three houses and one storage/refuse pit in the Labras Lake Mississippian component. This ware has been called "Caddoan" by some Cahokia archaeologists, but Hall (1980: 371) notes that the term should not be taken too literally. Similar ceramics have been found at other Mississippian sites on the American Bottom, and have been classified as tradeware from the Lower Mississippi Valley (Milner et al. 1984).

The ceramics associated with the Mississippian settlement at Labras Lake are mainly "Old Village" or "Early Mississippian" types that are now placed in the Stirling phase (A.D. 1050-1150) of the Cahokia ceramic chronology (Fowler and Hall 1975; Milner et al. 1984). Stumpware, juice presses, and hooded water bottles were not found at Labras Lake, and neither were the wide-rimmed or narrow-rimmed plate forms. The Fairmount and Lohmann phase ceramics that were present in the Labras Lake assemblage were in the minority, and there is about ten times as much shell-tempered as limestone-tempered pottery in the collection (Hall 1980: 368).

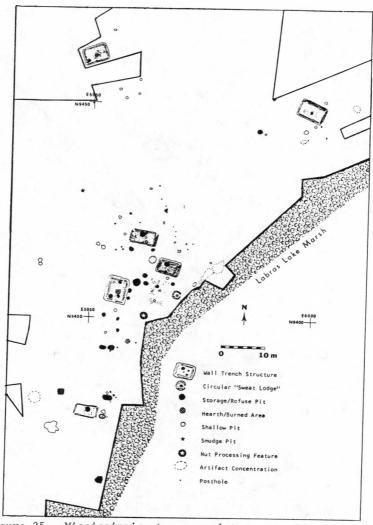

Figure 25. Mississippian houses and features at Labras Lake.

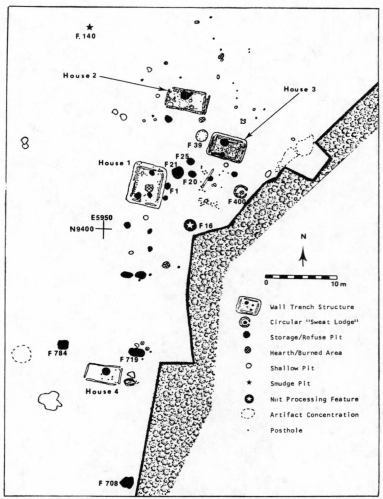

Figure 26. The central cluster of Mississippian houses and features.

Ten radiocarbon samples were taken from Mississippian features at Labras Lake and processed by Radiocarbon Ltd. The raw carbon dates were corrected for periodic variations in the amount of Carbon-14 originally available in the atmosphere by means of the University of Pennsylvania MASCA conversion charts (Ralph et al. 1973). Robert Hall (1986) employed several other correction factors in the analysis of the radiocarbon dates from the Labras Lake site. Hall normalized dates taken on carbonized maize for variations in isotopic content as determined by Carbon-13/Carbon-12 ratios, and he examined the variance ratio (F-test) between the mean variance of a series of radiocarbon dates and the variance among the dates in that series.

The ten uncorrected radiocarbon dates from the Labras Lake Mississippian component ranged from 1030+/-110 B.P. (RL-1284) to 630+/-110 B.P. (RL-1289). However, when the ten dates are placed in chronological order, their distribution approximates the cumulative probability distribution for a series of ten radiocarbon dates with a mean counting error (standard deviation) of +/-121 years (figure 27). The corrected radiocarbon dates from Labras Lake show that the Mississippian occupation lasted for several generations before and after the calendar date A.D. 1235.

This is nearly a century later than the end of the Stirling phase at Cahokia (A.D. 1050-1150), but this discrepancy may be due to errors in the typological dating of the Labras Lake Mississippian component, problems with the time frame for the Cahokia ceramic chronology, or to some combination of errors (Hall 1986). The range of fifteen uncorrectred radiocarbon dates from twelve Stirling phase features at three other sites in the American Bottom region was A.D. 890 to A.D. 1320 (Milner et al. 1984). This suggests that Stirling phase materials were in use at sites in this area prior to A.D. 1050 and after A.D. 1150.

It must be remembered that the time frame for the Stirling phase (as well as the other Cahokia ceramic phases) is based on limited excavations at a few localities within the Cahokia site limits and at a handfull of outlying sites on the American Bottom (Fowler and Hall 1975). It is possible that the ceramic assemblage that has been used to characterize the Stirling phase developed at a different rate at different parts of Cahokia, and at outlying sites. New interpretations of ceramic changes and cultural developments in the Cahokia settlement system must allow for the time-transgressive nature of these changes or fall victim to Hall's "blind men and the elephant" situation where "one's impression of Cahokia (or the Stirling phase) can be conditioned by the particular situation obtaining in the area of the site where one has worked" (Hall 1975: 25).

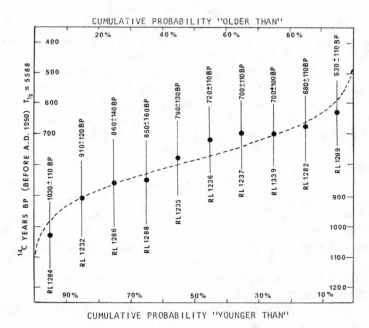

Figure 27. Distribution of ten radiocarbon dates from the
Mississippian component at Labras Lake compared to a cumulative probability ogive curve based on mean counting error
for the dates shown (after Hall 1986).

    Three of the six Mississippian wall-trench houses at Labras Lake; the two
circular structures; and most of the Mississippian pits, hearths, and
post-holes were clustered on a sandy silt ridge in the middle of the central
excavation block (figure 25).   Three additional Mississippian wall-trench
structures, each with several surrounding features, were located some distance
from this central cluster to the north, northeast, and south.   No
Mississippian features were found between the outlying houses and the central
house and feature cluster, and it is not known if all of these structures were
occupied at the same time.   Several ceramic cross-mends and lithic refits tie
together the houses and features in the central cluster, but there is only one

link between any of the outlying houses and the central group (figure 28). A single lithic refit ties House 4 to a pit near House 3 (Feature 797), and a match between lithic materials in the fill of House 3 and House 4 may also link those structures. There were no refits or cross-mends between any of the houses or features in the central area and House 5 or House 6. Sherds from House 4 and House 5 have been cross-mended however, and there are several matches between the lithics in House 5 and House 6. The absence of refit links between the households on the sandy silt ridge and the outlying houses does not prove that they were not contemporary. The patern of house location at Labras Lake may reflect segregation along social or kinship lines, with one kin group living in the central area while single families occupied the outlying households. Or the function of the houses may vary, with certain houses serving as dwellings or sleeping quarters while specific tasks were performed in the other structures.

Norris (1978) has suggested that different types of Mississippian houses were occupied by the same social group during different seasons of the year at the Lily Lake site (11-S-341). The Stirling phase occupation at the Lily Lake site (which is approximately 1.5 kilometers north of Labras Lake) consists of rectangular, semisubterranean pithouses with single posts that Norris believes were inhabited in the winter, and of shallow, rectangular wall-trench structures that Norris calls summer houses (1978: 32-33).

Rectangular, single-post houses are quite rare at the other excavated Stirling phase sites on the American Bottom, where over 90% of the structures were wall-trench houses (Milner et al. 1984). However, at sites occupied during the preceding Lohmann phase (A.D. 1000-1050), equal numbers of single-post and wall-trench houses were present (Esarey with Good 1981). A lack of radiocarbon dates and the paucity of seasonal information provided by floral and faunal remains from the structures at the Lily Lake site make it difficult to determine if the two types of Mississippian house were occupied by different social groups or if they represent winter and summer houses.

Small sites like Lily Lake and Labras Lake are the basic units in Fowler's (1978) Cahokia Settlement System and Porter's (1974) American Bottom settlement model. Fowler's system has Cahokia, the first-line community, as the seat of political, economic, and religious power in the Mississippian hierarchy of settlements.

Large sites (greater than 50 hectares) with several platform mounds are classified as second-line communities. Examples of these would be the Lundsford-Pulcher site, the East St. Louis or Metro site, the St. Louis mound

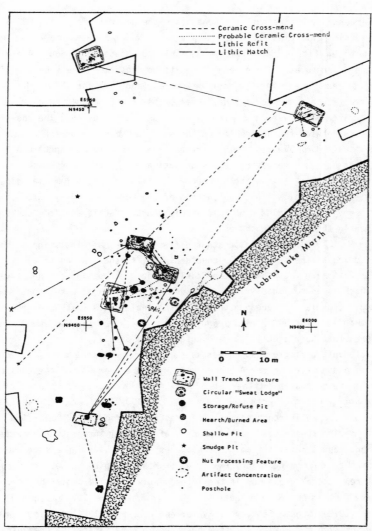

Figure 28. Refits and cross-mends between Mississippian features and houses at Labras Lake.

group, and the Mitchell site. These temple towns were all in direct communication with the Mississippi River (Fowler 1978: 472).

The third-line communities in Fowler's model are sites with single mounds that are usually located adjacent to oxbow lakes or sloughs. These may have been specialized food procurement and production sites that were most active during the earlier Mississippian phases (Gregg 1975).

Fourth-line communities are usually farmsteads or hamlets with no mounds. Fowler (1978: 471) believed fourth-line sites were primarily involved in maize agriculture, but others have included bluff-top mounds, specialized salt-procurement sites, and upland hunting camps as well as farmsteads in this settlement category (Gregg 1975: 74-75; Williams 1979).

Porter (1974) developed a chain settlement model for Late Woodland/Early Mississippian sites on the American Bottom that was supplanted by a "central place" model that had smaller Mississippian settlements dispersed around larger temple town centers. In the chain settlement model, villages with three or more mounds were spaced at 16 to 18 kilometer intervals along the American Bottom. Single mound sites that were located midway between the larger villages were surrounded by farmsteads in Porter's chain settlement system.

Porter believes the hexagonal "central place" settlement network marks the intrusion of a merchant class from the Lower Mississippi Valley that assumed control of the American bottom and surrounding area and developed what Porter has called "true" Mississippian Culture (1974: 30-31). In this model, the larger temple towns served both as ports of entry for exotic goods that were transported to the American bottom from distant sources and as redistribution centers for the surrounding farmstead sites.

The small Mississippian sites that were dispersed over the American Bottom have been labeled farmsteads or hamlets by both Fowler and Porter. They believe the Mississippian farmers who inhabited these sites without mounds grew the produce that fed the upper classes and supported the Cahokia settlement system.

Functional interpretations of these farmsteads have been based on surface data. The fact that there were many hoe fragments and chips, but few projectile points, bifacial knives, and end scrapers in the surface collections from fourth-line Mississippian communities led some archaeologists to conclude that cultivation of maize and other domesticates went on at these sites, while hunting activities were confined to upland campsites (Gregg 1975; Harn 1971; Munson 1971; Norris 1978; Porter 1974).

More recently, Muller (1978) has suggested that Mississippian farmsteads
were the minimum economic unit in the Kincaid settlement system on the Black
Bottom. One or more household groups inhabited these farmsteads all year
long, and they were basically involved in food production. The larger sites
in the Kincaid settlement system consisted of clusters of farmsteads combined
like building blocks. Butler (1977) developed a slightly different
settlement model for the Black Bottom, with farmsteads and hamlets linked
together in dispersed village networks.

Emerson and Milner (1982) applied the dispersed village and building
block models to Stirling phase settlements on the American Bottom. They
identified family farms at the Julien site that were occupied year-round, but
they also described clusters of Mississippian farmsteads and "nodal points"
(Riordan 1975), where sweat lodges and communal structures were present.
Emerson and Milner (1982: 3) believe the Labras Lake site is the archetypical
"nodal point" community, although sweat lodges and clusters of structures were
also found at Julien and Range during the Stirling phase. These authors
believe a local leader who had jurisdiction over several dispersed farmsteads
may have resided at nodal point sites such as Labras Lake (figure 29).

The main difference between Fowler's four-line hierarchy or Porter's
chain settlement/central place system and the dispersed village/building block
model is that in the former systems the Mississippian farmsteads were
single-function sites linked to larger communities, while in the latter models
the farmsteads are tied in with each other and are under some form of local
leadership (Emerson and Milner 1982).

Microwear analysis of chipped stone artifacts from the Mississippian
component at Labras Lake was undertaken to determine if the chipped stone
artifacts that were associated with the Stirling phase hamlet were used for a
different set of tasks than the implements found in the Late Archaic and Early
Bluff habitation areas. If different activities were associated with the
hunter-gatherer, hunter-gardener, and agricultural communities at Labras Lake,
were these differences related to economic and technological changes, or were
the site's inhabitants adjusting to a changing environment?

Changes in site utlization may also relate to changes in social structure
at the Labras Lake settlements. The Late Archaic and Late Woodland
occupations seem to have involved relatively egalitarian extended family
groups, and there is no evidence that exotic or status-oriented goods were
concentrated in a specific area of the site during those occupations.
However, it is possible that the Mississippian settlement at Labras Lake

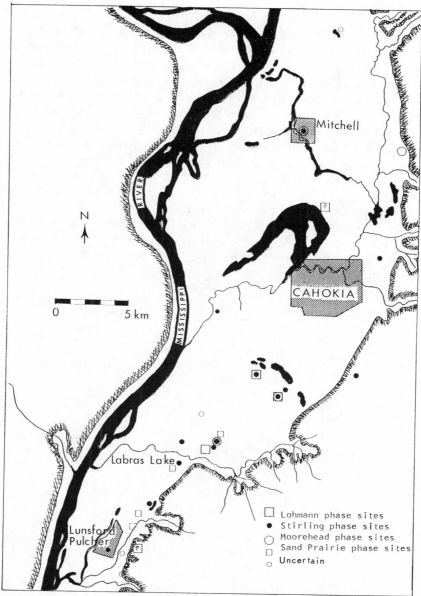

Figure 29. Excavated Mississippian sites on the American Bottom and adjacent bluffs.

served as a "nodal point" and the home of a regional leader. Some specialized activities beyond the normal agricultural regimen may have been performed at the site during this period.

If there is evidence that craft goods were produced at Labras Lake for exchange throughout the Mississippian settlement systems, and if "ceremonial" or status-related artifacts including the finer or more exotic ceramics (e.g., Ramey Incised and "Caddoan" wares) and "ceremonial" stone tools such as Ramey Knives, stone maces, and "spuds" are present but unequally distributed in the Mississippian artifact assemblage, then it is possible that we are not only witnessing the transition from a hunging-and-gathering economy to one based on collecting and plant tending and later on plant cultivation, but are also seeing changes in social organization and a shift in the structure and use of the Labras Lake site. The earliest settlements seem to have been seasonally occupied base camps that were inhabited by a family or band, but later, a small "nodal point" settlement may have been established that was occupied by a regional Mississippian leader who had some control over the affairs of the people inhabiting the surrounding farmsteads.

5 Bioarcheology at Labras Lake

Floral Remains

Plant remains were found in 156, or 56%, of the 279 Late Archaic features at Labras Lake. Carbonized nut husks dominated the Late Archaic floral assemblages, with 85.8 grams of nutshell present, along with five knotweed seeds (Polygonum erectum), three marsh elder seeds (Iva annua), two hawthorne seeds (Crataegus sp.), two seeds from a variety of goosefoot (Chenopodium sp.), and a single summac (Rhus sp.) seed. About 0.3 grams of carbonized maize were found in two Late Archaic pits, but this material is considered intrusive (F. B. King 1980).

Some 93% of the nutshell was identified as hickory, including shagbark (Carya ovata) and shellbark (C. laciniosa) species. However, hazelnut (Corylus americana), acorn (Quercus sp.), and black walnut (Juglans nigra) remains were also present. Black walnut husks are rare in Woodland and Mississippian floral samples from American Bottom sites (Johannessen 1983), and at Labras Lake, 94% of the black walnut remains came from Archaic contexts.

The four Late Archaic occupation areas at Labras Lake contained variable amounts of floral material (table 3). In the southwestern area, 69 grams of nutshell, 55 grams of charcoal, and seven carbonized seeds were recovered. The 69 grams of nutshell accounted for 80% of the nut remains found in Late Archaic contexts and these consisted of 67.2 grams of hickory nut, 0.9 grams of hazelnut, 0.6 grams of acorn, and 0.3 grams of black walnut shell fragments.

Two superimposed hearths inside Feature 1172, the large domestic area in the southwestern Late Archaic component (figure 14), contained 53 grams of hickory nuts, or 62% of the carbonized nuts in the entire Late Archaic floral assemblage from Labras Lake. The rest of the carbonized nuts were mainly found in the fill of roasting pits and storage/refuse pits located in the southwestern and north central Late Archaic areas.

All of the nut species present in the southwestern area floral sample would be available in the early fall, and could be found in both upland and bottomland habitats. Hazelnuts ripen slightly earlier than the other nut

TABLE 3. Carbonized floral remains recovered in flotation samples taken from features in the four Late Archaic components at the Labras Lake site.

	SOUTH CENTRAL	NORTH-WESTERN	SOUTH-WESTERN	NORTH CENTRAL	TOTAL ARCHAIC
NUTS: *Hickory*	2.3 grams	0.5 g	67.2 g	9.9 g	79.9 g
Hazelnut	-	0.2 g	0.9 g	0.3 g	1.4 g
Acorn	0.2 g	0.3 g	0.6 g	0.3 g	1.4 g
Black Walnut	0.1 g	0.1 g	0.3 g	2.6 g	3.1 g
TOTAL:	2.6 g	1.1 g	69.0 g	13.1 g	85.8 g
DENSITY*:	0.93	0.20	3.59	0.39	1.40
SEEDS: *Knotweed*	-	-	3 seeds	2 seeds	5 seeds
Marsh Elder	-	-	-	3	3
Chenopodium	-	-	2	-	2
Hawthorne	-	-	2	-	2
Summac	1	-	-	-	1
Maize**	-	-	2	1	3
Unidentifiable	-	-	-	-	1
TOTAL:	1	-	8	5	14 seeds
DENSITY*:	0.36	-	0.42	0.15	0.23
WOOD: *Hickory*	-	18.6 grams	22.3 g	6.9 g	47.8 g
Ash	-	-	10.0 g	1.5 g	11.5 g
Maple	-	-	3.5 g	-	3.5 g
Oak	-	-	2.0 g	-	2.0 g
Elm/Hackberry	-	-	0.5 g	1.0 g	1.5 g
Black Walnut	-	-	0.5 g	-	0.5 g
Cedar	0.3 g	-	-	-	0.3 g
Oak/Hickory	-	-	0.2 g	-	0.2 g
Honey Locust	-	-	0.1 g	-	0.1 g
Unidentifiable	2.3 g	9.2 g	15.9 g	34.4 g	61.8 g
TOTAL:	2.6 g	27.8 g	55.0 g	43.8 g	129.2 g
DENSITY*:	0.93	5.15	2.86	1.30	2.11
VOL. FLOATED:	28 liters	54 liters	192 lit.	337 lit.	611 lit.
*seeds/g nuts:	0.38	-	0.12	0.38	0.16
nuts/charcoal:	1.00	0.04	1.25	0.30	0.66

* DENSITY = number or weight per 10 liters of flotation-processed sediment.
** Maize remains were considered intrusive.

species (July-October), and are present in dense thickets at the edges of forests (F. B. King 1980; King and Roper 1976). The concentration of hickory nuts inside Feature 1172 may represent nut-processing activities inside that domestic area, but the nutshell may have been used as fuel. The charred remains of wild plants found in the southwestern area include knotweed, hawthorne, and Chenopodium. These plants were probably common weeds growing near the Late Archaic settlement.

There is 1.25 times as much carbonized nut matter as charcoal in the southwestern floral sample, which reflects the high concentration of nuts in the floral assemblage. The density of carbonized nutshell (grams of charred nuts found in every 10 litres of soil that was flotation processed) in the southwestern area was 3.59, the highest density for all of the Late Archaic components at the site.

The identified charcoal in the southwestern Late Archaic assemblage included seven different species. Hickory (Carya sp.) and ash (Fraxinus sp.) were the most common types, but maple (Acer sp.) and oak (Quercus sp.) were also well represented. Although more charcoal was recovered from the southwestern area than from any other Late Archaic area at Labras Lake (43% of all of the charcoal from Late Archaic features came from the southwestern area), the charcoal density per 10 liters of floated soil was 2.86. This value was greater than the density of charcoal for features from the north central and south central areas, but lower than the density of charcoal in the features in the northwestern area.

Late Archaic features in the north central area at Labras Lake contained 43.8 g of charcoal, 9.9 g of carbonized hickory nuts, 2.6 g of black walnut fragments, 0.3 g of hazelnut remains and 0.3 g of charred acorns. Three carbonized seeds identified as marsh elder, and two knotweed seeds were also found in features in the north central area (table 3).

The charred nuts to charcoal ratio for this area (0.30 times as much) shows a greater concentration of charcoal in the fill of the north central features (34% of the charcoal from all Late Archaic features at Labras Lake came from this component). The density of charcoal is 1.30, lower than the density of charcoal recorded for the southwestern area, and the density of carbonized nuts is 0.39, much lower than the density of nuts found in southwestern area features. However, the ratio of seeds (number) to nutshell (weight) in the north central floral sample is about four times what it was in the southwestern sample.

The marsh elder (<u>Iva</u> <u>annua</u> var. <u>macrocarpa</u>) seeds found in the north central Late Archaic area were too fragmentary to be measured, so it is not known if they were of the wild size or if they belonged to the larger domesticated variety (Yarnell 1972). Marsh elder and knotweed (<u>Polygonum</u> <u>erectum</u>-type) seeds ripen in late summer, but Francis B. King (1980) does not believe the knotweed seeds from Labras Lake were cultivated, although Asch and Asch (1978) have made a case for the domestication of this species in the Lower Illinois Valley.

The association of marsh elder, knotweed, and at least four species of wild nuts in the north central area suggests that several types of wild plants were exploited by the Late Archaic inhabitants, with a slim possibility that some starchy seed plants may have been cultivated.

The northwestern Late Archaic area contained the greatest number of hearths (or burned areas) found in any of the Late Archaic settlements at Labras Lake, and the density of charcoal in the features in this area (5.15) was the highest of all of the Late Archaic components. The high density is partly due to the lower volume of soil taken for flotation processing from the shallower features in the northwestern area, but it also shows that wood charcoal was fairly abundant in these burned areas.

The lowest density of charred nuts in any of the Late Archaic flotation samples from Labras Lake was recorded in the northwestern floral assemblage. The nut density was 0.20, and only 1.1 grams, or 1.3% of the total nut fragments (by weight) from Late Archaic contexts, came from the northwestern area. No seeds were recovered, and the charred nuts to charcoal ratio (only 0.04 times as much) indicates that nut processing was not an important activity.

In the south central area, only 2.6 grams of charred nuts were recovered in flotation samples, and an equal amount of charcoal was present. Almost all of the nuts (2.3 grams) were hickory, with 0.2 grams of acorn and 0.1 grams of black walnut making up the remainder of the total. A single summac seed was recovered in the south central area.

The density of nuts was relatively high (0.93), but the total weight of nut remains was low for this area. The low volume of soil taken for flotation samples probably accounts for the small amount of charred nuts found in the south central features. The density of charcoal is the lowest for all of the Late Archaic components, and this may indicate that the south central area was only occupied during the warmer months of the year. At the Aztalan site in Wisconsin, the amount of charcoal found in pits filled during different seasons (as determined by the seasonal analysis of fish scales found in the pit fill) decreased from winter to late summer. It is possible that charcoal density may serve as a rough approximation of the season of occupation at prehistoric sites located in temperate climates (Yerkes 1982).

The distribution of floral remains between the four Late Archaic areas at Labras Lake mirrors the functional patterns observed in the microwear samples (see chapter 6). The two older occupations (early Labras Lake phase) are marked by fewer varieties of stone tools, and fewer and more specialized activities are represented. The floral samples from both of these areas produced only a single carbonized seed. Charcoal was scarce in the south central area, but the density of nuts was rather high. Microwear revealed a lot of butchering and hide-working tools from the south central area, and the floral data indicate that some nut processing may have been going on there as well. Very little charcoal was recovered in this area, but the only piece of carbonized red cedar (Juniperus virginiana) recovered at Labras Lake came from a Late Archaic feature in the south central area.

The low density of nutshell, the absence of seeds, and the high density of charcoal in the northwestern area suggest that activities other than food preparation were conducted there. The microwear evidence indicates that the area was used for lithic manufacturing and repair, and there was an exceptionally high percentage of thermally altered chert artifacts in the northwestern lithic assemblage (76% of the total). The abundance of hearths and the high density of charcoal in this area reflects the use of fire in the lithic manufacturing process, not intensive food processing or cold weather habitation.

The more recent Late Archaic occupations in the southwestern and north central areas (late Labras Lake and early Prairie Lake phases) contain stone artifacts that represent a greater variety of activites than the older components, and the floral remains in these areas are more abundant. The densities of charcoal suggest these areas may have been occupied during the colder months. There is evidence for nut collecting and processing during the late summer and early fall months as well. Although only a small number of seeds were recovered, both southwestern and north central areas contained knotweed seeds, and some marsh elder, hawthorne, and Chenopodium were also present. These probably were weeds that grew near the Late Archaic camps, but incipient cultivation cannot be entirely ruled out. The interpretation of these younger Late Archaic areas as central base camps that were occupied for most of the year can be supported by the floral remains.

Caldwell viewed the Archaic period (7000-2000 B.C.) as a time when the nomadic inhabitants of the Eastern Woodlands became more efficient at hunting, fishing, and gathering wild plants and nuts. Gradual improvements in the subsistence system led to "primary forest efficiency" and a more sedentary lifestyle for the Archaic hunter-gatherers, with new food resources and established seasonal economic cycles (Caldwell 1958: 18).

Asch, Ford, and Asch (1972) believe that their analysis of the floral remains from Koster shows that a narrow range of food plants was utilized by the Middle Archaic inhabitants of that site, and this supports Caldwell's idea that Archaic subsistence patterns were conservative and efficient. Hickory nuts were the most abundant type of plant food represented throughout the Archaic horizons at Koster, and Asch, Ford, and Asch (1972: 27) interpret this as evidence for 3000 years of stability in the climate, vegetation, and human population density of the Lower Illinois Valley, with no change in prehistoric subsistence strategies. They maintain that the seasonal abundance, storability, caloric value, and protein content of hickory nuts led to their use as a "first-line" food by the Archaic populations at Koster, who did not make "serious demands on the carrying capacity of the environment," and who "lacked a good reason for diversifying their subsistence base" (Asch et al. 1972: 28).

These authors note that Caldwell failed to account for population dynamics in his model of the evolution of subsistence systems. Following Boserup (1965), they argue that the Archaic inhabitants of Koster concentrated on hickory nut collection and processing because a minimum of effort was required to obtain that "nutritionally complete" plant food, and the low level of human population in the Lower Illinois Valley would not seriously deplete the nut crop (1972: 28-30).

Population growth and pressure on local resources would lead to a shift in subsistence patterns and an increase in the variety of food plants, according to these authors, but since there is little variety in the floral remains from the Archaic levels at Koster, with 90% of the nutshell (by weight) identified as hickory, they assume that a stable population of hunter-gatherers was present in the area for three millennia (Asch et al. 1972).

If Asch, Ford, and Asch are correct, then the floral remains from the Late Archaic components at Labras Lake would indicate that a stable population of hunter-gatherers occupied that site between 1,500 and 3,500 years ago, since the floral assemblages show little variety and are dominated by hickory nutshell.   However, Lopinot (1982, 1983) has demonstrated that the abundance of hickory nutshell in archaeological floral samples from open-air sites in the Midwest may be due to the greater ability of hickory nutshell to resist thermal degradation and postdepositional attrition.

Less resilient, thinner-shelled varieties of nuts are often under represented in floral samples, and Lopinot (1982: 729) notes that archaeologists cannot assume that the proportions of recovered plant parts reflect their importance in the prehistoric diet. Certainly nutshell is more likely to be preserved than soft plant parts or seeds, and differential preservation will bias the interpretation of floral assemblages with an overemphasis on the importance of nuts in Archaic diets. The fact that hickory nuts are abundant in Late Archaic floral samples cannot be used to demonstrate "economic stability."

It is not clear if the evidence for a more diversified plant diet indicates higher levels of population during the Late Archaic period, but a case can be made for a more sedentary lifestyle based on the diversity of plant species represented at the Cahokia Interpretive Center Tract (Lopinot 1983).

Early Bluff Floral Remains

Features in the small Early Bluff component at Labras Lake contained 62.2 grams of charcoal, 7.4 grams of nuts, 0.2 grams of carbonized maize, and 26 charred seeds. Only hickory and hazelnuts were recovered from the Early Bluff features (table 4), and the low nuts to charcoal ratio (0.12 times as many nut remains), suggests that nut processing was less important during the Late Woodland occupation than it was during most of the Late Archaic habitation episodes (this ratio is similar to the nut/charcoal ratio for the lithic workshop in the northwestern Late Archaic area).

Starchy seeds assumed a greater importance in the Early Bluff diet, with eight marshelder, six Chenopodium, and four grass (maygrass?) seeds present, along with a single seed each of smartweed, summac, and wild pea (legume). Five unidentifiable seeds were also recovered (F. B.King 1980). It has been suggested that the transition from Archaic to Woodland subsistence patterns saw a shift from intensive nut collecting to the harvesting of plants with starchy and oily seeds (Asch et al. 1978; Johannessen 1983).

TABLE 4. Carbonized floral remains recovered in flotation samples from Late Archaic, Late Woodland, and Mississippian features at the Labras Lake site.

	LATE ARCHAIC	LATE WOODLAND	MISSISSIPPIAN	SITE TOTAL
NUTSHELL				
Hickory	79.9 grams	4.5 g	4638.8 g	4723.2 g
Hazelnut	1.4 g	2.9 g	1.2 g	5.5 g
Acorn	1.4 g	-	20.4 g	21.8 g
Black Walnut	3.1 g	-	0.2 g	3.3 g
TOTAL:	85.8 g	7.4 g	4460.6 g	4753.8 g
DENSITY*:	1.40	0.86	22.62	17.24
SEEDS				
Knotweed	5 seeds	-	6 seeds	11 seeds
Marsh Elder	3	8	51	62
Chenopodium	2	6	493	501
Hawthorne	2	-	-	2
Summac	1	1	1	3
Grasses	-	4	13	17
Smartweed	-	1	-	1
Tick-treefoil	-	-	9	9
Maygrass	-	-	7	7
Amaranth	-	-	5	5
Legume	-	1	2	3
Groundnut tuber	-	-	2	2
Sunflower	-	-	1	1
Squash rind	-	-	4	4
Persimmon	-	-	1	1
Bedstraw	-	-	1	1
Spurge	-	-	1	1
Unidentifiable	1	5	10	16
TOTAL:	14	26	607	647 seeds
DENSITY*:	0.23	3.02	2.95	2.35
MAIZE:	0.3 grams**	0.2 g	229+ g	229.5+ g
DENSITY*:	-	0.02	1.11	0.83

	LATE ARCHAIC	LATE WOODLAND	MISSISSIPPIAN	SITE TOTAL
WOOD CHARCOAL				
Hickory	47.8 grams	0.3 g	111.3 g	159.4 g
Honey Locust	0.1 g	-	108.7 g	108.8 g
Oak	2.0 g	17.0 g	50.5 g	69.5 g
Ash	11.5 g	12.5 g	34.8 g	58.8 g
Maple	3.5 g	-	27.1 g	30.6 g
Black Walnut	0.5 g	-	19.1 g	19.6 g
Elm/Hackberry	1.5 g	-	13.9 g	15.4 g
Poplar/Willow	-	-	4.2 g	4.2 g
Catalpa	-	3.5 g	-	3.5 g
Cedar	0.3 g	-	-	0.3 g
Oak/Hickory	0.2 g	-	-	0.2 g
Cane/Grass	-	-	5.6+g	5.6+g
Unidentifiable	61.8 g	28.9 g	238.0 g	328.7 g
TOTAL:	129.2 g	62.2 g	613.2+g	804.6+g
DENSITY*:	2.11	7.23	2.98	2.92
VOL. FLOATED:	611 liters	86 liters	2060 lit.	2757 lit.
seeds/g nuts:	0.16	3.51	0.13	0.14
nuts/charcoal:	0.66	0.12	7.60	5.90
PERCENTAGE OF FEATURES WITH:				
Nutshell	31 %	40 %	16 %	
Seeds	2 %	27 %	8 %	
Maize	<1 %**	7 %	14 %	
Wood Charcoal	39 %	60 %	23 %	

* DENSITY = number or weight per 10 liters of flotation-processed sediment.

** Maize remains in Late Archaic features were considered intrusive.

David Braun (1983) believes there are changes in Woodland ceramic technology that correspond to this dietary shift. Starchy seeds need to be boiled to the point of gelatinization in a liquid broth to improve their digestibility and palatability. This requires longer cooking times and higher cooking temperatures. Braun has shown that Woodland domestic jars change to a more globular shape with thinner vessel walls and finer temper between A.D. 200 and A.D. 800-900 (1983: 118). His experiments show that this trend in vessel morphology is a response to increased thermal stress that may be associated with the cooking of starchy seeds.

The floral data from the Late Archaic and Late Woodland components at Labras Lake seem to be in line with these interpretations, since the density of nut remains is 1.6 times greater in the Late Archaic flotation samples, while 13 times as many starchy and oily seeds are contained in each 10 liters of soil from the Late Woodland features (table 4).

Maize was only found in one of the fifteen Early Bluff features at Labras Lake (7%), but late summer and fall-ripening starchy seeds were present in 27% of the features. Some native cultigens are included in the sample of carbonized seeds. The fleshy parts of these plants could be collected and eaten in the spring and summer as well, so the Early Bluff habitation at Labras Lake may have spanned most of the warmer months. The high density of charcoal suggests a winter occupation, but no structures were found in the Early Bluff component at Labras Lake. However, construction activities during the Mississippian occupation at the site may have destroyed some Early Bluff houses.

The high charcoal density for the features in the Early Bluff component might also reflect the fact that 47% of the Early Bluff features were storage/refuse pits. In the Late Archaic components, only 10% of the features were classified as storage/refuse pits, while that type of deep pit feature accounted for only 4% of the Mississippian feature total, and only 10% of the features outside of the Mississippian wall-trench structures were storage/refuse pits (table 5). More organic refuse was present in storage/refuse pits than in any other type of feature, but since there were no more flotation samples taken from storage/refuse pits than from any other type of feature, the Early Bluff component, with its higher percentage of deep pits, would have a greater density of organic refuse.

TABLE 5. The number and percentage of different types of features in the
Late Archaic, Late Woodland, and Mississippian components at Labras Lake.

TYPE OF FEATURE	LATE ARCHAIC	LATE WOODLAND	MISSISSIPPIAN Outside Houses	Entire* Component
Hearth/Burned Area	15 (6%)	1 (7%)	8 (5%)	11 (2%)
Storage/Refuse Pit	27 (10%)	7 (47%)	17 (10%)	32 (4%)
Roasting Pit	7 (2%)	–	2 (1%)	2 (1%)
Shallow Pit	117 (42%)	1 (7%)	33 (20%)	65 (9%)
Artifact Concentration	24 (9%)	1 (7%)	7 (4%)	12 (2%)
Posthole	76 (27%)	3 (20%)	92 (55%)	545 (78%)
Structure/Domestic Area	8 (3%)	–	8 (5%)	5 (5%)
Oblong Pit	–	2 (13%)	–	–
Stain	3 (1%)	–	–	–
Wall Trench	1 (1%)	–	1 (1%)	35 (5%)
TOTAL:	278 (100%)	15 (101%)	168 (101%)	710 (101%)

* Entire component includes Mississippian features that were inside of the
six wall-trench houses.

Percentages may not sum to 100 due to rounding.

Mississippian Floral Remains

The Mississippian component at Labras Lake contained the greatest amounts of all types of floral remains, including 4660.6 grams of carbonized nuts, 229.0 grams of charred maize, 607 carbonized seeds, and 613.2 grams of carcoal. There are 7.6 times as many nut remains as charcoal in the entire Mississippian component, but 96% of the nuts came from a single pit, Feature 16, where 4,477.0 grams of hickory nuts were recovered.

Other species of nuts were not represented in the fill of Feature 16, although Chenopodium, marsh elder, and grass seeds were recovered along with some tubers, legumes, and a small quantity of charred maize (0.3 grams). This pit was obviously a nut-processing feature; and although maize cultivation may have been the most important part of the Mississippian economy at small farmsteads like Labras Lake, this feature shows that nuts still were being collected and processed in quantity.

The large numbers of Chenopodium (493) and marsh elder (51) seeds found in Mississippian features (along with a single sunflower seed) suggest that native domesticates continued to be cultivated by the Mississippians at Labras Lake, and they were not entirely displaced by exotic cultigens such as maize and squash (there were no domesticated beans recovered at Labras Lake).

The great variety of plant species represented in the Labras Lake Mississippian floral sample (four species of nuts and fifteen varieties of identifiable seeds in addition to the maize remains) seems to indicate that the site was occupied all year round, and that the inhabitants continued to collect wild plants and cultivate native and introduced domesticates. The Mississippian farmstead sites were not "specializing" in corn agriculture, but seem to have followed a broad spectrum-type of subsistence pattern that included the cultivation of mesoamerican domesticates as well as wild plant and nut collecting.

This conclusion is at variance with the axiom that Mississippian societies were dependent on maize horticulture and deliberately maintained a simplified ecosystem based on a few seasonally abundant species of animals and wild and domesticated plants (Cleland 1976; Ford 1977: 179-80; Smith 1978). In fact, Mississippian agriculture seems to be an example of the "polycultural" primitive cultivation defined by Harris (1972), rather than the seed-crop cultivation that is associated with early maize agriculture in mesoamerican or the southwestern United States. Polycultural agricultural systems are ecologically complex, and involve the alteration of selected components of the natural system rather than wholesale replacement. This leads to an ecosystem where a variety of preferred domesticated species are substituted for some wild species and integrated with others to simulate the structure and functional dynamics of the natural ecosystem (Harris 1972: 183). These polycultural systems may be less productive than simple seed-crop agriculture, but they are more stable (Flannery 1973).

Floral Remains: A Summary

Most of the archaeobotanical research that has been conducted in the eastern United States has focused on the origin and development of plant husbandry. Until Watson (1974) and her colleagues investigated the plant materials recovered in coprolites and flotation samples from dry caves in Kentucky, most workers believed that the cultivated plants used east of the Mississippi came from the tropics via the southwestern United States. Native North American cultigens such as <u>Iva annua</u>, <u>Helianthus annuus</u> (sunflower), <u>Phalaris caroliniana</u> (maygrass), and <u>Chenopodium</u> were found in association with the tropical cultigens squash and gourd (Watson et al. 1969; Yarnell 1976, 1978).

It was thought that members of this "Eastern Agricultural Complex" (Gilmore 1931) had been part of the aboriginal diet for some time, and that the adoption of plant husbandry was a gradual process that did not pick up steam until after 1500 B.C., when tropical domesticates were added to the complex (Jones 1936; Yarnell 1977: 867). More recent work (Asch and Asch 1979; Chapman and Shea 1977; Chomko and Crawford 1978; Cowan and Ford 1979; Kay et al. 1980; Marquardt and Watson 1977) has shown that tropical domesticates were present in eastern floral assemblages by 3000 B.C., and Ford (1981) has suggested that an "Early Eastern Mexican Agricultural Complex" consisting of gourds and squash originated in Mexico and diffused across Texas into the Southeast and Midwest before mesoamerican cultigens were introduced into the Southwest, and prior to the domestication of native North American plants.

The distribution of this early gourd and squash complex has been related to long-distance exchange networks (Kay et al. 1980; Marquardt and Watson 1983), and some have argued that Archaic sites with this complex may have been occupied all year long (Brown and Vierra 1983; Collins 1979); but most agree that squash and gourd cultivation had little impact on Archaic subsistence. Archaic groups in the Midwest continue to be characterized as efficient fisher-hunter-gatherers (Caldwell 1958) who "specialized" in nut harvesting, shellfish gathering, and deer hunting.

Johannessen (1983) believes plant exploitation patterns on the American Bottom changed from an emphasis on nut collecting by small Late Archaic populations to more intensive use of starchy and oily seed plants (that were probably cultivated) by Middle and Late Woodland groups who did not harvest many nuts. Mississippian groups are characterized as maize farmers who also exploited seeds but collected few nuts. Johannessen notes that Late Archaic floral assemblages from the American Bottom contain abundant nutshell and few seeds, with a low percentage of goosefoot, maygrass, knotweed, marsh elder, and sunflower (1983: 204).

At Labras Lake, the Late Archaic floral assemblages were dominated by nuts and had low seed densities (table 3). However, ten of the thirteen identified seeds (77%) were members of the starchy seed complex. The floral sample from the Cahokia Interpretive Center Tract contained a tremendous number of seeds and had a seed to nut ratio that is higher than any known Middle Woodland site and that matches or exceeds the ratios from most Late Woodland sites (Lopinot 1983). The variety of seeds represented in the Cahokia sample argues against any "specialized" seed harvesting, and the density of nutshell is 1.05 grams per 10 liters of flotation-processed soil, a figure that approaches the 1.40 nutshell density recorded for all of the Late Archaic components at Labras Lake and exceeds the total plant charcoal density for the Dyroff and MoPac #2 sites (Lopinot 1983).

Diversified subsistence, rather than specialized nut collecting, characterizes the Archaic occupation at Cahokia, and this pattern probably applies to other Late Archaic sites on the American Bottom as well. Several recent articles have commented on the variability of paleobotanical samples (Hally 1981) and the ambiguity of seed assemblages (Lopinot and Brussell 1982; Minnis 1981). The apparent shift from Late Archaic nut collecting to Woodland seed utilization may be more apparent than real, and the decline in nutshell and the rise in carbonzied seeds may reflect different methods of plant preparation and storage rather than economic changes.

A more realistic model for plant utilization on the American Bottom may be an additive pattern where starchy seeds and later maize were added to wild nut and plant utilization strategies that persisted through all cultural periods. Cultivated starchy seeds may not have "replaced" nuts in Middle and Late Woodland diets. Instead, these plants were added to the existing subsistence base, as maize was at a later date.

Faunal Remains

Bone preservation at Labras Lake was very poor, and although some 15,133 faunal elements were recovered, only 772 (5%) of the bone fragments could be identified to the genus or species level (Purdue and Styles 1980). Most of the bone fragments were found in the Late Archaic features (10,360, or 68% of all of the faunal remains from Labras Lake), but white-tailed deer (Odocoileus virginianus), elk (Cervus canadensis), and woodchuck (Marmota monax) were the only identified mammalian species, while sunfish (Centrachidae sp.) was the only identifiable fish species. Several turtle elements and a gastropod fragment were also present in the Late Archaic sample.

The majority of the faunal remains in the Late Archaic assemblage came from the south central area, where 8,222 bone fragments were recovered. These included the remains of white-tailed deer, elk, turtle, sunfish, and a nearly complete woodchuck skeleton. The sunfish was represented by a single scale that appears to have come from a fish caught in the summer months. The turtle remains suggest a summer habitation as well. The woodchuck skeleton may have been intrusive. Large game seem to have been the primary prey of the south central hunters. Most of the elk remains were teeth, illustrating the preservation problem that affected all of the faunal remains from Labras Lake. Nonetheless, the scanty faunal data do seem to agree with the interpretation that the south central Late Archaic area was occupied during the warmer months, possibly summer through fall, and served as a hunting camp.

The northwestern Late Archaic area contained very little faunal material. Only forty-four unidentifiable fragments were found there. The faunal remains also suggest that little food processing occurred in this area of the site, but that lithic manufacturing and repair were the primary activities in this component.

Relatively few faunal remains were recovered from the southwestern Late Archaic area (253 unidentifiable elements, and one deer sesamoid); however, it must be remembered that preservation was extremely poor in the clayey soils in that area of the site.

The north central area provided a relatively large faunal collection totaling 1,840 fragments, with white-tailed deer, small mammals, reptiles, turtles, and a gastropod identified from the poorly preserved material. Some of the species in this collection (e.g., the turtle and gastropod remains) suggest a warm-weather habitation. However, the majority of the faunal remains seem to belong to larger mammals, most likely deer.

Computer simulation experiments designed to test different methods of estimating the kill population (or death assemblage) from samples of faunal remains (Gilbert and Singer 1982) showed that counting the total number of fragments (TNF) or computing the relative frequency of bone types (RF) produced more accurate estimates of original species ratios than calculating the minimum number of individuals (MNI) represented by the faunal remains, and required smaller sample sizes to achieve the same degree of accuracy. However, Gilbert and Singer (1982: 32) caution that quantification of faunal data summarizes bone recovery frequencies, which may not correspond to the relative importance of different species in the prehistoric diet.

The Late Archaic faunal remains from Labras Lake were poorly preserved, but the features that did contain bone had an average of 191.8 fragments in their fill, which was the highest density of bone fragments per feature for all components at the site (Purdue and Syles 1980: 346). Of the 1,121 bones that could be identified to class, 1,115 (99%) were mammal bones, and most of these probably represent deer or elk (Purdue, personal communication).

Even though preservation problems preclude more detailed analyses, it is evident that large mammals were an important part of the Late Archaic diet, and the scanty seasonal evidence provided by the identified faunal elements is not at variance with interpretations presented earlier.

The Late Woodland faunal assemblage included 674 bone fragments, but only 13 could be identified to genus or species; while 143 more elements could be broken down to class. Nonetheless, some white-tailed deer and muskrat (Ondatra zibethicus) bones were identified along with some species of sunfish and catfish, a turtle, and several mussel shells. Even this small sample suggests a greater emphasis on aquatic species than the previous period. No fish scales from Late Woodland features could be used to determine the season of the year the fish were caught, but the presence of sunfish, catfish, mussel, and turtle remains suggests a warm-weather occupation by the Early Bluff population at Labras Lake.

The only evidence for cold-weather habitation is the relative abundance of charcoal in the Early Bluff features, but this may reflect the greater percentage of storage pits in the Late Woodland sample, and the concentration of refuse in those features. Other floral and faunal remains suggest a warm-weather occupation and an emphasis on aquatic animals, starchy seeds, and nuts. There is some evidence for cultivation or plant tending in the form of small amounts of carbonized maize, ground stone celts (used for forest clearance?), and a few fragments of chipped stone with "hoe polish" on them.

The greatest variety of animal species were identified in the faunal assemblage from the Mississippian component at Labras Lake. Some 3,335 bone fragments were recovered, and the 313 elements that could be identified to genus or species included white-tailed deer, muskrat, thirteen species of fish, an amphibian, a turtle, and a few mussels. Aquatic species continued to be well represented in the Mississippian sample, with many more fish remains present than there were in the Late Woodland faunal sample. Six fish scales from Mississippian contexts that were examined for seasonal information indicated that the fish were captured in late spring or summer (May-July). The fish species included those found in backwaters more often than in the channels of large rivers (Purdue and Styles 1980), so the exploitation of the abandoned meander scars near the site, as well as of the interior stream, is suggested. The mussels were too badly weathered to provide seasonal or habitat information, but their presence, along with the amphibians and turtles, suggests a summer occupation.

The diversity in the Mississippian faunal remains mirrors the pattern observed in the floral sample and suggests year-round occupation at the site. The broad spectrum Mississippian subsistence strategy is also corroborated by the wide variety of species represented in the poorly preserved faunal remains.

Bioarcheology: A Summary

Even though the vagaries of preservation hamper a detailed interpretation of the biotic remains from Labras Lake, some patterns do emerge from this analysis. The earliest Late Archaic occupations at the site have the fewest floral remains, and the least variety of species are represented. The low density of nuts, seeds, and faunal elements in the northwestern area (but the relative abundance of charcoal) suggests that while fires were built in that area of the site, little food processing went on there. Instead, this area seems to have served as a lithic workshop.

In the south central area, the occupation may have been contemporary with the northwestern habitation, but quite a different range of activities is represented. Late Archaic populations seem to have occupied this area during the summer and fall months for the purpose of hunting and butchering large animals, mainly deer and elk. Few plant remains were recovered from features in this component, but the density of nuts and seeds per 10 liters of flotation-processed soil is relatively high, the charcoal density is low, and there is no evidence for any structures.

The last Late Archaic occupations at Labras Lake were located in the southwestern and north central areas, where substantial amounts of charcoal and nuts were recovered. Specialized hickory nut processing seems to have gone on inside Feature 1172, the largest domestic area in the southwestern component, but few faunal remains were preserved in this area. More animal bones were found in the north central area, but fewer nut husks were recovered. Both the southwestern and north central areas produced a few seeds that may have come from weeds growing nearby, or there may have been some simple form of plant tending in these areas, since the majority of these seeds belong to the "starchy or oily" complex. Both areas seem to have been occupied during the colder months of the year.

These terminal Late Archaic occupations seem to have been base camps where a group of hunter-gatherers established themselves during the fall and winter months and sent out collecting parties to obtain plant and animal foods from the surrounding floodplain and upland habitats.

During all of the Late Archaic occupations, the emphasis seems to have been on large game and nuts, but the recovered floral and faunal remains may not reflect the relative importance of different plant and animal species in the aboriginal diet. Nonetheless, the Late Woodland group who returned to the Labras Lake site after a 1,700-year hiatus in the occupation record, seem to have utilized more aquatic animals and more starchy seed plants. Their stay at the site seems to have been limited to the warmer months, and they may have been engaged in plant tending or gardening activities as well as hunting and gathering. There is also some scant evidence for maize cultivation.

The final prehistoric habitation at Labras Lake involved a Mississippian population, and it was marked by a year-round occupation that involved farming, hunting, and gathering. A broad spectrum of terrestrial and aquatic animals were captured and processed, along with nuts, seeds, tubers, and other wild plants. Maize, squash, and sunflowers were cultivated; and it seems that Chenopodium, marsh elder, knotweed, and maygrass may have been grown or tended as well.   The site does not seem to have been used as a specialized agricultural settlement during Mississippian times, but resembles a self-sufficient community that exploited a variety of wild and domesticated plants and several species of wild animals.

Artifact Function and Activity
Patterns at Labras Lake

Microwear Analysis

When experimental stone tools are used for specific tasks, microscopic examination reveals that distinctive polishes, striations, and damage scars form on their edges. Diagnostic microwear patterns are associated with specific worked materials and different methods of tool use.

Most agree that microwear analysis of stone tools will yield valid functional information, but there has been some disagreement over which method should be employed in these investigations (Gerwitz 1980). A low-power microwear technique that uses reflected light and a stereomicroscope with a magnification range between 10x and 100x has been championed by George Odell (1975, 1980), although several others have also tried this approach (Ahler 1971; Frison 1968; Tringham et al. 1974). Edge damage scars receive most of the attention in low-power analysis, and distinctions between different worked materials are limited to hard (resistant) and soft (yielding).

Several microwear analysts have used scanning electron microscopes (or SEMs) that have magnification ranges greater than 400x (Anderson 1980; Del Bene 1979; Fedje 1979; Mansur 1982). Most of their work has concentrated on striation patterns, with the exception of Anderson (1980), who has used an SEM to examine the organic residues that are preserved on the edges of stone tools.

The study of striations can lead to an understanding of motor functions (Fedje 1979) and the "scratching agents" responsible for striation formation (Mansur 1982), but the SEM approach does not allow one to differentiate between specific types of worked material (Gerwitz 1980).

A method of incident light microscopy employing a magnification range between 50x and 400x, has been developed by Lawrence Keeley (1974, 1977, 1980). Keeley's technique involves the examination of microwear polishes, striations, and edge damage, in order to determine the area of a tool that was used, the method of use, and the material that was worked. Distinctive microwear polishes form on stone implements that are used to work hide, meat, bone, antler, shell, wood, and soft plant material. The incident light mode of illumination described by Keeley (1980) makes these polishes visible at magnifications between 100x and 400x.

Some claim that the low-power methods recognize all "available wear traces," require less time, and use less expensive equipment (Ahler 1982; Odell 1982); but the low-power techniques do not allow the microwear analyst to discriminate between different worked materials (Odell 1982: 20). The only method that provides a means to that end is the incident light technique developed by Keeley.

A pair of independent blind tests have shown that the incident light method of microwear analysis can be used to determine the functions of chipped stone tools accurately (Keeley and Newcomer 1977; Gendel and Pirnay 1982). In these tests, one researcher manufactured and used a set of flint tools and then sent the used tools to another for microwear analysis.

In the Keeley-Newcomer test, Keeley was able to identify the used area on fourteen of the sixteen tools in the test (88%), while he recognized the activity performed by Newcomer 76.5% of the time, and he identified the specific worked material in 62% of the cases. Keeley was able to recognize how most of the experimental tools were used, even though his performance in the test was hampered by Newcomer's use of a wooden cutting board in some of the butchering and hide-cutting experiments, and by the use of "seasoned" wood and dry antler for some of the other tasks.

Gendel could recognize the part of the implement that was used nine times out of ten (or in 91% of the cases), and he correctly determined the motion that Pirnay had used with 84% of the tools in his test. Gendel was correct in his identification of the material that was worked in 74% of the cases.

This degree of accuracy was attained by both microwear analysts (Keeley and Gendel) even though the only preconditions in these tests were that (1) both retouched and unretouched implements would be used;(2) the tools would be used in tasks relevant to prehistoric hunters; (3) no "trick" specimens would be used; and (4) the test results would be published regardless of the results (Gendel and Pirnay 1982; Keeley 1981; Keeley and Newcomer 1977).

When Odell performed a similar blind test using the low-power technique of microwear analysis (Odell and Odell-Vereeken 1980), he was able to determine the used area of the tool 84% of the time. He recognized the activity 68% of the time, and he identified specific worked material 32% of the time. Odell's rate of success in identifying the area of the tool that was used and the activity involved approached the rates achieved by Keeley and Gendel; but he could only guess the specific worked material about one third of the time, while Keeley was correct nearly two thirds of the time, and Gendel properly identified the worked material three times out of four.

Keeley's experimental results have been replicated by nearly a dozen workers, and his method has been used in a number of functional studies that have involved different types of lithic raw material (Akoshima 1979; Anderson 1980; Bamforth 1985; Binneman 1981; Cahen et al. 1979; Gendel 1982; Gerwitz 1980; Keeley and Toth 1981; Moss 1983; Sabo 1982; Symens 1980; Vaughan 1985; Yerkes 1983).

Archeologists often establish relationships between artifacts and specific prehistoric activities a priori, by assigning artifacts to function-al categories that are based on tool morphology or ethnographic analogy, instead of using experimentation and edge-wear analysis to determine how the tools were used.

American Bottom site reports often contain artifact descriptions that include a priori functional classifications such as the following: Morphologically, it is suggested that very few of these are thin enough for cutting meat efficiently, and their very uneven sinuous edges suggest that they would not have been adequate for scraping hides. One function they may have served, however, is as hefty cutting tools for dismembering primary joints of game animals. Their size suggests that they would have been inefficient for large-scale processing of larger animals, but they may well have served for processing smaller, medium-sized game such as turtle, fish, rodents, and fowl. (McElrath 1981:135)

In order to avoid this kind of rampant speculation and dubious functional attribution, Laura Gerwitz (1980) examined thirty three lithic artifacts from Labras Lake for microwear traces. Formal tool types such as bifaces, drills, sidescrapers, denticulates, and notches, as well as retouched and unretouched flakes, were included in this preliminary study. Hide-cutting and scraping tools, wood boring, whittling, and sawing tools, meat-cutting tools, and shell-drilling tools were identified using Keeley's method of microwear analysis (Gerwitz 1980: 304-5).

A more extensive microwear study was conducted by the author to gain a better understanding of the primary economic activities that went on at Labras Lake during each occupational episode.

The Labras Lake Microwear Sample

Some 35,552 lithic artifacts were recovered during the University of Illinois at Chicago excavations at Labras Lake, but 8,672 of these could not be assigned to a cultural component (table 6). The stone artifacts in the three components included tools, unretouched chert blanks, and lithic debris.

The debris amounted to 18,174 items, or 68% of the artifact total. The debris included chert chips whose greatest dimension was less than one centimeter, and blocky, amorphous chunks of chert that did not appear to have been used or modified to produce tools.

TABLE 6. The Labras Lake microwear sample.

35,552	*The total number of chipped stone artifacts recovered at the Labras Lake site*
- 8,672	*Artifacts that could not be assigned to a cultural component*
26,880	
-18,174	*Artifacts that were classified as debris**
8,706	
- 118	*Hoe chips*
8,588	
- 104	*Projectile points*
8,484	***Artifacts that were suitable for microwear analysis***
1,009	Artifacts examined for microwear traces, or 12 % of the suitable artifacts from the Labras Lake site
376	*Artifacts from the four Late Archaic components*
+ 100	*Artifacts from the Late Woodland component*
+ 533	*Artifacts from the Mississippian component*
1,009	

* *Debris* includes chips (lithic flakes whose greatest dimension is less than one cm) and chunks (blocky fragments of chert with little or no evidence of human modification).

Preliminary analysis of small samples of lithic debris from the Labras Lake site did not reveal any microscopic wear traces, and Lawrence Keeley (personal communication) has noted that small chips of flint or chert almost never show any microwear on their edges. Chert chunks and chips less than 1 centimeter long were not analyzed in the present study, because it was believed that very little functional information could be obtained by examining this lithic debris.

The 118 "hoe chips" that were recovered at Labras Lake were not included in this study either, since the glazed polish on their edges is visible without magnification. The "corn gloss" polish on hoes and hoe chips has been associated with cultivating prairie soils or cutting grasses (Witthoff 1967).

Nor were the 104 projectile points that could be assigned to a cultural component examined, since they obviously functioned as dart or arrow points. Preliminary microwear analysis on a sample of 6 Labras Lake projectile points showed no use wear other than than impact fractures. However, larger hafted bifacial "knives" were included in this study.

Some 8,484 chipped stone tools and unretouched artifacts from three cultural components were large enough to be analyzed, and 1,009 of these (12%) were actually examined for microwear traces. The Labras Lake microwear sample included 376 artifacts that were taken from Late Archaic contexts, 100 stone implements from the Late Woodland component, and 533 lithic items associated with Mississippian features (table 7).

Representative chert tools and unretouched blanks found in or near the Late Archaic domestic areas and associated features, the Late Woodland (Early Bluff) feature clusters and the Mississippian wall trench houses and surrounding pits, were assembled, and the microwear samples were selected by picking out representative tools and unretouched artifacts from the lithic collections associated with each concentration of features.
Usually 50-100% of the tools in each class were selected for microwear analysis, while at least 5% of the artifacts in each blank category were studied. The number of artifacts examined here (1,009) is larger than the sample sizes found in most published microwear studies.

The feature concentrations at Labras Lake resemble the groups of houses, graves, and pits that occur at Formative Oaxacan sites. Winter called these concentrations "household clusters," or the "material manifestations of prehistoric households" (1976: 25).However, Flannery (1982) has labeled them "household units." Although Winter has not been able to demonstrate that a specific segment of Formative society was responsible for the features and artifacts found within a household cluster (unit), both he and Flannery have shown that the household unit concept is a productive means of organizing archaeological data at an analytical level between the house or activity area and the settlement or component (Flannery 1976).

In this study, the primary data from all components at the Labras Lake site have been segregated into feature clusters or household units, and microwear analysis was performed on samples drawn from specific clusters, not from entire components. The number of artifacts in each lithic assemblage varies: 10,917 for the Late Archaic, 1,489 for the Late Woodland, and 14,474 for the Mississippian.

TABLE 7. Total lithic artifacts from each component at Labras Lake and the number and percentage of different artifact types in the microwear sample.

TOOL TYPE	LATE ARCHAIC			LATE WOODLAND		
	Total Artifacts	In Sample NO.	%	Total Artifacts	In Sample NO.	%
End Scraper	4	4	100%	-	-	-
Side Scraper	1	1	100%	2	2	100%
Burin	5	4	80%	-	-	-
Notched Flake	20	10	50%	4	3	75%
Denticulate	10	4	40%	4	4	100%
Perforator	7	7	100%	-	-	-
Truncation	6	1	17%	-	-	-
Multiple Tool	64	6	25%	1	1	100%
Biface	63	43	68%	2	2	100%
Retouched Flake	262	79	30%	40	20	50%
Total Tools	**402**	**159**	**40%**	**53**	**32**	**60%**

BLANK TYPE

	LATE ARCHAIC			LATE WOODLAND		
Primary Flake	60	12	20%	14	14	100%
Secondary Flake	2723	168	6%	262	28	11%
Blade	52	20	38%	6	6	100%
Core Trimmer	26	4	15%	10	10	100%
Core	43	2	5%	3	2	67%
Broken Core	19	1	5%	2	2	100%
Biface Fragment	73	10	14%	6	6	100%
Total Blanks:	**2996**	**217**	**7%**	**303**	**68**	**22%**
GRAND TOTAL:	**3398**	**376**	**11%**	**356**	**100**	**28%**

TABLE 7, continued

| TOOL TYPE | MISSISSIPPIAN | | | ALL COMPONENTS | | |
	Total Artifacts	In Sample NO.	%	Total Artifacts	In Sample NO.	%
End Scraper	11	11	100%	15	15	100%
Side Scraper	11	11	100%	14	14	100%
Burin	4	3	75%	9	7	78%
Notched Flake	40	30	75%	64	43	67%
Denticulate	14	11	78%	28	19	68%
Perforator	15	15	100%	22	22	100%
Truncation	4	4	100%	10	5	50%
Multiple Tool	20	10	50%	45	17	38%
Biface	17	11	65%	82	56	68%
Retouched Flake	403	85	21%	705	184	26%
Total Tools:	**539**	**191**	**35%**	**994**	**382**	**38%**
BLANK TYPE						
Primary Flake	495	41	8%	569	67	12%
Secondary Flake	3518	243	7%	6503	439	7%
Blade	38	29	76%	96	55	57%
Core Trimmer	21	21	100%	57	35	61%
Core	52	4	8%	98	8	8%
Broken Core	8	0	-	29	3	10%
Biface Fragment	59	4	7%	138	20	14%
Total Blanks:	**4191**	**342**	**8%**	**7490**	**627**	**8%**
GRAND TOTAL:	**4730**	**533**	**11%**	**8484**	**1009**	**12%**

The Mississippian lithic assemblage is nearly ten times larger than the Late Woodland inventory; while the Late Archaic collection is seven times larger than the Late Woodland, and three-fourths the size of the Mississippian assemblage. Direct comparisons of microwear samples drawn from total assemblages may be misleading. Functional variation between the three assemblages may be due to the disparity in their sizes, not to activity differences that reflect contrasting site utilization strategies during the different occupational episodes. To avoid problems of scale in interassemblage comparisons, the household was used as the basic analytical unit in this study.

While 159 (or 40%) of the 402 tools found in Late Archaic contexts at Labras Lake were examined for microwear traces (table 7), only 238 of those tools were found inside Late Archaic features (table 8). In the south western area, 29 of the 71 tools recovered from Late Archaic features were examined (41%), and these included between 50% and 100% of each of nine formal tool types (defined by Phillips 1980) such as end scrapers, side scrapers, burins, and perforators (table 8). In addition, 31% of the retouched pieces (defined as chert flakes that had been further shaped by percussion or pressure flaking) were examined.

TABLE 8. Total lithic artifacts found inside and outside of Late Archaic features at Labras Lake and the number and percentage of each type in the microwear sample.

| | SOUTHWESTERN LATE ARCHAIC COMPONENT | | | | | |
| | *Inside Features* | | | *Outside Features* | | |
TOOL TYPE	Total Artifacts	In Sample NO.	%	Total Artifacts	In Sample NO.	%
End Scraper	-	-	-	1	1	100%
Burin	2	1	50%	-	-	-
Notched Flake	4	2	50%	-	-	-
Denticulate	2	2	100%	-	-	-
Perforator	-	-	-	1	0	-
Truncation	1	1	100%	1	1	100%
Multiple Tool	3	3	100%	1	0	-
Biface	4	3	75%	3	0	-
Retouched Flake	55	17	31%	25	1	4%
Total Tools:	71	29	41%	35	3	9%
BLANK TYPE						
Primary Flake	7	3	43%	4	0	-
Secondary Flake	466	45	10%	462	0	-
Blade	12	5	42%	5	0	-
Core Trimmer	1	0	-	3	0	-
Core	5	0	-	8	0	-
Broken Core	3	0	-	5	0	-
Biface Fragment	9	2	22%	-	-	-
Preform	1	0	-	-	-	-
Total Blanks:	504	55	11%	487	0	-
GRAND TOTAL:	575	84	15%	522	3	<1%

TABLE 8, continued

LATE ARCHAIC COMPONENTS IN THE CENTRAL BLOCK

TOOL TYPE	Inside Features			Outside Features		
	Total Artifacts	In Sample NO.	%	Total Artifacts	In Sample NO.	%
End Scraper	1	1	100%	2	2	100%
Side Scraper	-	-	-	1	1	100%
Burin	1	1	100%	2	2	100%
Notched Flake	12	7	58%	4	1	25%
Denticulate	4	2	50%	3	1	33%
Perforator	4	4	100%	2	2	100%
Truncation	-	-	-	4	0	-
Multiple Tool	5	3	60%	13	0	-
Biface	40	40	100%	16	0	-
Retouched Flake	100	60	60%	82	1	1%
Total Tools:	**167**	**118**	**71%**	**129**	**10**	**8%**

BLANK TYPE

	Total Artifacts	In Sample NO.	%	Total Artifacts	In Sample NO.	%
Primary Flake	15	9	60%	34	0	-
Secondary Flake	1072	123	11%	723	1	<1%
Blade	27	15	56%	8	0	-
Core Trimmer	11	4	36%	11	0	-
Core	8	2	25%	22	0	-
Broken Core	4	1	25%	7	0	-
Biface Fragment	61	7	11%	-	-	-
Preform	1	1	100%	1	0	-
Total Blanks:	**1199**	**162**	**14%**	**806**	**1**	**<1%**
GRAND TOTAL:	**1366**	**280**	**20%**	**935**	**11**	**1%**

In the central excavation block, 118 (or 71%) of the 167 tools found in Late Archaic features were analyzed. (In the original analysis [Phillips et al. 1980], the Late Archaic features in the central excavation block were treated as a single component, and the lithic data were compiled for the entire unit. In this study the features in the central excavation block have been subdivided into three areas, but data on the number of lithic artifacts found outside of features in each of these three areas are unavailable.)

In all, 147 (or 62%) of the 238 tools found in the Late Archaic features at Labras Lake were examined for use wear. Only 13 (or 8%) of the 164 Late Archaic tools that were found outside of features were included in the microwear sample (table 8). These tools were selected from features associated with the four Late Archaic household and pit clusters because it was believed that they would reveal the most information about the activities that went on in those areas of the site.

All of the unretouched blanks selected for microwear analysis (except one secondary flake recovered near the Feature 138 domestic area) were found inside of features. Blanks include **primary flakes** that were removed from a block of stone when it was being "roughed out" (primary flakes have some cortex on their surfaces); unretouched **secondary flakes** that show no cortex and were removed from a tool during the final stages of manufacture; **blades**, which are flakes that are twice as long as they are wide, have parallel edges, and often show the traces of previous parallel removals; **core trimmers** or flakes that have been removed from a core in the course of preparing or rejuvenating it; **cores**, and **broken cores**, which are blocks of lithic raw material from which flakes and blades are detached; **biface fragments**; and **preforms**, or roughed out, unused tool blanks generally shaped by pressure flaking (Crabtree 1972; Phillips 1980; Tixier 1974).

The 5 cores, 3 broken cores, 1 preform, and the lone core trimming flake from the southwestern area features were not examined, since it was assumed that these artifacts were associated with lithic manufacturing activities. Three of the 7 primary flakes (43%), 45 of the 466 unretouched secondary flakes (10%), 5 of the 12 blades (42%), and 2 of the 9 biface fragments (22%) were selected after the entire southwestern Late Archaic lithic assemblage was laid out on a laboratory table. Different types of blanks were randomly selected from pits found in this part of the site.

A similar selection process was used on the Late Archaic blanks from the central excavation block. In that area, 162 of the 1,199 unretouched artifacts found in Late Archaic features (14%) were included in the microwear sample, while between 11% and 100% of each different blank type were examined for wear traces (table 8). In all, 217 (or 13%) of the 1,703 blanks found in Late Archaic features at Labras Lake were analyzed, and out of the 1,941 Late Archaic artifacts found in features, 364 (or 19%) were included in the microwear study.

The Early Bluff lithic assemblage is smaller, and probably represents a single occupation episode. The microwear sample included 32 of the 53 tools assigned to the Early Bluff component (60%), and 68 of the 303 blanks in that assemblage (22%). In all, 100 of the 356 Early Bluff artifacts (or 28% of the total) were examined for use wear (table 7).

The Mississippian microwear sample includes 35% of the tools assigned to that component, and 8% of the blanks., However, the artifacts selected for analysis were drawn from the lithic assemblages associated with the six Mississippian wall trench houses at Labras Lake (table 9). In fact, between

TABLE 9. Total lithic artifacts from the Mississippian houses at Labras Lake and the number and percentage of each type in the microwear sample.

	HOUSE 1			HOUSE 2			HOUSE 3					
							Upper Level			Lower Level		
TOOL TYPE	Tot. Art.	Sample NO.	%	Tot. Art.	Sample NO.	%	Tot. Art.	Sample NO.	%	Tot. Art.	Sample NO.	%
End Scr.	5	5	100%	-	-	-	3	3	100%	-	-	-
Side Scr.	2	2	100%	1	1	100%	-	-	-	-	-	-
Burin	-	-	-	3	3	100%	-	-	-	-	-	-
Notch	4	4	100%	9	9	100%	3	3	100%	1	1	100%
Dent.	-	-	-	4	4	100%	-	-	-	2	2	100%
Perf.	3	3	100%	5	5	100%	2	2	100%	2	2	100%
Trunc.	-	-	-	-	-	-	-	-	-	-	-	-
Mult. Tool	-	-	-	2	2	100%	-	-	-	1	1	100%
Biface	3	3	100%	5	5	100%	2	2	100%	-	-	-
Ret'd Fl.	88	21	24%	62	15	24%	53	10	19%	29	9	32%
Total	**105**	**29**	**36%**	**91**	**44**	**48%**	**63**	**20**	**32%**	**35**	**15**	**43%**

BLANK TYPE

Prim. Fl.	10	5	50%	287	15	5%	24	5	21%	14	3	21%
Sec'd. Fl.	213	23	11%	728	91	13%	245	26	10%	269	26	11%
Blade	5	5	100%	4	4	100%	2	2	100%	1	1	100%
Core Tr.	6	6	100%	9	9	100%	4	4	100%	1	1	100%
Core	4	2	50%	6	1	17%	9	0	-	1	0	-
Biface Fr.	1	1	100%	-	-	-	-	-	-	1	1	100%
Total	**239**	**42**	**18%**	**1034**	**120**	**12%**	**284**	**37**	**13%**	**287**	**32**	**11%**
GR. TOT.	**344**	**80**	**23%**	**1125**	**164**	**15%**	**347**	**57**	**16%**	**322**	**47**	**15%**

TABLE 9, continued

TOOL TYPE	HOUSE 4			HOUSE 5			HOUSE 6			MISS. TOTAL		
	Tot. Art.	Sample NO.	%	Tot. Art.	Sample NO.	%	Tot. Art.	Sample NO.	%	Tot. Art.	Sample NO.	%
End Scr.	-	-	-	2	2	100%	-	-	-	11	11	100%
Side Scr.	1	1	100%	3	3	100%	2	2	100%	11	11	100%
Burin	-	-	-	-	-	-	-	-	-	4	3	75%
Notch	5	5	100%	4	4	100%	4	4	100%	40	30	75%
Dent.	-	-	-	1	1	100%	4	4	100%	14	11	78%
Perf.	1	1	100%	-	-	-	1	1	100%	15	15	100%
Trunc.	1	1	100%	2	2	100%	1	1	100%	4	4	100%
Mult.Tool	-	-	-	5	5	100%	2	2	100%	20	10	50%
Biface	-	-	-	2	1	50%	-	-	-	17	11	65%
Ret'd Fl.	21	12	57%	20	7	35%	21	6	29%	403	85	21%
Total	**29**	**20**	**69%**	**39**	**25**	**64%**	**35**	**20**	**57%**	**539**	**191**	**35%**

BLANK TYPE

	HOUSE 4			HOUSE 5			HOUSE 6			MISS. TOTAL		
Prim. Fl.	14	5	36%	8	4	50%	4	3	75%	495	41	8%
Sec'd. Fl.	313	34	11%	120	19	16%	154	18	12%	3526	243	7%
Blade	10	10	100%	3	3	100%	3	3	100%	38	29	76%
Core Tr.	1	1	100%	-	-	-	-	-	-	21	21	100%
Core	5	0	-	3	0	-	4	1	25%	52	4	8%
Biface Fr.	-	-	-	2	2	100%	-	-	-	59	4	7%
Total	**343**	**50**	**15%**	**136**	**28**	**20%**	**165**	**25**	**15%**	**4191**	**342**	**8%**
GR. TOT.	**367**	**57**	**19%**	**175**	**53**	**30%**	**200**	**45**	**22%**	**4730**	**533**	**11%**

32% and 69% of the tools found in each Mississippian household cluster were examined, while between 11% and 20% of the blanks were analyzed. Table 9 shows that all of each type of formal tool in each house were usually studied, while between 19% and 54% of the retouched flakes were examined. Between 11% and 100% of the samples of each type of blank found in the houses were also included in the microwear study.

The microwear samples used in this study were large enough to reveal the range of activities that went on at each household cluster at Labras Lake, and included almost all of the "formal" tools that were recovered. While it may not be possible to quantify the subsistence and maintenance activities that ere performed with the analyzed artifacts, the functional information provided by the microwear analysis is more specific than any data that could be obtained from the analysis of tool and feature morphology.

Refitting and Cross-mending

The lithic and ceramic artifacts from Labras Lake were examined for possible refits and cross-mends during the UIC Labras Lake investigations, and the lithic refitting was continued as part of this study. Refitting is not a new technique, but Daniel Cahen and Lawrence Keeley have shown that when piece plotting, refitting, and microwear analysis are used in combination, the manufacture, use, and disposal of stone implements can be studied within a dynamic structural framework. The "life histories" of stone tools can be documented with these techniques, and the examination of "tool kits" and "activity areas" can be undertaken using functional as well as spatial information (Audouze et al. 1981; Cahen et al. 1979).

Unfortunately, the refitting program at Labras Lake failed to produce many large lithic blocks that could be used to study tool production and use in the fashion of Cahen and Keeley at the sites of Meer and Verberie; but refits were used to link features and study spatial patterning in the lithic assemblages. A number of excavated features at Labras Lake contained no diagnostic material, but several of these pits could be assigned to a specific cultural component because they were linked to a "dated" feature by lithic refits. Refit patterns were also used to establish the boundaries of household or feature clusters, and some insights into tool production were also provided by blocks that contained several refits.

Late Archaic Microwear Samples I. Southwestern Area

A total of 4,100 lithic artifacts were recovered in the southwestern area of the Labras Lake site. There were 115 tools (3% of the total), 995 un-retouched blanks (24%), and 2,990 chips and chunks classified as debris (73%). Most of the tools were retouched pieces, while most of the blanks were unretouched secondary flakes.

Microwear traces were observed on 21 of the 32 tools that were examined (66%), but only 14 of the 55 blanks (25%) appear to have been used. Ten of the utilized artifacts were meat knives (25%), and 11 were used to work hides (28%). Eight tools (20%) were used to work wood; 9 artifacts (22%) were used on bone or antler material; and 2 implements (5%) had wear traces that could not be identified (table 10). A total 87 implements from the southwestern component were microscopically examined, and 35 (or 40%) had visible wear traces on their edges. Five of the tools were used in more than one activity, so 40 separate tasks are represented in the southwestern microwear sample.

TABLE 10. Summary of tool functions in microwear samples from four Late Archaic components at the Labras Lake site.

TOOL FUNCTION	SOUTH CENTRAL NO.	%	NORTH-WESTERN NO.	%	SOUTH-WESTERN NO.	%	NORTH CENTRAL NO.	%	TOTAL ARCHAIC NO.	%
Meat Knife	13	45%	1	7%	10	25%	4	16%	28	25%
Hide Knife	-	-	-	-	3	8%	1	4%	4	4%
Hide Scraper	6	21%	3	20%	7	18%	8	32%	24	22%
Hide Awl/Reamer	1	3%	1	7%	1	2%	2	7%	5	5%
Wood Saw	-	-	-	-	3	8%	-	-	3	3%
Wood Scraper	1	3%	3	20%	4	10%	1	4%	9	8%
Wood Borer	-	-	-	-	-	-	1	4%	1	1%
Wood Graver	-	-	1	7%	1	2%	-	-	2	2%
Bone/Antler Saw	-	-	-	-	3	8%	-	-	3	3%
B/A Scraper	3	10%	3	20%	2	5%	5	20%	13	12%
B/A Graver	-	-	-	-	4	10%	-	-	4	4%
Unknown Use	5	17%	3	20%	2	5%	3	12%	13	12%
Total Tasks:	29	99%	15	101%	40	101%	25	99%	109	101%
Total Tools:	27		15		35		24		101	

TOOL CATEGORY

	SOUTH CENTRAL NO.	%	NORTH-WESTERN NO.	%	SOUTH-WESTERN NO.	%	NORTH CENTRAL NO.	%	TOTAL ARCHAIC NO.	%
BUTCHERY	13	45%	1	7%	10	25%	4	15%	28	25%
HIDE-WORKING	7	24%	4	27%	11	28%	11	28%	33	30%
WOOD-WORKING	1	3%	4	27%	8	20%	2	7%	15	13%
BONE/ANTLER WORKING	3	10%	3	20%	9	22%	5	18%	20	18%

Note: percentages may not sum to 100% due to rounding errors.

Microwear analysis showed that at least eleven different activities were performed by the Late Archaic inhabitants of the southwestern area (table 10), but there does not appear to be a good correspondence between the form of the utilized tools and their functions. Implements from several different formal classes were used to perform the same task, while a single formal class of tools often contained artifacts that served a variety of functions. For example, denticulates, notches, retouched flakes, unretouched blades, and secondary flakes were all used to cut meat; while the formal class "notched flake" included a meat knife, a dry-hide scraper, and a hide knife.

Artifact Form and Function

It must be remembered, however, that the artifact typology used in the Labras Lake investigations was morphological and was not designed to provide functional descriptions of the artifacts (Phillips 1980). If formal/functional relationships are to be addressed, the lithics from Labras Lake must be classified under a system that uses tool morphology, not microwear traces, as the basis for determining the function of chipped stone tools.

An artifact typology developed by Carr (1982) uses edge angles, edge shape, knapping techniques, size, and macroscopic edge damage to assign chipped stone implements to functional classes. In Carr's typology, artifacts are divided into retouched and unretouched classes; then the retouched pieces are divided into bifacially and unifacially retouched forms, which are each classified as knives or scrapers, depending on the edge angle (an edge angle less than or equal to 61 degrees is diagnostic of a knife, while an edge angle greater than 61 degrees makes it a scraper). Further classification of the tools depends on the amount and location of edge damage ("wear"), the shape of the edge, and further consideration of edge angles.

When the chipped stone artifacts from the southwestern area that had visible use-wear traces were classified using Carr's system, and the functional interpretations based on morphology and microwear were compared, it was found that they were in agreement in seven out of thirty-three cases (21%). There was partial agreement in eight of thiry-three cases (24%), and disagreement in eighteen of the thirty-three cases, or 55% of the time (table 11).

The high incidence of disagreement is not surprising, because any morphological typology that is used for functional interpretations assumes that tools were manufactured with specific tasks in mind, and that all the tools in a class will conform to the same set of formal specifications.

TABLE 11. Number and percentage of cases when the results of functional analyses of artifacts from Labras Lake based on tool morphology (Carr 1982) and microwear traces were in agreement.

COMPONENT	n	PARTIALLY AGREE		COMPLETELY AGREE		DISAGREE	
		NO.	%	NO.	%	NO.	%
Late Archaic							
Southwestern	33	7	21%	8	24%	18	55%
North Central	21	1	5%	6	28%	14	67%
Northwestern	12	1	8%	3	25%	8	67%
South Central	22	2	9%	3	14%	17	77%
Archaic Total	**88**	**11**	**12%**	**20**	**23%**	**57**	**65%**
Late Woodland	**15**	**1**	**7%**	**4**	**26%**	**10**	**67%**
Mississippian							
House 1	25	2	8%	3	12%	20	80%
House 2	30	2	7%	4	13%	24	80%
House 3 Upper	12	1	8%	1	8%	10	84%
House 3 Lower	10	2	20%	5	50%	3	30%
House 4	11	0	-	4	36%	7	64%
House 5	12	2	17%	4	33%	6	50%
House 6	12	1	8%	2	17%	9	75%
Other Features	10	1	10%	2	20%	7	70%
Miss. Total	**122**	**11**	**9%**	**25**	**20.5%**	**86**	**70.5%**
GRAND TOTAL	**225**	**23**	**10%**	**49**	**22%**	**153**	**68%**

Ethnographic work among modern stone tool users has shown that tools are rarely manufactured with a single task in mind. Instead, stone tools are viewed as pieces of stone, parts of which may be used for different activities (Gould et al 1971; Hayden 1977; Odell 1981; White 1967; White and Thomas 1972).

Microwear analysis of the Late Archaic artifacts from Labras Lake indicates that stone tools were not being "mass produced" by "experts," and that the implements were used for a variety of tasks. Still, some workers maintain that there is a high correlation between tool form and function. Frison and Bradley (1980) claim that even if it can be shown that the implements in a single class of tools were used to perform different tasks, the artifacts that were not used in the way that class of tools was "intended to be used" are functionally aberrant. They go on to cite Francois Bordes's infamous "housewife using a screwdriver" analogy as an example of how formal tools that are functionally specific may be misused. But this suggests that there is little difference in the manufacture and use of stone and metal tools, and that regardless of the raw material involved, both stone and metal tools are specialized and designed to be used for the same task over and over again.

In fact, stone tools are not at all like metal tools, and while the fresh edge of a stone implement may be sharper than its metal equivalent, most stone tools soon become dull, require frequent sharpening, and break more easily than metal tools. The durability of metal tools was recognized by stone tool users who readily accepted them and soon added them to their tool kits. Because lithic tools were rapidly replaced with metal ones, there are few good ethnographic accounts of stone tool technology. Odell (1981) notes that some ethnographic studies of stone tool form and function do show that hafted tools were sometimes made in specific shapes for specific tasks, but unhafted stone tools were casually selected by stone tool users from the odd pieces of stone that were lying around the area where they were working.

Most of the tools in prehistoric midwestern lithic assemblages are unhafted, and were probably not transported between sites in anticipation of future use (Binford 1973) or "disposed of" when a haft was "retooled" (Keeley 1982). Instead, unhafted tools were probably selected as needed from available flakes and were disposed of at or near the place that they were used.

Nonetheless when Carr developed his functional typology, he assumed that if a tool had a distinctive shape, it was produced intentionally by a prehistoric flint knapper who had a specific task in mind. For example, Carr believes notches were designed to smooth wooden shafts, but he also thinks that they were occasionally used to smooth other wooden and bone items (1982: 261-62). Three notches from the southwestern area of the Labras Lake site had polishes and striations indicated that one had been used to scrape dry hide, one had been used to cut meat or fresh hide, and the other had been used to scrape hide and wood (table 12).

Carr believes that unifacially retouched scrapers were used to work wood, bone, and hides. He used the location of edge damage on the piece, the shape of the edge, and the edge angle to distinguish between scrapers that were used on each of these materials (1982: 280-82).According to Carr, straight-edged scrapers would not have been used on hide, since their sharp corners could accidentally pierce the skins that were being worked. Straight-edged scrapers used on hard wood and bone would need to have steeper edge angles (74-84 degrees) than those used on softer materials (61-73 degrees), but both kinds

TABLE 12. Comparison of the results of functional analyses of chipped stone artifacts from the southwestern Late Archaic area based on tool morphology (Carr 1982) and microwear traces.

		ARTIFACT CLASSIFICATION		
LOT NO.	CONTEXT	Phillips (1980)	Carr (1982)	"V" NO.
2786-2	Unit 21	End Scraper	Unifacial Endscraper	V 37
3027-4	F. 778	Burin	N/A	–
3032-2	F. 779	Notched Flake	Notch	V 47
1512(a)	Fea. 72	Primary Flake	Notch	V 48
3034-2	F. 778	Denticulate	Denticulate	V 50
862(a)	Unit 6	Perforator	Drill	V 53
3730-6	F. 1172	Truncation	Lamellar Blade (prox.)	V 58
3025-3	F. 778	Multiple Tool	Chipped Stone Celt	V 98
1515(a)	F. 227	Multiple Tool	Bifacial Knife	V108
3025-1	F. 778	Biface (broken)	Bifacial Knife	V108
3025-2	F. 778	Biface (broken)	Bifacial Knife	V108
3730-20	F. 900	Retouched Flake	Straight-edged Knife	V 84
3730-21	F. 900	Retouched Flake	Straight-edged Knife	V 84
3726-9(26)	F. 896	Retouched Flake	Straight-edged Knife	V 84
3718-1	F. 910	Retouched Flake	Round-edged Knife	V 87a
3723-3	F. 910	Blade	Lamellar Blade	V 11a
3724-1	F. 901	Blade (broken)	Lamellar Blade	V 11b
3025-4	F. 778	Retouched Flake	Round-edged Knife	V 87a
3031-1	F. 779	Retouched Flake	Straight-edged Knife	V 84
2835-2	F. 767	Unretouched Flake	Lamellar Blade	V 11b
1523(a)	F. 272	Notched Flake	Notch	V 45
3993-1	F. 1172	Retouched Flake	Unifacial Scraper	V 75
3700-1	F. 941	Unretouched Flake	Round-edged Knife	V 87a
3023-3	F. 779	Unretouched Flake	Lamellar Blade	V 11b
4045-3	F.941/946	Retouched Flake	Denticulate	V 50
4145-1	F. 944	Retouched Blade	Saw	V 57
2942	Unit 21	Retouched Blade	Saw	V 57
3724-2	F. 901	Unretouched Flake	Lamellar Blade	V 11a
3730-50	F. 1172	Unretouched Flake	Notch	V 47
1509(a)	F. 271	Unretouched Flake	Lamellar Blade	V 11b
2950-3	F. 777	Unretouched Flake	Spur	V 52
4048-1	F. 946	Unretouched Flake	Straight-edged Knife	V 84
3726-4	F. 899	Unretouched Flake	Spur	V 51
3730-38	F. 1172	Unretouched Flake	Chipping Debris	V 15
3032-1	F. 779	Retouched Flake	Concave-edged Knife	V 88
4049-2	F. 910	Unretouched Flake	Lamellar Blade (prox.)	V 58

TABLE 12, continued

	FUNCTIONAL INTERPRETATION		Agree/
LOT NO.	Carr (1982)	Microwear Analysis	Disagree
2786-2	work soft wood	scrape dry hide	disagree
3027-4	N/A	engrave bone/antler	N/A
3032-2	work wood	scrape dry hide	disagree
1512(a)	smoothing wood/bone	scrape dry hide/wood	(agree)
3034-2	scrape plants/hide	cut meat/fresh hide	disagree
862(a)	drill wood/bone	bore or ream dry hide	disagree
3730-6	groove wood/bone	unknown	N/A
3025-3	scrape bark/soft wood	scrape dry hide	disagree
1515(a)	scrape (grain) hide	cut and scrape dry hide	agree
3025-1	scrape (grain) hide	saw bone/antler	disagree
3025-2	scrape (grain) hide	scrape dry hide	agree
3730-20	whittle wood/bone/horn	cut meat/fresh hide	disagree
3730-21	whittle wood/bone/horn	cut meat/fresh hide	disagree
3726-9(26)	whittle wood/bone/horn	cut meat/fresh hide	disagree
3718-1	cut meat/skin/sinew	cut meat/fresh hide	agree
3723-3	whittle wood/bone	cut meat/fresh hide	disagree
3724-1	cut meat/hide/plants	cut meat/fresh hide	(agree)
3025-4	cut meat/skin/sinew	scrape bone	disagree
3031-1	whittle wood/bone/horn	cut meat/fresh hide	disagree
2835-2	cut meat/hide/plants	cut meat/fresh hide	(agree)
1523(a)	smooth wood	cut meat/fresh hide	disagree
3993-1	scrape wood	scrape dry hide	disagree
3700-1	cut meat/skin/sinew	cut dry hide	agree
3023-3	cut meat/hide/plants	cut dry hide	(agree)
4045-3	scrape plants/hide	saw wood	disagree
4145-1	work wood/bone	saw wood/bone	agree
2942	work wood/bone	saw wood/bone	agree
3724-2	whittle bone/wood	whittle or scrape wood	(agree)
3730-50	work wood	whittle or scrape wood	agree
1509(a)	cut meat/hide/plants	whittle wood	disagree
2950-3	work hard wood/bone	chisel or engrave wood	(agree)
4048-1	whittle wood/bone/horn	Whittle bone	(agree)
3726-4	work hard wood/bone	engrave bone/antler	(agree)
3730-38	lithic manufacturing	engrave bone/antler	disagree
3032-1	dehair hide	engrave bone/antler	disagree
4049-2	groove wood/bone	unknown	N/A

V NO. = Variable number (Carr 1982: 212-308)

of straight-edged scrapers would have edge damage on their unretouched faces. Round-edged scrapers or slightly concave-edged scrapers would be classified as hide-working tools in Carr's system, since those shapes would conform to the contours of the hides being scraped (Carr 1982: 281).

Cantwell (1979) has argued that artifact weight and bit-thickness can be used to separate unifacial scrapers that were used on wood from those that were used on hide. She took a sample of sixty-four heat-treated chert scrapers from the Middle Woodland Dickson Camp and Pond sites, and examined their edges for wear using a stereo zoom microscope. She did not state the explicit criteria she used in identifying the wear traces (1979: 6), but based on her unstated wear criteria, she noted that hardwood scrapers were larger, heavier, and had thicker bits than the hide scrapers. In addition she noted that the edge angles on the hardwood scrapers tended to be steeper.

It is not clear if Cantwell included both broken and complete scrapers in her sample, but in her report on the two sites, she illustrates some examples of hardwood and hide scrapers. While the hardwood scrapers in these figures seem to be complete specimens, the hide scrapers are broken (Cantwell 1980: figures 5.17, 5.18, 5.19). This may account for the difference in mean weight between the two classes of scrapers.

Two of the tools in the microwear sample from the southwestern area of the Labras Lake site were classified as unifacial scrapers by Phillips (1980); and the same two, plus an additional implement, would fit Carr's criteria for scrapers. In Carr's system, these tools would be interpreted as softwood scrapers. Using Cantwell's method, the edge angles would indicate that these three scrapers were all used on hide, while the size and bit-thickness of two out of three of the southwestern scrapers would suggest they were hardwood scrapers.

Microwear analysis showed that all three were used to scrape dry hide (table 12). By following the classification procedures outlined by Carr and Cantwell, scrapers can be subdivided into formal classes that are based on morphological criteria, but it does not follow that these morphological differences can be used to determine how the tools were used.

Carr used similar morphological attributes to classify bifacial tools, and suggest their functions. Edge shape, edge angles, and edge damage were again used to distinguish bone scrapers, plant-working tools, hide-working tools, and butchering tools. However, the functional interpretations of the tools from the southwestern area that were based on microwear rarely agreed with the functional interpretations derived from the morphological attributes in Carr's system.

More than a decade ago, Winters stated that "no **individual** artifact can be classified with any certainty as to function, but . . .the individual specimen can be assigned to a [functional] class on the basis of statistical tendency rather than on the basis of absolute identification of the function of each specimen" (1969: 31). Microwear analysis provides a means to identify the function of individual artifacts and to determine what kinds of activities went on at an archaeological site, rather than how tools were **likely** to have been used and what the most **probable** activities were. There are limitations to the application of microwear studies, but if the goal is to determine the function of artifacts and to document the activities that were performed at a site, interpretations based on evidence derived from use wear are superior to those based on speculation and analogy.

Microwear traces on twenty-one artifacts, or 53% of the used tools in the southwestern Late Archaic sample, indicated they were used to butcher animals and work hides. Hunting and animal processing were obviously important economic activities, even though very few animal remains were recovered from the southwestern area of the Labras Lake site. Wood-, bone-, and antler-working tools were also present in the microwear sample, suggesting that a number of nonlithic tool production and maintenance activities were performed during the Late Archaic occupation here, despite the fact that not a single bone, antler, or wooden tool was recovered during the course of the UIC excavations.

Late Archaic Microwear Samples: II. North Central Area

The feature distribution in the north central area resembles the pattern observed in the southwestern habitation area, and the lithic assemblages from the two areas are similar. A total of fifty-seven tools and fifty-one blanks from the north central area were microscopically examined, and eighteen tools (32%) and six blanks (12%) had wear traces on their edges. The twenty-four utilized implements were used to perform twenty-seven different tasks. Eleven artifacts (41%) were used to work hide; four implements (15%) were used to cut meat, and two artifacts (7%) served as wood-working tools. Five implements (18%) were used on bone or antler material, but the microwear traces on three artifacts (11%) could not be identified. Two "hoe flakes" with distinctive "corn gloss" turned up in this sample. The hoe chips are probably associated with later Mississippian or Late Woodland cultivation in the north central area.

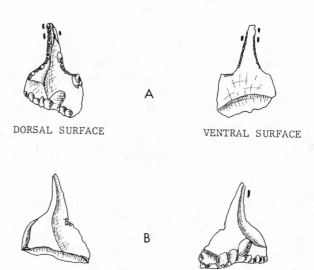

Figure 30. Perforators from the north central Late Archaic area at Labras Lake. A. Lot #1269(a), Feature 172, the tip of this tool was "stained" red. B. Lot #2030(d), Feature 599 (a storage/refuse pit inside of Feature 171), dark lines show the location of the hide polish.

The majority of the artifacts in the north central microwear sample were used to process hides. Eight hide scrapers, a hide knife, and two hide reamers chipped stone gravers that Nero (1957) identified as wood- or bone-engraving tools (although he mentioned that they may have been used in tatooing or other piercing operations).

Winters (1969) recovered microperforators at Riverton Culture sites, and noted that these tools occur at other Late Archaic sites throughout the Midwest and South. According to Winters, microperforators were made on free flakes, with a "perforating, or possibly a graving, spur with scraping edges, pigment stains on some specimens, and use polish confined to the tip" (1969: 53-55).

A search of the ethnographic literature revealed that the Omaha fabricated arrow shafts by whittling branches to the proper size and removing all the knots. Next they smoothed the arrows and grooved or engraved their shafts (Fletcher and LaFlesche 1911, cited in Winters 1969). This suggested a possible function for the microperforators to Winters, who believed the concave scraping edges on these implements may have served as shaft smoothers, while the sharp tips were used to engrave or groove finished atlatl darts (Winters 1969: 54).

Carr classified microperforators as spurs (which he distinguished from gravers or because spurs are retouched to a point). He cited several ethnographic accounts that describe the aboriginal use of spurs during the production of wooden dart or arrow shafts, bone needles, and antler implements, but he also noted that they may have been used to "pierce holes in leather while sewing." However, based on the spatial associations between spurs and other artifacts that he believed were used to work wood and bone, Carr concluded that spurs were used to groove hardwood and bone (1982: 264-65).

Two artifacts from the north central area of the Labras Lake site resembled spurs, and one of these had a reddened tip. However, when a series of experiments were conducted with replicas of these tools, the microwear patterns that were produced when wood, bone, and antler material were scraped and engraved did not resemble the observed use wear on the archaeological specimens.

When experimental perforators were used to bore or ream out holes in dry hide, the wear patterns on the replicas were similar to the microwear traces on the microperforators from the north central area. These two perforators were found in and near Feature 171, a large domestic area, and were nearly identical in form (figure 30). Both had dry-hide polish on their tips, but one of the tools was retouched and had a reddened tip, while the other was unretouched, without the discolored appendage. The red-tipped perforator was not coated with ochre or any other pigment; and the discoloration, which resembles the color change associated with thermal pretreatment of chert (Price et al. 1982: 469), may be the result of friction during dry-hide boring and reaming activities.

The hide polish on the red-tipped perforator was well-developed, and the tool was probably used for a longer period of time than the other hide reamer; but more experiments are needed to prove that prolonged dry-hide boring and reaming will cause the tips of these perforators to become discolored.

Microwear analysis has shown that the perforators from the north central portion of the Labras Lake site were not used to produce wooden atlatl shafts or to engrave bone or antler, but there is evidence that these materials had been worked by the inhabitants of the north central area. Two wood-working tools and five bone and antler scrapers were found in the north central area, even though no wood, bone, or antler artifacts were recovered. In fact, no bone or antler tools were found during the UIC excavations at Labras Lake; and none have been found at any of the excavated Late Archaic sites on the American Bottom.

Bone and antler implements were an integral part of Riverton tool assemblages (Winters 1969), and tools made of these materials have been recovered at contemporary sites in the South and Midwest. Their absence at Late Archaic sites on the American Bottom is more likely the result of poor preservation than of cultural or technological exclusion.

Butchering tools and wood-working implements were less common in the north central microwear sample than they were in the southwestern assemblage (table 10), but a number of different activities are represented in both microwear samples. However, when the used artifacts in the north central microwear sample were classified using Carr's system, and functional determinations were made using morphological attributes, only 5% of the morphological interpretations agreed with the microwear results. There was partial agreement in 28% of the cases, and disagreement 67% of the time. The only case where the morphological interpretation matched the microwear evidence involved a drill used to bore wood. The functional morphological classifications of several scrapers and knives that had been used on hides were in partial agreement with the microwear results, but the functions that were assigned to two-thirds of the tools when Carr's system was employed were quite different from those based on microwear analysis (table 13).

Late Archaic Microwear Samples III: Northwestern Area

Some thirty-four tools and thirty-six blanks from the northwestern area were examined for microwear traces. Eleven of the tools (32%) and four of the blanks (11%) were used. Four of the artifacts (27%) were used on hide, while another four were used to work wood. Three implements were used to scrape bone or antler (20%), and a single artifact was used to cut meat (7%). Three implements had microwear traces that could not be identified (table 10).

When the fifteen used implements in the northwestern microwear sample were classified using Carr's system, the functional interpretation of one tool agreed with the microwear evidence (an unretouched flake, or "round-edged knife," used to scrape hide), while there was partial agreement in three cases (25%), and disagreement in eight others (65%). The cases of partial agreement involved a denticulate used to scrape hide and two wood-working tools (table 13).

Several tasks are represented by the microwear traces on the fifteen used artifacts in the northwestern area, but lithic manufacture and repair seem to have been the primary activities that were performed in this part of the site. Three of the used tools seem to have been hafted during use, and three others are broken. These hafted and broken tools may have been discarded in this area after they were replaced with newly made tools (Keeley 1982).

Late Archaic Microwear Samples: IV. South Central Area

Some fourty-two tools and sixty-nine blanks from the south central Late Archaic component at Labras lake were examined for microwear traces. Fifteen of the tools (36%) and twelve of the blanks (17%) were used. Twenty-nine tasks were performed with these twenty-seven utilized tools, which included thirteen

TABLE 13. Comparison of the results of functional analyses of chipped stone artifacts from the north central and northwestern Late Archaic areas based on tool morphology (Carr 1982) and microwear traces.

North Central Area
ARTIFACT CLASSIFICATION

LOT NO.	CONTEXT	Phillips (1980)	Carr (1982)	"V" NO.
3478-3	F. 857	Retouched Flake	Straight-edged Knife	V 84
3229-1	F. 831	Retouched Flake	Straight-edged Knife	V 85
3313-7	F. 841	Biface	Bifacial Knife	V108
3679-1	F. 885	Biface (broken)	Bifacial Knife	V108
1984(b)	F. 557	Retouched Flake	Straight-edged Knife	V 85
2030(a)	F. 559	End Scraper	Straight-edged Knife	V 85
2030(b)	F. 559	End Scraper	St.-edged Scraper	V 75
1272(b)	F. 173	Unretouched Flake	Unretouched Blade	V 11a
3477-1	F. 857	Retouched Flake	Concave-edged Knife	V 88
3085-1	F. 831	Multiple Tool	Notch	V 45
3050-1	F. 821	Multiple Tool	Notch/Scraper	47/81
1859(a)	F. 174	Biface (broken)	Straight-edged Knife	V 83
3670-1	F. 887	Unretouched Flake	Round-edged Knife	V 87a
1269(a)	F. 172	Perforator	Drill	V 54
2030(c)	F. 559	Perforator	Drill	V 54
3085-3	F. 831	Core Trimmer	Chipping Debris	V 15
1826	F. 555	Perforator	Drill	V 54
1872(b)	F. 171	Biface (broken)	Cache Blade/Notch	42/47
1268(a)	F. 171	Retouched Flake	Notch/St.-edged Knife	46/85
1272(f)	F. 173	Unretouched Flake	Chipping Debris	V 15

LOT NO.	CONTEXT	Phillips (1980)	Carr (1982)	"V" NO.
3312-1	F. 841	Biface	Cache Blade	V 41
1708(a)	F. 246	Retouched Flake	Round-edged Knife	V 87a
1663(a)	F. 249	Biface	Cache Blade	V 42
3651-1	F. 894	Biface (broken)	Cache Blade	V 41

North Central Area
FUNCTIONAL INTERPRETATION

LOT NO.	Carr (1982)	Microwear Analysis	Agree/ Disagree
3478-3	whittle wood/bone/horn	cut meat/fresh hide	disagree
3229-1	dehair hide	cut meat/fresh hide	disagree
3313-7	scrape (grain) hide	cut meat/fresh hide	disagree
3679-1	scrape (grain) hide	cut meat/fresh hide	disagree
1984(b)	dehair hide	scrape dry hide	(agree)
2030(a)	dehair hide	scrape dry hide	(agree)
2030(b)	scrape wood	scrape dry hide	disagree
1272(b)	whittle wood/bone	scrape dry hide	disagree
3477-1	dehair hide	scrape dry hide	(agree)
3085-1	smooth wooden shafts	scrape dry hide	disagree
3050-1	work wood/bone/hide	scrape hide/bone/antler	(agree)
1859(a)	dehair hide	scrape dry hide	(agree)
3670-1	cut meat/skin/sinew	cut dry hide	(agree)
1269(a)	drill soft wood	bore or ream dry hide	disagree
2030(c)	drill soft wood	bore or ream dry hide	disagree
3085-3	lithic manufacturing	scrape wood	disagree
1826	drill soft wood	drill wood	agree
1872(b)	work hide/wood	scrape bone/antler	disagree
1268(a)	work wood/hide	scrape bone/antler	disagree
1272(f)	lithic manufacturing	scrape bone/antler	disagree
3312-1	animal dismembering	scrape bone/antler	disagree
1708(a)	cut meat/skin/sinew	unknown	N/A
1663(a)	deflesh hide	unknown	N/A
3651-1	animal dismembering	unknown	N/A

Northwestern Area
ARTIFACT CLASSIFICATION

LOT NO.	CONTEXT	Phillips (1980)	Carr (1982)	"V" NO.
768(b)	Fea. 57	Unretouched Flake	Chipping Debris	V 15
1816(a)	Unit 14	Denticulate	Denticulate	V 49
1157(q)	Fea. 52	Unretouched Flake	Round-edged Knife	V 87b
651(a)	Fea. 45	Biface	Cache Blade	V 41
566(a)	Unit 7	Perforator	Drill	V 53
687(a)	Unit 7	Side Scraper	Concave-edge Scraper	V 89b
566-7	Unit 7	Notch	Notch	V 48

Table 13, continued

Northwestern Area
ARTIFACT CLASSIFICATION

LOT NO.	CONTEXT	Phillips (1980)	Carr (1982)	"V" NO.
687-1	Unit 7	Perforator	Drill	V 54
566-2	Unit 7	Retouched Flake	Spur	V 51
905(b)	Fea. 52	Biface Fragment	Chopper (fragment)	V 92
684(c)	Fea. 52	Unretouched Flake	Chipping Debris	V 15
767	Fea. 57	Unretouched Flake	Notch	V 47
1174(a)	Fea. 52	Retouched Flake	Drill	V 54
1157(g)	F. 52	Retouched Flake	Straight-edged Knife	V 84
814(h)	F. 52	Perforator	Drill	V 53

FUNCTIONAL INTERPRETATION

LOT NO.	Carr (1982)	Microwear Analysis	Agree/Disagree
768(b)	lithic manufacturing	cut meat/fresh hide	disagree
1816(a)	scrape plants/hide	scrape dry hide	(agree)
1157(q)	deflesh hide	scrape hide	agree
651(a)	animal dismembering	scrape hide	disagree
566(a)	drill wood/bone	bore or ream dry hide	disagree
687(a)	scrape (grain) hide	scrape wood	disagree
566-7	shape wood/bone shafts	scrape wood	(agree)
687-1	drill soft wood	scrape wood	disagree
566-2	work wood/bone	engrave wood	(agree)
905(b)	rough wood-working	scrape bone/antler	disagree
684c	lithic manufacturing	scrape bone/antler	disagree
767	work wood	scrape bone/antler	disagree
1174(a)	drill soft wood	unknown	N/A
1157(g)	whittle wood/bone/horn	unknown	N/A
814(h)	drill wood/bone	unknown	N/A

V NO. = Variable number (Carr 1982: 212-308);   (agree) = partial agreement

meat knives (45%), seven hide-working tools (24%), and three implements (10%) that were used on bone or antler. One tool (3%) was used to whittle wood, and five of the artifacts (17%) had microwear traces that could not be identified (table 10).

Functional interpretations of the twenty-seven used tools that were based on Carr's morphological system were in agreement with the microwear results in only two cases (9%): a retouched flake/round-edged knife that was used to cut meat, and another of these tools that was used to scrape dry hide. There were three cases of partial agreement (14%), and seventeen cases of disagreement (77%) between the two systems (table 14).

The thirteen tools with microwear traces that indicated they had been used to cut meat were classified as wood working tools (6), dry-hide scrapers (2), and lithic manufacturing debris (3) in Carr's system. Only two of the thirteen implements with meat polish on their edges had the morphlogical attributes that Carr believes are diagnostic of meat knives.

TABLE 14. Comparison of the results of functional analyses of chipped stone artifacts from the south central Late Archaic area based on tool morphology (Carr 1982) and microwear traces.

South Central Area
ARTIFACT CLASSIFICATION

LOT NO.	CONTEXT	Phillips (1980)	Carr (1982)	"V" NO.
2505-1	F. 700	Notched Flake	Notch	V 45
2506-1	F. 700	Biface	Cache Blade	V 43a
2528-1	F. 700	Retouched Flake	Notch/Concave Knife	45/88
2638-4	F. 700	Unretouched Flake	Chipping Debris	V 15
2638-6	F. 700	Unretouched Flake	Notch	V 45
2809-4	F. 746	Retouched Flake	Straight-edged Knife	V 84
2789-7	F. 746	Blade	Lamellar Blade	V 11
2807-8	F. 746	Unretouched Flake	Notch/Round Knife	47/108
2809-9	F. 746	Unretouched Flake	Chipping Debris	V 15
3274-1	F. 835	Retouched Flake	Round-edged Knife	V 87a
393a	Fea. 27	Unretouched Flake	Chipping Debris	V 15
1182	F. 145	Retouched Flake	Round-edged Knife	V108
1797a	F. 298	Retouched Flake	Straight-edged Knife	V 84
2638-2	F. 700	Unretouched Flake	Notch/Spur	47/51
2807-11	F. 746	Notched Flake	Notch	V 48
2807-9	F. 746	Retouched Flake	Round-edged Knife	V108
2628-1	F. 750	Retouched Flake	Round-edged Scraper	V 82
3348-1	Unit 26	End Scraper	Round-edged Knife	V 87a
2720-1	F. 712	Unretouched Flake	Chipping Debris	V 15
2507-4	F. 702	Unretouched Flake	Straight-edged Knife	V 85
2698-4	F. 700	Unretouched Flake	Chipping Debris	V 15
2507-5	F. 702	Multiple Tool	Notch	V 46
2638-5	F. 700	Unretouched Flake	Chipping Debris	V 15
2809-6	F. 746	Retouched Flake	Straight-edged Knife	V 84
2807-10	F. 746	Retouched Flake	Round-edged Knife	V 87a
2717-9	F. 712	Biface Fragment	Notch	V 47
2688-2	F. 712	Unretouched Flake	Chipping Debris	V 15

TABLE 14, continued

South Central Area

LOT NO.	FUNCTIONAL INTERPRETATION Carr (1982)	Microwear Analysis	Agree/ Disagree
2505-1	smooth wooden shafts	cut meat/fresh hide	disagree
2506-1	scrape (grain) hide	cut meat/fresh hide	disagree
2528-1	work wood/hide	cut meat/fresh hide	disagree
2638-4	lithic manufacturing	cut meat/fresh hide	disagree
2638-6	smooth wooden shafts	cut meat/fresh hide	disagree
2809-4	whittle wood/bone/horn	cut meat/fresh hide	disagree
2789-7	cut meat/hide/plants	cut meat/fresh hide	(agree)
2807-8	work wood/dry hide	cut meat/fresh hide	disagree
2809-9	lithic manufacturing	cut meat/fresh hide	disagree
3274-1	cut meat/skin/sinew	cut meat/fresh hide	agree
393a	lithic manufacturing	cut meat/fresh hide	disagree
1182	scrape (grain) hide	cut meat/fresh hide	disagree
1797a	whittle wood/bone/horn	cut meat/fresh hide	disagree
2638-2	work wood/bone	work hide/bone/antler	(agree)
2807-11	scrape wood/bone	scrape dry hide	disagree
2807-9	scrape (grain) hide	scrape dry hide	agree
2528-1	scrape dry hide/wood	scrape dry hide	(agree)
3348-1	cut meat/skin/sinew	scrape dry hide	disagree
2720-1	lithic manufacturing	scrape dry hide	disagree
2507-4	dehair hide	whittle wood	disagree
2698-4	lithic manufacturing	scrape bone/antler	disagree
2507-5	smooth wooden shafts	scrape bone/antler	disagree
2638-5	lithic manufacturing	unknown	N/A
2809-6	whittle wood/bone/horn	unknown	N/A
2807-10	cut meat/skin/sinew	unknown	N/A
2717-9	work wood	unknown	N/A
2688-2	lithic manufacturing	unknown	N/A

V NO. = Variable number (Carr 1982: 212-308); (agree) = partial agreement

Quite a lot of butchering and meat processing seems to have gone on in the south central Late Archaic habitation area, but Carr's morphological system of assessing tool function and site activities would have indicated that wood working, not butchering, was the primary activity (table 15). However, the high density of animal bones in the south central area would corroborate the microwear interpretation. Some 8,222 fragments, or more than 80% of the faunal remains that were recovered from Late Archaic contexts at Labras Lake, came from the south central area. A single pit in this habitation unit, Feature 746, contained 4,110 bone fragments, more than the

TABLE 15. Summary of functional analysis of samples of chipped stone artifacts taken from Late Archaic components at Labras Lake based on tool morphology (Carr 1982) and microwear traces.

TOOL FUNCTION	SOUTHWESTERN AREA				NORTH CENTRAL AREA			
	Carr (1982)		Microwear		Carr (1982)		Microwear	
	No.	%	No.	%	No.	%	No.	%
Meat Knife	7	12%	10	25%	5	17%	4	15%
Hide Knife	-	-	3	8%	-	-	1	4%
Hide Scraper	6	11%	7	18%	10	33%	8	30%
Hide Awl/Reamer	-	-	1	2%	-	-	2	7%
Wood Saw	2	4%	3	8%	-	-	-	-
Wood Scraper	14	25%	4	10%	7	23%	1	4%
Wood Borer	1	2%	-	-	3	10%	1	4%
Wood Graver	4	7%	1	2%	-	-	-	-
Bone/Antler Saw	2	4%	3	8%	-	-	-	-
B/A Scraper	8	10%	2	5%	3	10%	5	18%
B/A Graver	4	7%	4	10%	-	-	-	-
B/A Borer	1	2%	-	-	-	-	-	-
Plant Knife	4	7%	-	-	-	-	2	7%
Plant Shredder	2	4%	-	-	-	-	-	-
Lithic Manufact.	1	2%	-	-	2	7%	-	-
Unknown Use	-	-	2	5%	-	-	3	11%
Total Tasks:	56	100%	40	101%	30	100%	27	100%
Total Tools:	35		35		24		24	

TOOL CATEGORY

BUTCHERY	7	12%	10	25%	5	17%	4	16%
HIDE-WORKING	6	11%	11	28%	10	33%	11	44%
WOOD-WORKING	21	38%	8	20%	10	33%	2	8%
BONE/ANTLER	15	27%	9	22%	3	10%	5	20%
PLANT-WORKING	6	11%	-	-	-	-	-	-
LITHIC MANUFACT.	1	2%	-	-	2	7%	-	-

TOOL FUNCTION	ALL LATE ARCHAIC COMPONENTS			
	Carr (1982)		Microwear	
	No.	%	No.	%
Meat Knife	18	12%	28	25%
Hide Knife	-	-	4	4%
Hide Scraper	25	17%	24	21%
Hide Awl/Reamer	-	-	5	4%
Wood Saw	2	1%	3	3%
Wood Scraper	37	29%	9	8%
Wood Borer	8	6%	1	1%
Wood Graver	6	4%	2	2%
Bone/Antler Saw	2	1%	3	3%
B/A Scraper	18	12%	13	12%
B/A Graver	6	4%	4	4%
B/A Borer	3	2%	-	-
Plant Knife	5	3%	-	-
Plant Shredder	3	2%	-	-
Lithic Manufact.	12	8%	-	-
Unknown Use	-	-	13	12%
Total Tasks:	**145**	**101%**	**111**	**101%**
Total Tools:	**101**		**101**	

TOOL CATEGORY

BUTCHERY	18	12%	28	25%
HIDE-WORKING	25	17%	33	30%
WOOD-WORKING	53	37%	15	13%
BONE/ANTLER	29	20%	20	18%
PLANT-WORKING	8	6%	-	-
LITHIC MANUFACT.	12	8%	-	-

TABLE 15, continued

TOOL FUNCTION	NORTHWESTERN AREA				SOUTH CENTRAL AREA			
	Carr (1982)		Microwear		Carr (1982)		Microwear	
	No.	%	No.	%	No.	%	No.	%
Meat Knife	2	10%	1	7%	4	10%	13	45%
Hide Knife	-	-	-	-	-	-	-	-
Hide Scraper	2	10%	3	20%	7	18%	6	21%
Hide Awl/Reamer	-	-	1	7%	-	-	1	3%
Wood Saw	-	-	-	-	-	-	-	-
Wood Scraper	4	19%	3	20%	12	32%	1	3%
Wood Borer	4	19%	-	-	-	-	-	-
Wood Graver	1	4%	1	7%	1	3%	-	-
Bone/Antler Saw	-	-	-	-	-	-	-	-
B/A Scraper	2	10%	3	20%	5	13%	3	10%
B/A Graver	1	4%	-	-	1	3%	-	-
B/A Borer	2	10%	-	-	-	-	-	-
Plant Knife	-	-	-	-	1	3%	-	-
Plant Shredder	1	4%	-	-	-	-	-	-
Lithic Manufact.	2	10%	-	-	7	18%	-	-
Unknown Use	-	-	3	20%	-	-	5	17%
Total Tasks:	21	100%	15	101%	38	100%	29	99%
Total Tools:	15		15		27		27	

TOOL CATEGORY

BUTCHERY	2	10%	1	7%	4	10%	13	45%
HIDE-WORKING	2	10%	4	27%	7	18%	7	24%
WOOD-WORKING	9	43%	4	27%	13	34%	1	3%
BONE/ANTLER	5	24%	3	20%	6	16%	3	10%
PLANT-WORKING	1	4%	-	-	1	3%	-	-
LITHIC MANUFACT.	2	10%	-	-	7	18%	-	-

Note: percentages may not sum to 100% due to rounding errors.

combined total of all of the faunal elements from the other three Late Archaic components.

Most of the tools in the south central microwear sample were used to process meat, and butchering was an important activity in this habitation area, but implements with morphological attributes that are commonly associated with meat cutting and dismemberment did not dominate the south central lithic assemblage.

Late Archaic Microwear Samples: A Summary

Microwear traces on samples of chipped stone artifacts from four Late
Archaic habitation areas at the Labras Lake site reveal different activity
patterns for each locality. Radiocarbon dates from features in these four
areas suggest that each component was occupied at a different time. The two
earlier occupation episodes fall within the early part of the Labras Lake
phase (1850-1400 b.c.), a time when the Horseshoe Lake meander and the ancient
channel beneath Goose Lake were active reaches of the Mississippi River. These
habitation areas were in the northwestern and south central portions of the
central excavation block at Labras Lake on a slight elevation between the
Prairie Lake and Goose Lake meander scars.

The northwestern and south central occupation episodes are contemporary
with Riverton Culture settlements in the Wabash Valley (which lies some 300
kilometers to the east of the American Bottom). The projectile points
associated with these components are similar to Riverton types such as Trimble
side-notched and Merom expanding-stemmed.

Most of the features in the northwestern area are large artifact
concentrations and small hearths. It is presumed that the small hearths
served as facilities where chipped stone cores and bifaces were heated, since
the percentage of thermally altered chert artifacts (76%) in the lithic
assemblage from the northwestern area is greater than the other late Archaic
areas (56-60%). The lack of floral and faunal remains in the hearths
indicates that they were not used in food-processing activities.

In the Late Archaic settlement system Winters (1969) developed for the
Riverton Culture, the northwestern component at Labras Lake would be
classified as a transient camp. There were seventeen projectile points found
in this 1,200-square-meter area, or 38% of the Late Archaic projectile points
in the central excavation block at Labras Lake, a relatively high incidence of
points. However, few storage pits were found and only a single domestic area
was present in the northwestern area. Winters argues that a foraging mode of
subsistence was practiced by the Late Archaic inhabitants of transient camps
during the fall and spring seasons, when deer and migratory waterfowl were
hunted, nuts and seed-bearing plants were gathered, and fishing was practiced
(1969: 137).

Nassaney and colleagues (1983: 110) have argued that Late Archaic
"extractive camps" that were occupied for a short period of time by small
bands of hunter-gatherers would be characterized by (1) a low density of

cultural material, (2) little variety in the types of features present, (3) a limited range of tool types, (4) debitage representing primarily the later stages of tool production and repair, and (5) features lacking multiple-season floral indicators. Based on the results of the 1982 excavations at the Cahokia Interpretive Center Tract, these authors suggest that a series of short-duration, seasonally specific occupations took place during the Prairie Lake phase at Cahokia.

Many of the characteristics of Late Archaic "extractive camps" are found in the northwestern habitation area at Labras Lake, but Phillips (1986) believes this area of the site was occupied by Late Archaic hunter-gatherers during the winter months, when they "geared up" for subsequent seasonal activities by maintaining and building structures, processing and storing food, and manufacturing and repairing stone tools and other equipment. Phillips cites several ethnographic sources that suggest that these retooling activities are restricted to the winter months in hunter-gatherer societies that inhabit temperate woodlands (also see Binford 1980 and Keeley 1982).

The artifact and feature distribution pattern in the northwestern area suggests that lithic manufacture and repair were the primary activities, but the microwear analysis showed that hide working, wood working, and bone and antler working may have gone on there also. Hunting activities are minimally represented in the northwestern microwear sample by a lone knife, even though a large number of projectile points were recovered.

If tool repairing and manufacturing were winter activities, then the Late Archaic occupation in the northwestern area of the Labras Lake site probably represents a winter encampment by a single family of hunter-gatherers. However, the evidence at hand does not allow us to rule out the "transient camp" or "extractive camp" interpretations. It is also possible that this area of the Labras Lake site was where Late Archaic people who resided elsewhere at the site came to manufacture and repair stone tools.

The other early Labras Lake phase occupation area was located in the south central portion of the site and was characterized by an abundance of faunal remains, even though these were poorly preserved. There were no domestic areas or structures in this area, but several pit clusters were present. The south central area has been interpreted as a hunting camp, even though the density of projectile points in this component is not exceptionally high (there were nine complete and broken points in the south central area, or 20% of the total for the central excavation block).

Microwear analysis showed that 45% of the tools in the south central sample were used to butcher animals. The percentage of meat-processing tools in this sample is about twice as large as the proportion of butchering tools in the entire Late Archaic microwear assemblage, and the greatest concentration of faunal remains (80% of the Late Archaic total) was found in the south central area. The microwear data, not the relative abundance of projectile points, seem to be the better index of hunting and butchering activity in the Late Archaic habitation areas.

Deer and elk seem to have been the primary prey of the inhabitants of the south central area, and a fall season of occupation has been postulated based on the faunal remains, the absence of structures, the scarcity of storage facilities, and the low density of charcoal in the features in the south central areas (Yerkes and Phillips in press).

Most of the evidence suggests that the south central area of the Labras Lake site was periodically used as a hunting camp by several Late Archaic groups, but an alternative explanation would be that this part of the site represents a number of butchering and hide-processing activity areas that were associated with households located in other areas of the site. The fact that there is little variety in its features, and no domestic areas, may indicate that the south central area was only inhabited for short periods of time.

More domestic areas and large pits were found in the late Labras Lake phase habitation areas at the southwestern and north central parts of the site than in the older occupation areas. The "roasting pit" features are only found in these areas, and the density and variety of features are greater. The southwestern and north central areas seem to represent more sedentary Late Archaic settlements than the older components at Labras Lake.

Microwear analysis of lithic samples from the southwestern and north central areas revealed that a greater variety of activities went on at both of these localities than at the older Late Archaic settlements at the Labras Lake site. The southwestern habitation area contained the largest domestic area at the site, and the lithic assemblage associated with that structure and the surrounding features contained twice as many used tools as the microwear samples associated with the other three Late Archaic components. The large domestic area in the north central component (Feature 171) also contained a large number of tools, and these were used for a variety of tasks.

It has been suggested that the late Labras Lake and early Prairie Lake phase settlements at the site represent base camps or base locales occupied by as many as fifty individuals for most of the year (Phillips and Gladfelter

1983; Yerkes and Phillips in press). The Late Archaic hunter-gatherers who occupied the southwestern and north central areas lived as collectors, rather than as foragers, and supplied themselves with "specific resources through specially organized task groups," and "are characterized by storage of food and logistically organized food procurement parties" (Binford 1980: 9).

While the early Labras Lake phase occupations seem to have been less sedentary than the later habitation episodes, they do not resemble the camps of highly mobile foragers, since they contain some storage pits and at least one domestic structure. The later occupation areas have more storage facilities than the older components, and they include large food-processing features (roasting pits). The Late Archaic households that occupied the southwestern and north central areas of the Labras Lake site seem to have exploited deer, elk, wild nuts, and other wild plants and animals that were available on the floodplain and adjacent bluffs. They established central base camps that were inhabited by part of each group for most of the year.

The evidence for long-term, centrally based occupation includes the greater number of lithic refits and matches that link several feature clusters in the southwestern and north central areas (figures 16, 31). More refuse accumulated in these areas, and lithic artifacts that once belonged to a single block of chert were distributed between a number of different features. In the northwestern and south central areas, less debris was encountered, and fewer refits and matches could be made. More refits may indicate that there was more tool repair and replacement going on, and a longer period of habitation in the north central and southwestern Late Archaic areas.

The density of floral remains is also greater in features from the southwestern and north central areas. There were only two hearths in the southwestern area, but 82% of the nuts, 54% of the carbonized seeds, and 43% of the charcoal found in Late Archaic contexts at Labras Lake came from this area. The north central area contained one hearth, but 14% of the nut remains, 38% of the seeds, and 33% of the charcoal was found there. The older Late Archaic components together only accounted for 4% of the nuts, 8% of the seeds, and 24% of the charcoal.

Knotweed, marsh elder, hawthorn, and Chenopodium seeds were found in Late Archaic features in the southwestern and north central areas, while only a single summac seed came from the other areas. However, the remains of hickory nuts, acorns, and black walnuts were found in all four of the Late Archaic components, and hazelnuts were present everywhere except the south central component. The nuts identified in the Late Archaic floral samples have the

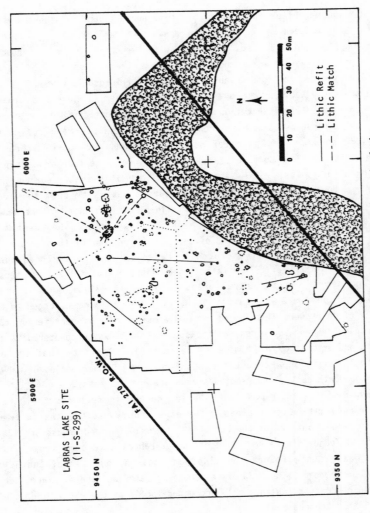

Figure 31. Lithic refits and matches between Late Archaic features in the central excavation block at Labras Lake.

potential for long-term storage and thus do not serve as very accurate seasonal indices; however, the great density of nut remains and the presence of several species of edible seeds in the southwestern and north central floral assemblages argue for a longer period of habitation in those areas.

Active channels of the Mississippi River may have occupied the Pittsburg Lake and Prairie Lake meander scars during the late Labras Lake phase, and Goose Lake could have been an oxbow lake at this time. The spring-fed stream flowed past the site throughout the entire Labras Lake phase. The habitation of the southwestern component of the Labras Lake site was restricted to the late Labras Lake phase, and may have occurred when the area was drier than it is at present. The poor condition of faunal remains from the Late Archaic habitation areas precludes any evaluation of the importance of aquatic species in the aboriginal diet, but the paleohydrology suggests that a variety of wetland habitats would have existed near the site, even though they may have been less extensive than they were during later time periods.

Microwear analysis revealed that during the Labras Lake and Prairie Lake phases several different groups of Late Archaic people performed a variety of activities at four different habitation areas of the Labras Lake site. It is not perfectly clear if the functional variability in the stone tool assemblages represents activity differences or temporal differences (Parkington 1980). However, it is more likely that the four Late Archaic components at the site represent temporally distinct occupational episodes, since the radiocarbon dates from features in each of the spatially separate habitation areas form four separate clusters (figure 11).

The functional interpretations of the Late Archaic chipped stone artifacts from Labras Lake that were based on microwear analysis were rarely in agreement with the functional determinations that were based on morphological attributes.

Even though Carr (1982) had used a variety of ethnographic sources and several earlier investigations of the relationships between tool form and function when he devised his classification scheme (Binford and Binford 1966; Semenov 1964; Sonnefield 1962; Wilmsen 1970; Winters 1969), the functional interpretations of the Labras Lake artifacts based on his system did not often agree with the results based on use-wear and experimentation.

There are many reasons for this disagreement, including the "Frison effect" (Frison 1968; Jelinek 1976: 22), in which stone tools ultimately abandoned at a site, and later classified by the archeologist, have been modified during use and may not have the same form as unused tools. Even if different types of stone tools were designed for certain tasks and were manufactured to fit certain specifications, the form of these tools would change as they were used and repaired. This effect would not always be the same for all types of tools, and consequently, the form of some tool types may correspond more closely to their "supposed" function than others (Odell 1982:29).

Lithic analysts have long been concerned with questions of artifact form and function, and microwear studies have been undertaken in an attempt to determine how formal attributes are related to tool use (Ahler 1971; Odell 1981; Seitzer 1977-78). Despite Jelinek's rather pessimistic pronouncement that "the best that can be hoped for [in microwear studies] is the identification of general sets or categories of resistant materials that produce particular effects during particular kinds of contact with the stone tools" (1976: 32), and Dunnell's (1975) argument that the only justifiable product of use-wear analysis is the enumeration of aggregates of attributes that correspond to wear types, microwear studies have produced concrete evidence backed up by replicable experiments that have helped us understand the relations between stone tool form and function.

Instead of producing endless delineations of tool taxa based on wear patterns (Dunnell 1975; Meltzer 1981), microwear studies have shown that specific tools were used for certain tasks. Since these used tools were found in specific contextual situations, it is possible to examine the nature and location of activity areas within a given site. With more precise functional information in hand, archaeologists can examine how prehistoric populations have adapted to changes in technology, environment, and culture. This can be done because, as George Odell has put it, "function relates to people, whereas wear, as employed by Dunnell, does not" (1982: 27).

Some sort of formal classification of lithic artifacts is necessary before further analyses can be undertaken, but classification can become an end in itself; and when employed in the fashion advocated by Dunnell (1975) and Meltzer (1981), it can actually hinder the investigation of past human behavior. Instead of attempting to learn more about prehistoric tool production and use by examining the evidence preserved on the working edges of chipped stone implements, Dunnell advocates the isolation and definition of certain patterns of wear, which can be used to classify and compare lithic assemblages (1975: 54). The archaeologist can say that several sites contain artifacts that possess the same wear characteristics in similar or disparate proportions by using Dunnell's system, but there is no way of determining how the wear traces formed, how the tools were used, or what activities went on at these sites (also see Odell 1982: 27).

Several of Carr's morphological attributes did seem to correlate with the functions of the Late Archaic tools from Labras Lake (as determined by microwear analysis). Steep-edged tools are likely to be scrapers, but larger, heavy, straight-edged scrapers were not exclusively used on wood, and lighter, smaller round-edged scrapers were not always used on hide, despite the claims of Carr (1982) and Cantwell (1979) that weight and edge-shape are diagnostic of the function of scraping tools. Microwear patterns on scrapers from the Labras Lake Late Archaic samples were similar to those reported by Plisson (1982), who examined ninety-five small end scrapers from the Azilian levels at La Tourasse and concluded that different typological forms were used without discrimination on wood, bone, antler, and hide.

The Late Woodland Microwear Sample

There were 59 tools and 303 blanks in the Early Bluff lithic assemblage from the Labras Lake site. Some 1,128 pieces of lithic debris were also found. The tools included a corner-notched projectile point, and the bases of 4 expanding-stemmed points that suggest a "Lowe-like" point type. A projectile point tip was found. Two bifaces or preforms were recovered, along with 2 side scrapers, 4 notches, 4 denticulates, a combination denticulate and graver, and 40 retouched flakes.

Six blades, 14 primary flakes, 10 core trimming flakes, 3 cores, 2 broken cores, and 6 biface fragments were among the blanks found in the Late Woodland features at Labras Lake, and 262 unretouched secondary flakes were also recovered.

A sample consisting of 60% of the tools and 22% of the blanks in the Early Bluff lithic assemblage was microscopically examined (table 7). Fifteen (40%) of the 38 tools had use-wear traces on their edges. However, only 3 of the 62 blanks (5%) showed any evidence of use. In the four Late Archaic microwear samples, between two and four times as many blanks showed evidence of use. However, the percentage of used tools in the Early Bluff collection is about the same as it was in the Archaic microwear samples.

The used artifacts included 6 hide scrapers (33%); 2 meat knives (11%); 4 bone-or antler-working tools (22%), and one wood scraper (6%). One plant knife was identified, as well as a reworked "hoe" fragment with silica gloss (Witthoff 1967) still visible. Three of the implements (17%) had polishes what could not be identified.

When the used tools were classified under Carr's functional/ morphological scheme, the function of only one tool (a round-edged knife or retouched flake used to cut meat or fresh hide) was found to be in agreement with the microwear evidence. Four tools were in partial agreement (26%), while the function derived from morphological attributes did not agree with the microwear results in ten cases, or 67% of the sample total (table 16).

The cases of partial agreement between Carr's system and microwear analysis involved a unifacial side-scraper whose form suggested that it was used to deflesh hides, while microwear traces indicated it had been used to scrape dry hide; two denticulates that could have been used to shred plants or scrape hide, but were only used to scrape dry hide; and a multiple tool that included a spur that should have been used to work wood and bone, but was actually used to saw and engrave bone or antler.

When the functional interpretations based on the morophological and microwear analyses are compared, it can be seen that while about the same number of butchering tools, bone or antler-working tools, and plant-processing tools are present in each assemblage, hide-working tools are slightly underrepresented in the morphological sample while wood-working tools are overrepresented. Nonetheless, the correspondence between form and function in the general tool-use categories is much better for the Late Woodland lithic assemblage than it was in the Late Archaic samples from Labras Lake.

The number of tools in the Early Bluff assemblage was small, but several activities were represented. Hide-and bone-or antler-working tools were the most common types, and only one wood-working tool was noted. In addition there were two butchering and two plant-processing tools in the sample.

The plant-processing tools represent a functional type that was not found in the Late Archaic microwear samples, but it is not clear whether they were used on mesoamerican cultigens or on native cultivated or wild plants. Only 0.2 gram of charred maize was recovered from Early Bluff features at Labras Lake, and maize is a rare commodity at Early Bluff sites on the American Bottom.

Faunal remains were poorly preserved in the Early Bluff component, and no worked bone or antler was found. However, four chipped stone tools in the Early Bluff microwear sample had wear traces that showed they had been used to engrave, scrape, saw, and whittle bone or antler material.

Microwear analysis of the Early Bluff lithic assemblage from Labras Lake failed to reveal specialized or restricted activities at the site. Hide working and tool maintenance occurred at the site, since dry-hide scraping

TABLE 16. Comparison of the results of functional analyses of Late Woodland lithic artifacts based on tool morphology (Carr 1982) and microwear traces.

		ARTIFACT CLASSIFICATION		
LOT NO.	CONTEXT	Phillips (1980)	Carr (1982)	"V" NO.
1278	F. 169	Retouched Flake	Spur	V 52
408(a)	Fea. 8	Retouched Flake	Round-edged Knife	V 87a
1359(a)	F. 169	Side Scraper	Unifacial Scraper	V 73
1359(b)	F. 169	Side Scraper	Unifacial Scraper	V 39
389	Fea. 7	Retouched Flake	Round-edged Knife	V 87a
1491(a)	F. 170	Denticulate	Denticulate	V 49
1491(b)	F. 170	Unretouched Flake	Straight-edged Knife	V 84
3209-1	F. 785	Denticulate	Denticulate	V 50
1491-12	F. 170	Core Trimmer	Chipping Debris	V 15
431(a)	Fea. 8	Broken Biface	Turtlebacked Scraper	V 71
1360(c)	F. 169	Biface	Bifacial Knife	V108
3513-3	F. 785	Multiple Tool	Spur	V 51
2817-1	F. 745	Unretouched Flake	Chipping Debris	V 15
408(g)	Fea. 8	Retouched Flake	Lamellar Blade	V 58
690(c)	Fea. 8	Unretouched Flake	Chipping Debris	V 15
396-1	Fea. 7	Retouched Flake	Concave-edge Scraper	V 89b
408(b)	Fea. 8	Biface Fragment	Bifacial Knife	V108
392(a/c)	Fea. 49	Retouched Flake	Straight-edged Knife	V 84
1467	Fea. 92	Retouched Flake	Concave-edge Scraper	V 89b

	FUNCTIONAL INTERPRETATION		Agree/
LOT NO.	Carr (1982)	Microwear Analysis	Disagree
1278	work wood/bone	cut meat/fresh hide	disagree
408(a)	cut meat/skin/sinew	cut meat/fresh hide	agree
1359(a)	scrape hard wood	scrape dry hide	disagree
1359(b)	deflesh hide	scrape dry hide	(agree)
1491(a)	cut meat/skin/sinew	scrape dry hide	disagree
1491(b)	whittle wood/bone/horn	scrape dry hide	disagree
3209-1	scrape plants/hide	scrape dry hide	(agree)
1491-12	lithic manufacturing	cut plant material	disagree
431(a)	scrape wood	digging/plant processing	disagree
1360(c)	scrape (grain) hide	scrape wood	disagree
3513-3	work wood/bone	saw and engrave bone	(agree)
2817-1	lithic manufacturing	scrape bone/antler	disagree
408(g)	groove wood/bone	scrape bone/antler	disagree
690(c)	lithic manufacturing	scrape bone/antler	disagree
396-1	scrape (grain) hide	unknown	N/A
408(b)	scrape (grain) hide	unknown	N/A
392(a/c)	whittle wood/bone/horn	unknown	N/A
1467	scrape (grain) hide	unknown	N/A

tools and bone-and antler-working tools were identified in the microwear sample; and the presence of four projectile point bases suggests that arrows or darts were being rearmed. Plant-processing, gardening, animal-butchering, and wood-working tools are also represented in the microwear sample.

It would appear that a small group of hunter-gatherer-gardeners inhabited the site around A. D. 900. They exploited the available wild plant and animal resources and perhaps engaged in some form of shifting cultivation or plant tending. Aquatic animals such as muskrat, fish, and mussels were captured and processed at the site, and hickory and hazelnuts were obtained along with wild starchy plants and native cultigens. Maize was only a very minor element in the Early Bluff subsistence economy.

The Early Bluff inhabitants at Labras Lake did not stay long, and the absence of substantial dwellings could indicate that they only remained there during the warmer months of the year. Their subsistence base seems to have been expanded, but their settlement pattern is not too different from the Late Archaic groups who established base camps at Labras Lake some 1,600 years before.

The Mississippian Microwear Sample

There were 14,474 lithic items recovered from Mississippian contexts at Labras Lake. These included 709 tools (5% of the total), 4,259 blanks (29%), and 9,506 chips and chunks that were classified as lithic debris (66%). Only 4,720 of these artifacts were suitable for microwear analysis, and 533 (11%) of them were actually examined under the microscope. All but 16 of the lithic artifacts in the Mississippian microwear sample came from the household clusters associated with the six wall-trench houses at Labras Lake (table 9).

The six Mississippian households at Labras Lake can be subdivided into a central cluster and two or three outlying structures. More tools and blanks were associated with the three central houses, and microwear analysis revealed that a greater variety of activities were performed in and around these structures (table 17). All six of the Mississippian houses contained domestic implements used to cut meat, scrape hide, and work wood, bone, and antler; but shell drills, wood saws, bone/antler saws, and plant knives were only recovered from households in the central area.

Microwear traces on the majority of the chipped stone artifacts found in each of the six Mississippian households showed that they had been used on hide. The hide-working tools included scrapers, knives, and combination tools that were used to cut and scrape hide. However, only one chipped stone hide awl or reamer was present in the entire Mississippian microwear sample (five of these tools were present in the Late Archaic microwear assemblage).

Bone- or antler-working tools were usually ranked second in the tool inventories. Bone or antler scrapers were the most common element in this functional class, although saws used on these materials were present in the central structures, and bone- or antler gravers and drills were found in houses in the central and outlying areas (table 17).

Knives that were used to cut meat or fresh hide were usually third on the list of functional tool classes, showing that hunting and animal processing were important activities at Mississippian farmstead sites. Wood-working tools were less common, ranking behind hide-working, bone- or antler-working, and butchering tools in the household assemblages. Wood-scraping or whittling tools were the most common type, but boring and sawing tools were also present in the Mississippian microwear samples. The least common tools were the shell drills and the plant knives, which were restricted to the three central Mississippian households at Labras Lake.

Sixteen of the chipped stone artifacts in the Mississippian microwear sample did not come from the household clusters. However, several of these implements were found in the fill of features located near one of the wall-trench houses, and some of these features were linked to specific households by ceramic cross-mends or lithic refits.

Ten of these sixteen artifacts had been used. A dry hide scraper and a meat knife were included in the fill of Feature 20, one of three storage/refuse pits that were located between House 1 and House 3. Another of these storage/refuse pits, Feature 21, contained a perforator that was used to saw and engrave bone or antler material. Feature 21 has been linked to House 1 by a ceramic cross-mend. A bone/antler scraper was found in the fill of Feature 25, the third storage/refuse pit in this area.

One of the sweat houses at Labras Lake, Feature 400, contained a meat knife; and Feature 16, the roasting pit located southeast of House 1, contained a possible hide scraper (figure 26).

Three rectangular pits were located near House 4. Scrapers used on bone or antler material were found in two of these pits, Features 719 and 784. The third rectangular pit, Feature 708, has been linked to House 4 by a ceramic cross-mend. This rectangular pit contained a combination knife and scraper that was used on meat or fresh hide.

TABLE 17. Summary of tool functions in microwear samples taken from six
Mississippian households at the Labras Lake site.

TOOL FUNCTION	HOUSE 1 NO.	%	HOUSE 2 NO.	%	HSE.3 UPPER NO.	%	HSE.3 LOWER NO.	%
Meat Knife	6	20%	5	13%	4	25%	1	7%
Hide Knife	2	7%	6	15%	1	6%	1	7%
Hide Scraper	8	27%	13	33%	3	19%	5	36%
Hide Awl/Reamer	1	3%	-	-	-	-	-	-
Shell Drill	1	3%	2	5%	1	6%	1	7%
Wood Saw	1	3%	1	3%	1	6%	1	7%
Wood Scraper	2	7%	-	-	-	-	2	14%
Wood Borer	-	-	1	3%	-	-	-	-
Wood Graver	-	-	-	-	-	-	-	-
Plant Knife	1	3%	1	3%	2	13%	-	-
Bone/Antler Saw	3	10%	1	3%	-	-	-	-
B/A Scraper	4	13%	4	10%	2	13%	1	7%
B/A Graver	-	-	-	-	1	6%	2	14%
B/A Borer	-	-	2	5%	-	-	-	-
Unknown Use	1	3%	3	8%	1	6%	-	-
Total Tasks:	30	99%	39	101%	16	100%	14	99%
Total Tools:	26		33		13		10	

TOOL CATEGORY

	HOUSE 1 NO.	%	HOUSE 2 NO.	%	HSE.3 UPPER NO.	%	HSE.3 LOWER NO.	%
BUTCHERY	6	20%	5	13%	4	25%	1	7%
HIDE-WORKING	11	37%	19	49%	4	25%	6	43%
SHELL-WORKING	1	3%	2	5%	1	6%	1	7%
WOOD-WORKING	3	10%	2	5%	1	6%	3	21%
PLANT CUTTING	1	3%	1	3%	2	12%	-	-
BONE/ANTLER WORKING	7	23%	7	18%	3	19%	3	21%

TOOL FUNCTION	HOUSE 4 NO.	HOUSE 4 %	HOUSE 5 NO.	HOUSE 5 %	House 6 NO.	House 6 %	Miss. NO.	Total %
Meat Knife	2	17%	2	12%	3	20%	26	17%
Hide Knife	1	8%	3	19%	-	-	14	9%
Hide Scraper	6	50%	7	44%	5	33%	51	33%
Hide Awl/Reamer	-	-	-	-	-	-	1	1%
Shell Drill	-	-	-	-	-	-	5	3%
Wood Saw	-	-	-	-	-	-	4	3%
Wood Scraper	-	-	1	6%	1	7%	6	4%
Wood Borer	1	8%	-	-	-	-	2	1%
Wood Graver	-	-	-	-	1	7%	1	1%
Plant Knife	-	-	-	-	-	-	4	3%
Bone/Antler Saw	-	-	-	-	-	-	4	3%
B/A Scraper	2	17%	2	12%	2	13%	20	13%
B/A Graver	-	-	1	6%	-	-	5	3%
B/A Borer	-	-	-	-	1	7%	3	2%
Unknown Use	-	-	-	-	2	13%	7	4%
Total Tasks:	12	100%	16	99%	15	100%	153	100%
Total Tools:	11		12		14		129	

TOOL CATEGORY

	HOUSE 4 NO.	HOUSE 4 %	HOUSE 5 NO.	HOUSE 5 %	House 6 NO.	House 6 %	Miss. NO.	Total %
BUTCHERY	2	17%	2	12%	3	20%	26	17%
HIDE-WORKING	7	58%	10	63%	5	33%	66	43%
SHELL-WORKING	-	-	-	-	-	-	5	3%
WOOD-WORKING	1	8%	1	6%	2	13%	13	8%
PLANT CUTTING	-	-	-	-	-	-	4	3%
BONE/ANTLER WORKING	2	17%	3	19%	3	20%	32	21%

Note: percentages may not sum to 100% due to rounding errors.

Between ten and thirty-three used artifacts were identified in the microwear samples from the three central Mississippian households, and a number of different domestic activities are represented in each assemblage. More restricted sets of activities are represented in the smaller tool assemblages from the outlying houses. House 4 contained eleven used tools, twelve used tools were associated with House 5, and House 6 had fourteen used implements in its fill.

When the used artifacts in the microwear samples from the Mississippian component are classified using Carr's system, the functional interpretations are often at variance with the use wear evidence. Only 9% of the functional designations that were based on the morphology of the Mississippian artifacts are in agreement with the microwear data, while partial agreement exists in 20.5% of the cases, and there is disagreement 70.5% of the time.

In the House 1 microwear sample, the functions of twenty-five implements could be derived from microwear evidence, but the morphological/functional classifications of only two of these artifacts agreed with the use-wear data. These artifacts included a retouched round-edged knife that had been used to cut meat or fresh hide, and a "turtlebacked" end scraper that had served as a wood-scraping tool (table 18).

Microwear analysis indicated that 37% of the used artifacts in the House 1 microwear sample had been used on hide, but the formal attributes of only 15% of these tools suggested that function.

The morphology of most of the tools in the House 1 sample indicated that they were wood-working tools (26% of the total), but microwear traces that are associated with wood-working tools were present on only 10% of the used implements from that structure. Plant-processing tools (excluding hoes and hoe chips) were overrepresented in the morphological/functional classification system, while meat-cutting and bone- or antler-working tools were underrepresented (table 19).

Shell-working tools are not included in Carr's classification scheme, so none of the shell drills in the Mississippian assemblage from Labras Lake would be recognized if his system was used to determine artifact function. Carr did suggest that drills in his classes V53 and V54 could have been used to drill hide, bone, wood, or shell (1982: 266), but because these drills were found on the surface of the Crane site in close proximity to other tools that he believes were used to work wood and bone, he classified them as wood-or bone-drilling implements.

TABLE 18. Comparison of the results of functional analyses of samples of lithic artifacts from House 1 in the Mississippian component at Labras Lake based on tool morphology (Carr 1982) and microwear traces.

		ARTIFACT CLASSIFICATION		
LOT NO.	CONTEXT	Phillips (1980)	Carr (1982)	"V" NO.
520(a)	Fea. 22	Side Scraper	Straight-edged Knife	V 85
551(a)	Fea. 22	Retouched Flake	Straight-edged Knife	V 84
572(a)	Fea. 22	Retouched Flake	Round-edged Knife	V 87a
615(b)	Fea. 22	Core Trimmer	Chipping Debris	V 15
896(a)	Fea. 77	Unretouched Flake	Chipping Debris	V 15
846(a)	Fea. 76	Unretouched Flake	Chipping Debris	V 15
474-24	Fea. 22	Unretouched Flake	Chipping Debris	V 15
645(a)	Fea. 22	End Scraper	Round-edged Scraper	V 82
432(b)	House 1 Floor	End Scraper	Rectangular Celt	V100
432(c)	House 1 Floor	End Scraper	Unifac'l Scraper/Spur	39/51
331(a)	House 1 Fill	Retouched Flake	Round-edged Knife	V 87a
382(b)	House 1 Fill	Retouched Flake	Denticulate	V 49
572-1	Fea. 22	Side Scraper	Dent./St. edge Scraper	49/75
474-9	Fea. 22	Unretouched Flake	Chipping Debris	V 15
474-21	Fea. 22	Unretouched Flake	Chipping Debris	V 15
376(a)	House 1 Fill	Microdrill	Drill	V 54
407(a)	House 1 Fill	Unretouched Flake	Chipping Debris	V 15
474-4/8	Fea. 22	End Scraper	Turtlebacked Scraper	V 71
722(a)	House 1 Fill	Retouched Flake	Notch	V 45
615(c)	Fea. 22	Retouched Flake	Denticulate	V 50
474-6	Fea. 22	Core Trimmer	Chipping Debris	V 15
474-25	Fea. 22	Unretouched Flake	Notch	V 47
474-14	Fea. 22	Notch	Notch	V 48
474-10	Fea. 22	Core Trimmer	Chipping Debris	V 15
474-11	Fea. 22	Unretouched Flake	Chipping Debris	V 15
474-15	Fea. 22	Unretouched Flake	Chipping Debris	V 15

TABLE 18, continued

LOT NO.	FUNCTIONAL INTERPRETATION Carr (1982)	Microwear Analysis	Agree/ Disagree
520(a)	dehair hide	cut meat/fresh hide	disagree
551(a)	whittle wood/bone/horn	cut meat/fresh hide	disagree
572-2	cut meat/skin/sinew	cut meat/fresh hide	agree
615(b)	lithic manufacturing	cut meat/scrape bone	disagree
896(a)	lithic manufacturing	cut meat/fresh hide	disagree
846(a)	lithic manufacturing	cut meat/fresh hide	disagree
474-24	lithic manufacturing	cut dry hide	disagree
645(a)	scrape hide/wood	scrape dry hide	(agree)
432(b)	scrape bone	scrape dry hide	disagree
432(c)	work fr. hide/wood/bone	scrape, bore dry hide	disagree
331(a)	cut meat/skin/sinew	scrape dry hide	disagree
382(b)	scrape plants/ fresh hide	scrape dry hide	disagree
572-1	scrape plants/hide/wood	scrape, cut hide/plants	(agree)
474-9	lithic manufacturing	scrape dry hide	disagree
474-21	lithic manufacturing	scrape dry hide	disagree
376(a)	drill soft wood	drill shell	disagree
407(a)	lithic manufacturing	saw wood	disagree
474-4/8	scrape wood	scrape wood	agree
722(a)	smooth wooden shafts	whittle wood	disagree
615(c)	scrape plants/hide	saw bone/antler	disagree
474-6	lithic manufacturing	saw bone/antler	disagree
474-25	work wood	saw bone/antler	disagree
474-14	work wood/bone	scrape bone/antler	(agree)
474-10	lithic manufacturing	scrape bone/antler	disagree
474-11	lithic manufacturing	scrape bone/antler	disagree
474-15	lithic manufacturing	unknown	N/A

TABLE 19. Summary of functional analysis of samples of chipped stone artifacts taken from the three central Mississippian houses at Labras Lake based on tool morphology (Carr 1982) and microwear traces.

TOOL FUNCTION	*House 1*				*House 2*			
	Carr (1982)		Microwear		Carr (1982)		Microwear	
	No.	%	No.	%	No.	%	No.	%
Meat Knife	6	6%	6	20%	-	-	5	13%
Hide Knife	-	-	2	7%	1	2%	6	15%
Hide Scraper	5	15%	8	27%	12	27%	13	33%
Hide Awl/Reamer	-	-	1	3%	-	-	-	-
Shell Drill	-	-	1	3%	-	-	2	5%
Wood Saw	-	-	1	3%	1	2%	1	3%
Wood Scraper	7	20%	2	7%	5	11%	-	-
Wood Borer	1	3%	-	-	5	11%	1	3%
Wood Graver	1	3%	-	-	-	-	-	-
Bone/Antler Saw	-	-	3	10%	-	-	1	3%
B/A Scraper	4	12%	4	13%	2	5%	4	10%
B/A Graver	-	-	-	-	-	-	-	-
B/A Borer	-	-	-	-	2	5%	2	5%
Plant Knives	-	-	1	3%	-	-	1	3%
Plant Shredders	3	9%	-	-	6	13%	-	-
Lithic Manufact.	11	32%	-	-	11	24%	-	-
Unknown Use	-	-	1	3%	-	-	3	8%
Total Tasks:	**34**	**100%**	**30**	**99%**	**45**	**100%**	**39**	**101%**
Total Tools:	**26**		**26**		**33**		**33**	

TOOL CATEGORY

BUTCHERY	2	6%	6	20%	-	-	5	13%
HIDE-WORKING	5	15%	11	37%	13	29%	19	49%
SHELL-WORKING	-	-	1	3%	-	-	2	5%
WOOD-WORKING	9	26%	3	10%	11	24%	2	5%
BONE/ANTLER	4	12%	7	23%	4	9%	7	18%
PLANT-WORKING	3	9%	1	3%	6	13%	1	3%
LITHIC MANUFAC.	11	32%	-	-	11	24%	-	-

TABLE 19, continued

TOOL FUNCTION	HOUSE 3 UPPER LEVEL				HOUSE 3 LOWER LEVEL			
	Carr (1982)		Microwear		Carr (1982)		Microwear	
	No.	%	No.	%	No.	%	No.	%
Meat Knife	2	12%	4	25%	–	–	1	7%
Hide Knife	–	–	1	6%	1	7%	1	7%
Hide Scraper	3	17%	3	19%	3	20%	5	36%
Hide Awl/Reamer	–	–	–	–	–	–	–	–
Shell Drill	–	–	1	6%	–	–	1	7%
Wood Saw	–	–	1	6%	–	–	1	7%
Wood Scraper	3	17%	–	–	2	13%	2	14%
Wood Borer	2	12%	–	–	1	7%	–	–
Wood Graver	–	–	–	–	2	13%	–	–
Bone/Antler Saw	–	–	–	–	–	–	–	–
B/A Scraper	1	6%	2	13%	–	–	1	7%
B/A Graver	–	–	1	6%	2	13%	2	14%
B/A Borer	2	12%	–	–	1	7%	–	–
Plant Knife	1	6%	2	13%	–	–	–	–
Plant Shredder	–	–	–	–	1	7%	–	–
Lithic Manufact.	3	17%	–	–	2	13%	–	–
Unknown Use	–	–	1	6%	–	–	–	–
Total Tasks:	17	99%	16	100%	15	100%	14	99%
Total Tools:	13		13		10		10	

TOOL CATEGORY

BUTCHERY	2	12%	4	25%	–	–	1	7%
HIDE-WORKING	3	17%	4	25%	4	27%	6	43%
SHELL-WORKING	–	–	1	6%	–	–	1	7%
WOOD-WORKING	5	29%	1	6%	5	33%	3	21%
BONE/ANTLER	3	17%	3	19%	3	20%	3	21%
PLANT-WORKING	1	6%	2	13%	1	7%	–	–
LITHIC MANUFACT.	3	17%	–	–	2	13%	–	–

TOOL FUNCTION	CENTRAL MISSISSIPPIAN HOUSES TOTAL			
	Carr (1982)		Microwear	
	No.	%	No.	%
Meat Knife	4	4%	16	16%
Hide Knife	2	2%	10	10%
Hide Scraper	23	21%	29	29%
Hide Awl/Reamer	-	-	1	1%
Shell Drill	-	-	5	5%
Wood Saw	1	1%	4	4%
Wood Scraper	17	15%	4	4%
Wood Borer	9	8%	1	1%
Wood Graver	3	3%	-	-
Bone/Antler Saw	-	-	4	4%
B/A Scraper	7	6%	11	11%
B/A Graver	2	2%	3	3%
B/A Borer	5	4%	2	2%
Plant Knife	1	1%	4	4%
Plant Shredder	10	9%	-	-
Lithic Manufact.	27	24%	-	-
Unknown Use	-	-	5	5%
Total Tasks:	111	100%	99	99%
Total Tools:	82		82	

TOOL CATEGORY

BUTCHERY	4	4%	16	16%
HIDE-WORKING	25	22%	40	40%
SHELL-WORKING	-	-	5	5%
WOOD-WORKING	30	27%	9	9%
BONE/ANTLER	14	13%	20	20%
PLANT-WORKING	11	10%	4	4%
LITHIC MANUFACT.	24	24%	-	-

Note: percentages may not sum to 100% due to rounding errors.

It may be argued that because Carr's sytem was used for a Middle Woodland collection, he would not consider shell drills as a distinctive class of artifacts. However, since Mason and Perino (1961) described the Mississippian Cahokia "microdrills," and suggested that these drills were used to produce shell beads, the formal attributes of the Labras Lake microdrills could be used to deduce their function in lieu of use-wear analysis.

All of the shell drills from Labras Lake do not resemble the Cahokia microdrills defined by Mason and Perino, and in fact only a single microdrill was recognized in the preliminary analysis of the Labras Lake assemblage (Yerkes 1980). However, in the present study eleven possible microdrills were considered; six of them showed evidence of use, and five of these were used to drill shell. The Labras Lake microdrills were not all rod-shaped like the Cahokia tools, and some were not made of Burlington chert (figure 32). All of them would not have automatically been classified as shell microdrills if the formal criteria defined by Mason and Perino (1961) were used.

In Carr's system, some 32% of the used artifacts from House 1 at Labras Lake would not have been classified as tools, but as lithic chipping debris. However, microwear traces on the edges of these unretouched flakes indicated that they had been used to cut meat and dry hide, scrape dry hide, saw wood, bone, or antler materials, and scrape bone or antler.

In the sample from House 2, there was agreement between the classification scheme developed by Carr and the microwear data in less thanone case out of twelve. Of the thirty-three used implements, only a wood drill and a side scraper or knife used on hide were assigned the same function (table 20) .Meat knives, wood saws, plant knives, and shell drills were not included in the formal/functional classification of the House 2 artifacts, and only 29% of the implements were interpreted as hide-working tools in that system. Microwear data showed that nearly half of the artifacts in the House 2 sample (49%) had been used on hide.

Wood-working and plant-processing tools were also overrepresented when Carr's morphological method was used to classify the House 2 artifacts, and 24% of the used implements in the sample were designated as chipping debris.

The lithic artifacts from House 3 were divided between the upper and lower levels of that structure in this analysis. The upper level of House 3 was a larger wall-trench house that was superimposed on the smaller, lower wall-trench structure that had occupied the same house basin (figures 33, 34). The closest agreement between the microwear data and the morphological/ functional classifications was found in the sample of ten used artifacts from

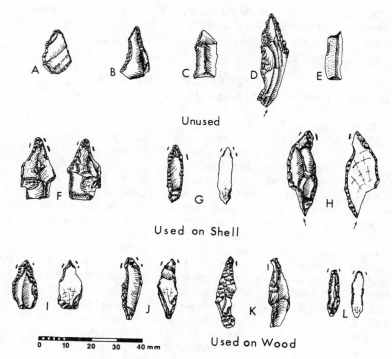

Unused

Used on Shell

Used on Wood

Figure 32. Microdrills from the Mississippian component at
Labras Lake. A. House 1 fill, Burlington chert (BC);
B. House 1 north wall trench (BC); C. House 2 fill, Mill
Creek(?) chert; D. House 2 fill, heat-treated chert;
E. House 3, Feature 133 (BC); F. House 1 fill, tan chert;
G. House 2 fill, heat-treated chert; H. House 2 fill (BC);
I. House 3 upper floor (BC); J. House 3 lower floor (BC);
K. House 4, Feature 703, heat-treated chert; L. "Typical"
microdrill from the Cahokia site. A-E: unused; F-J, L: used
on shell; K: used on wood (H also used on bone/antler). D and
H would be classified as burins. Thick lines indicate the
location of microwear polishes.

TABLE 20. Comparison of the results of functional analyses of samples of lithic artifacts from House 2 in the Mississippian component at Labras Lake based on tool morphology (Carr 1982) and microwear traces.

		ARTIFACT CLASSIFICATION		
LOT NO.	CONTEXT	Phillips (1980)	Carr (1982)	"V" NO.
1679-14	House 2 Fill	Notch	Notch	V 45
1415-14	House 2 Fill	Retouched Flake	Straight-edged Knife	V 85
1303(a)	House 2 Fill	Primary Flake	Straight-edged Knife	V 85
1013(a)	House 2 Fill	Unretouched Flake	Straight-edged Knife	V 83
997(b)	House 2 Fill	Unretouched Flake	Chipping Debris	V 15
2154(a)	Fea. 591	Retouched Blade	Lamellar Blade	V 11
1439-1	House 2 Floor	Unretouched Flake	Straight-edged Knife	V 84
1096(a)	House 2 Fill	Side Scraper	Straight-edged Knife	V 83
2049(a)	Fea. 425	Notch	Notch	V 47
2009(a)	Fea. 404	Denticulate	Denticulate	V 50
1281(a)	House 2 Fill	Multiple Tool	Dent./C'cave Scraper	50/89b
1015(a)	House 2 Fill	Retouched Flake	Straight-edged Knife	V 85
1013(a)	House 2 Fill	Retouched Flake	Straight-edged Knife	V 86
290(a)	House 2 Fill	Primary Flake	Chipping Debris	V 15
2155(a)	Fea. 591	Unretouched Flake	Chipping Debris	V 15
891(b)	House 2 Fill	Unretouched Flake	Chipping Debris	V 15
1471(a)	House 2 Fill	Unretouched Flake	Chipping Debris	V 15
1634-14	House 2 Fill	Unretouched Flake	Chipping Debris	V 15
2259-2	Fea. 445	Unretouched Flake	Chipping Debris	V 15
2033(a)	Fea. 410	Unretouched Flake	Notch/St.-edge Knife	45/85
2003-12	House 2 Fill	Microdrill	Drill	V 53
995(a)	House 2 Fill	Burin/Microdrill	Drill	V 53
1627-4	House 2 Fill	Perforator	Drill	V 54
804(a)	House 2 Fill	Multiple Tool	Denticulate/Drill	50/54
1229-3	House 2 Floor	Primary Flake	Chipping Debris	V 15
1535-4	House 2 Fill	Unretouched Flake	Denticulate	V 50
1463(a)	House 2 Fill	Perforator	Drill	V 54
2129(a)	House 2 Fill	Retouched Flake	Straight-edged Knife	V 85
1229-1	House 2 Fill	Core Trimmer	Chipping Debris	V 15
381(d)	House 2 Fill	Unretouched Flake	Chipping Debris	V 15
1628-1	Fea. 293	Retouched Flake	Concave-edge Scraper	V 89b
804-2	House 2 Fill	Core Trimmer	Chipping Debris	V 15
804(d)	House 2 Fill	Unretouched Flake	Notch/Denticulate	47/50

LOT NO.	FUNCTIONAL INTERPRETATION Carr (1982)	Microwear Analysis	Agree/ Disagree
1679-14	smooth wooden shafts	cut meat/fresh hide	disagree
1415-14	dehair hide	cut meat/fresh hide	disagree
1303(a)	dehair hide	cut meat/fresh hide	disagree
1013(a)	dehair hide	cut meat/fresh hide	disagree
997(b)	lithic manufacturing	cut meat/fresh hide	disagree
2154(a)	whittle wood/bone	cut dry hide	disagree
1439-1	whittle wood/bone/horn	cut dry hide	disagree
1096(a)	dehair hide	scrape dry hide	agree
2049(a)	work wood	scrape dry hide	disagree
2009(a))	scrape plants/hide	scrape dry hide	(agree)
1281(a)	scrape plants/hide	scrape dry hide/bone	(agree)
1015(a)	dehair hide	scrape, cut dry hide	(agree)
1013(a)	shred plants/sinew	scrape dry hide	disagree
290(a)	lithic manufacturing	scrape dry hide	disagree
2155(a)	lithic manufacturing	scrape, cut dry hide	disagree
891(a)	lithic manufacturing	scrape, cut dry hide	disagree
1471(a)	lithic manufacturing	scrape dry hide	disagree
1634-14	lithic manufacturing	scrape dry hide	disagree
2259-2	lithic manufacturing	scrape dry hide	disagree
2033(a)	work wood/hide	scrape dry hide	(agree)
2003-12	drill wood/bone	drill shell	disagree
995(a)	drill wood/bone	drill shell/antler?	disagree
1627-4	drill soft wood	drill wood	agree
804(a)	scrape plants/hide/wood	saw wood	disagree
1229-3	lithic manufacturing	cut plants	disagree
1535-4	scrape plants/hide	saw bone	disagree
1463(a)	drill soft wood	drill antler	disagree
2129(a)	dehair hide	scrape bone/antler	disagree
1229-1	lithic manufacturing	scrape bone/antler	disagree
381(d)	lithic manufacturing	scrape bone/antler	disagree
1628-1	scrape (grain) hide	unknown	N/A
804-2	lithic manufacturing	unknown	N/A
804(d)	work wood/plants/hide	unknown	N/A

(agree) = partial agreement

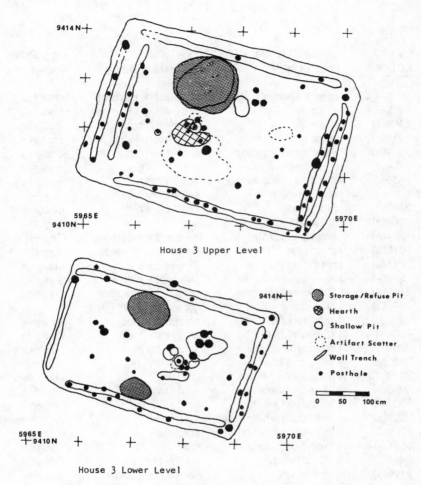

House 3 Upper Level

House 3 Lower Level

Figure 33.   House 3 upper and lower levels (plan view).

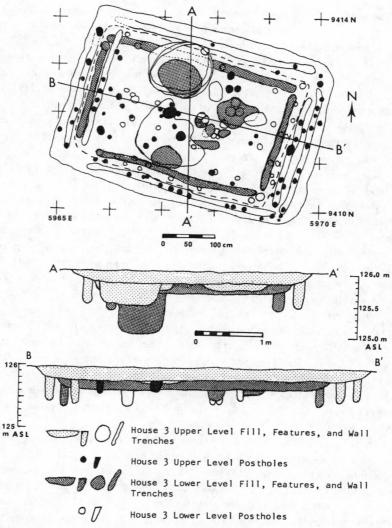

Figure 34. Cross-sections through House 3.

the lower level of House 3. However, the incidence of agreement between the
two systems in the upper level sample from House 3 was more in line with the
samples from the other Mississippian houses at Labras Lake.

Most of the used tools in the lower level of House 3 had served as
scrapers, gravers, or cutting tools, and they had been used on hide, wood,
bone, or antler (table 21). With the exception of the shell drill and the
unretouched tools that Carr would classify as chipping debris, there was
complete or partial agreement between the functional interpretations of the
used artifacts from the lower level of House 3 that were based on formal
attributes and on microwear traces.

There were fewer chipped stone artifacts associated with the outlying
wall-trench houses at Labras Lake, and a smaller range of activities were
represented in their use-wear samples, but the functional designations based
on formal attributes were rarely in agreement with the microwear data. In the
samples from House 4, House 5, and House 6, wood-working and plant-
processing tools are overrepresented in the morphological classifications,
while meat-cutting and hide-working tools are underrepresented, but the
percentage of bone- or antler-working tools are nearly equal in both
classification systems (tables 22, 23).

Functional data derived from microwear analysis do not depend on
spatial associations or ethonographic analogy. Studies of the spatial
relationships between artifacts often assume that artifacts that where found
each other during excavation had been used to perform the same prehistoric
activities. But it has not been shown that spatially associated artifacts
really represent "toolkits." In fact, refitting studies and microwear
analysis may be the only way to determine if artifacts from the same spatial
contexts were used in the same manner.

In this study, activities at Labras Lake were reconstructed based on the
physical evidence of use that has been preserved on the edges of chipped stone
tools. While all of the activities that went on at Labras Lake cannot be
derived from the functions of chipped stone tools, and while the relative
numbers of tools used for different tasks may not be directly proportional to
the relative importance of those tasks in the prehistoric economy, the
evidence provided by microwear traces and confirmed by experimentation is
still more sound than inferences about tool function based on morphology and
spatial associations.

Microwear analysis of lithic samples from the six Mississippian households
at Labras Lake revealed that a variety of activities were performed in

TABLE 21. Comparison of the results of functional analyses of samples of lithic artifacts from Houses 3 and 4 in the Mississippian component at Labras Lake based on tool morphology (Carr 1982) and microwear traces.

House 3 Upper Level
ARTIFACT CLASSIFICATION

LOT NO.	CONTEXT	Phillips (1980)	Carr (1982)	"V" NO.
887(a)	Upper Fill	Retouched Flake	Straight-edged Knife	V 35
1003(a)	Upper Fill	Blade (broken)	Lamellar Blade	V 11a
859(a)	Upper Fill	Unretouched Flake	Lamellar "Blade"	V 11b
1405(a)	Fea. 239	Unretouched Flake	Chipping Debris	V 15
1481(a)	Fea. 600	Notch	Notch	V 47
812(a)	Upper Fill	End Scraper	Straight-edged Knife	V 83
833(a)	Upper Floor	Notch	Notch	V 47
728(a)	Upper Fill	End Scraper	Unifacial Endscraper	V 39
893(a)	Upper Floor	Microdrill	Drill	V 53
692(a)	Upper Fill	Retouched Flake	Hoe Fragment	V 10
599(a)	Upper Fill	Unretouched Flake	Chipping Debris	V 15
839(a)	Upper Floor	Retouched Flake	Straight-edged Knife	V 85
1208(a)	Fea. 133	Perforator	Drill	V 53

FUNCTIONAL INTERPRETATION

LOT NO.	Carr (1982)	Microwear Analysis	Agree/ Disagree
887(a)	dehair hide	cut meat/fresh hide	disagree
1003(a)	whittle wood/bone	cut meat/fresh hide	disagree
859(a)	cut meat/hide/plants	cut meat/fresh hide	(agree)
1405(a)	lithic manufacturing	cut meat/fresh hide	disagree
1481(a))	work wood	cut dry hide	disagree
812(a)	dehair hide	scrape dry hide	agree
833(a)	work wood	scrape, grave bone/hide	disagree
728(a)	deflesh fresh hide	scrape dry hide	disagree
893(a)	drill wood/bone	drill shell	disagree
692(a)	re-sharpen hoes	cut plants	disagree
599(a)	lithic manufacturing	cut plants/soft wood	disagree
839(a)	dehair hide	scrape bone/antler	disagree
1209(a)	drill wood/bone	unknown	N/A

House 3 Lower Level
ARTIFACT CLASSIFICATION

LOT NO.	CONTEXT	Phillips (1980)	Carr (1982)	"V" NO.
1256(b)	Lower Floor	Multiple Tool	Notch/Round Knife	47/87b
1607(b)	Fea. 290	Retouched Flake	Unifacial Endscraper	V 36b
1073(a)	Lower Fill	Retouched Flake	Straight-edged Knife	V 85
1124(a)	Lower Fill	Core Trimmer	Chipping Debris	V 15
1231(a)	Lower Fill	Unretouched Flake	Chipping Debris	V 15
1256(a)	Lower Floor	Microdrill	Drill	V 53
1650(a)	Fea. 290	Denticulate	Notch/Denticulate	45/50
1073(c)	Lower Fill	Retouched Flake	Straight-edge Scraper	V 77a
1607(a)	Fea. 290	Perforator	Spur	V 51
1832(a)	Fea. 366	Unretouched Flake	Spur	V 52

FUNCTIONAL INTERPRETATION

LOT NO.	Carr (1982)	Microwear Analysis	Agree/ Disagree
1256(b)	work wood/ hide	scrape dry hide	(agree)
1607(b)	work hide	scrape dry hide	agree
1073(a)	dehair hide	scrape dry hide	agree
1124(a)	lithic manufacturing	scrape, cut dry hide	disagree
1231(a)	lithic manufacturing	scrape dry hide, cut meat	disagree
1256(a)	drill wood/bone	drill shell	disagree
1650(a)	work wood/plants/hide	saw, scrape wood	(agree)
1073(c)	scrape wood	scrape wood/bone	(agree)
1607(a)	work wood/bone	engrave bone/antler	(agree)
1832(a)	work wood/bone	engrave bone/antler	(agree)

House 4
ARTIFACT CLASSIFICATION

LOT NO.	CONTEXT	Phillips (1980)	Carr (1982)	"V" NO.
2749-1	House 4 Fill	Unretouched Flake	Chipping Debris	V 15
2588-5	Fea. 703	Unretouched Flake	Chipping Debris	V 15
2620-5	Fea. 703	Notch	Notch	V 46
2692-1	House 4 Fill	Notch	Notch	V 47
2682-1	Fea. 721	Retouched Flake	Str./Concave Scraper	75/89b
2749-2	House 4 Fill	Retouched Flake	Denticulate	V 50
2890-3	Fea. 728	Retouched Flake	Straight-edged Knife	V 87a
3085-2	Fea. 728	Retouched Flake	Straight-edge Scraper	V 79a
2547-3	Fea. 703	Perforator	Drill	V 53
2588-1	Fea. 703	Retouched Flake	Straight-edged Knife	V 84
2998-3	Fea. 730	Retouched Flake	Straight-edged Knife	V 85

FUNCTIONAL INTERPRETATION

LOT NO.	Carr (1982)	Microwear Analysis	Agree/ Disagree
2749-1	lithic manufacturing	cut meat/fresh hide	disagree
2588-5	lithic manufacturing	cut meat/fresh hide	disagree
2620-5	smooth wooden shafts	scrape, cut dry hide	disagree
2692-1	work wood	scrape dry hide	disagree
2682-1	scrape wood/hide	scrape dry hide	(agree)
2749-2	scrape plants/hide	scrape dry hide	(agree)
2890-3	cut meat/skin/sinew	scrape dry hide	disagree
3058-2	chop hard wood	scrape dry hide	disagree
2547-3	drill wood/bone	drill wood	(agree)
2588-1	whittle wood/bone/horn	scrape bone/antler	(agree)
2998-3	dehair hide	scrape bone/antler	disagree

(agree) = partial agreement

TABLE 22. Summary of functional analysis of samples of chipped stone artifacts taken from the three outlying Mississippian houses at Labras Lake based on tool morphology (Carr 1982) and microwear traces.

TOOL FUNCTION	House 4				House 5			
	Carr (1982)		Microwear		Carr (1982)		Microwear	
	No.	%	No.	%	No.	%	No.	%
Meat Knife	1	7%	2	17%	1	6%	2	12%
Hide Knife	-	-	1	8%	-	-	3	19%
Hide Scraper	3	20%	6	50%	3	16%	7	44%
Hide Awl/Reamer	-	-	-	-	-	-	-	-
Shell Drill	-	-	-	-	-	-	-	-
Wood Saw	-	-	-	-	1	6%	-	-
Wood Scraper	4	26%	-	-	6	33%	1	6%
Wood Borer	1	7%	1	8%	-	-	-	-
Wood Graver	-	-	-	-	-	-	-	-
Bone/Antler Saw	-	-	-	-	1	6%	-	-
B/A Scraper	1	7%	2	17%	2	11%	2	12%
B/A Graver	-	-	-	-	-	-	1	6%
B/A Borer	1	7%	-	-	-	-	-	-
Plant Knives	-	-	-	-	1	6%	-	-
Plant Shredders	1	7%	-	-	2	11%	-	-
Lithic Manufact.	2	13%	-	-	1	6%	-	-
Unknown/Other	1*	7%	-	-	-	-	-	-
Total Tasks:	15	101%**	12	100%	18	101%	16	99%
Total Tools:	11		11		12		12	

TOOL CATEGORY

BUTCHERY	1	7%	2	17%	1	6%	2	12%
HIDE-WORKING	3	20%	7	58%	3	16%	10	63%
SHELL-WORKING	-	-	-	-	-	-	-	-
WOOD-WORKING	6*	40%	1	8%	7	39%	1	6%
BONE/ANTLER	2	13%	2	17%	3	16%	3	18%
PLANT-WORKING	1	7%	-	-	3	16%	-	-
LITHIC MANUFAC.	2	13%	-	-	1	6%	-	-

TOOL FUNCTION	HOUSE 6				OUTLYING HOUSES TOTAL			
	Carr (1982)		Microwear		Carr (1982)		Microwear	
	No.	%	No.	%	No.	%	No.	%
Meat Knife	1	5%	3	20%	3	6%	7	16%
Hide Knife	-	-	-	-	-	-	4	9%
Hide Scraper	4	21%	5	33%	10	19%	18	42%
Hide Awl/Reamer	-	-	-	-	-	-	-	-
Shell Drill	-	-	-	-	-	-	-	-
Wood Saw	-	-	-	-	1	2%	-	-
Wood Scraper	4	21%	1	7%	14	27%	2	5%
Wood Borer	1	5%	-	-	2	4%	1	2%
Wood Graver	1	5%	1	7%	1	2%	1	2%
Bone/Antler Saw	-	-	-	-	1	2%	-	-
B/A Scraper	2	11%	2	13%	5	10%	6	14%
B/A Graver	1	5%	-	-	1	2%	1	2%
B/A Borer	-	-	1	7%	1	2%	1	2%
Plant Knife	-	-	-	-	1	2%	-	-
Plant Shredder	2	11%	-	-	5	10%	-	-
Lithic Manufact.	3	16%	-	-	6	11%	-	-
Unknown Use	-	-	2	13%	1*	2%	2	5%
Total Tasks:	**19**	**100%**	**15**	**100%**	**52**	**101%****	**43**	**99%**
Total Tools:	**14**		**14**		**37**		**37**	

TOOL CATEGORY

	HOUSE 6				OUTLYING HOUSES TOTAL			
BUTCHERY	1	5%	3	20%	3	6%	7	16%
HIDE-WORKING	4	21%	5	53%	10	19%	22	51%
SHELL-WORKING	-	-	-	-	-	-	-	-
WOOD-WORKING	6	32%	2	14%	19*	35%	4	9%
BONE/ANTLER	3	16%	3	20%	8	15%	8	19%
PLANT-WORKING	2	11%	-	-	6	12%	-	-
LITHIC MANUFACT.	3	16%	-	-	6	11%	-	-

| TOOL FUNCTION | ENTIRE MISSISSIPPIAN COMPONENT | | | |
| | Carr (1982) | | Microwear | |
	No.	%	No.	%
Meat Knife	8	5%	26	17%
Hide Knife	3	2%	14	9%
Hide Scraper	36	21%	51	33%
Hide Awl/Reamer	-	-	1	1%
Shell Drill	-	-	5	3%
Wood Saw	2	1%	4	3%
Wood Scraper	24	14%	6	4%
Wood Borer	13	8%	2	1%
Wood Graver	5	3%	1	1%
Bone/Antler Saw	2	1%	4	3%
B/A Scraper	14	8%	20	13%
B/A Graver	4	2%	5	3%
B/A Borer	6	4%	3	2%
Plant Knife	2	1%	4	3%
Plant Shredder	15	9%	-	-
Lithic Manufact.	34	20%	-	-
Unknown Use	1*	1%	7	4%
Total Tasks:	**169**	**100%**	**153**	**100%**
Total Tools:	**129**		**129**	

TOOL CATEGORY

BUTCHERY	8	5%	26	17%
HIDE-WORKING	39	23%	66	43%
SHELL-WORKING	-	-	5	3%
WOOD-WORKING	45*	27%	13	8%
BONE/ANTLER	26	15%	32	21%
PLANT-WORKING	17	10%	4	3%
LITHIC MANUFACT.	34	20%	-	-

* wood-chopping tool from House 4 (included in the wood-working category)
** percentages may not sum to 100% due to rounding errors.

TABLE 23. Comparison of the results of functional analyses of chipped stone artifacts from House 5, House 6, and several external features in the Labras Lake Mississippian component based on tool morphology (Carr 1982) and microwear traces.

House 5
ARTIFACT CLASSIFICATION

LOT NO.	CONTEXT	Phillips (1980)	Carr (1982)	"V" NO.
4035-1	Fea. 1024	End Scraper	Turtleback Scraper	V 71
3892-4	Fea. 958	Unretouched Flake	Chipping Debris	V 15
3961-1	Fea. 911	Side Scraper	Saw/Str.-edge Knife	57/86
4005-1	Fea. 926	Side Scraper	Unifacial Endscraper	V 37
3758-1	House 5 Fill	Multiple Tool	Endscraper/Dent.	37/50
3815-2	House 5 Fill	Multiple Tool	Straight-edge Scraper	V 73
3846-1	House 5 Fill	Multiple Tool	Dent./C'cave Scraper	50/89b
4015-6	Fea. 912/916	Retouched Flake	Straight-edged Knife	V 85
4035-2	Fea. 1024	Notched Flake	Notch	V 46
3847-1	Fea. 917	Multiple Tool	Notch/St.-edge Knife	46/84
4005-3	Fea. 926	Blade	Lamellar Blade	V 11a
4015-1	Fea. 912/916	Biface (broken)	Cache Blade	V 42

FUNCTIONAL INTERPRETATION

LOT NO.	Carr (1982)	Microwear Analysis	Agree/ Disagree
4035-1	scrape wood	cut meat, scrape hide	disagree
3892-4	lithic manufacturing	cut meat/fresh hide	disagree
3961-1	cut wood/bone/plants	scrape dry hide	disagree
4005-1	work soft wood	scrape dry hide	disagree
3758-1	work wood/plants/hide	cut, scrape dry hide	(agree)
3815-2	scrape hard wood	scrape, cut dry hide	disagree
3846-1	scrape plants/hide	scrape, cut dry hide	(agree)
4015-6	dehair hide	scrape dry hide	agree
4035-2	smooth wooden shafts	whittle wood	agree
3847-1	work wood/bone/horn	scrape bone/antler	(agree)
4005-3	whittle wood/bone	scrape bone/antler	(agree)
4015-1	deflesh hide	engrave bone/antler	disagree

House 6
ARTIFACT CLASSIFICATION

LOT NO.	CONTEXT	Phillips (1980)	Carr (1982)	"V" NO.
3907-5	House 6 Fill	Blade	Lamellar Blade	V 11a
3866-21	House 6 Fill	Unretouched Flake	Spur	V 52
3862-5	House 6 Fill	Unretouched Flake	Chipping Debris	V 15
4112-6	Fea. 982	Side Scraper	Straight-edged Knife	V 83
3900-1	House 6 Fill	Retouched Flake	Denticulate	V 50
3907-11	House 6 Fill	Primary Flake	Decortication Flake	V 14
3883-1	House 6 Fill	Unretouched Flake	Round-edged Knife	V 87a
4217-1	Fea. 1102	Side Scraper	Concave-edge Scraper	V 89b
4100-2	Fea. 981	Retouched Flake	Notch	V 46
4092-8	House 6 Fill	Perforator	Drill	V 54
3907-1	House 6 Fill	Denticulate	Denticulate	V 50
3910-1	House 6 Floor	Multiple Tool	Notch	V 48
4724-1	House 6 Floor	Multiple Tool	Notch	V 46
4111-6	Fea. 1039	Primary Flake	Decortication Flake	V 14

FUNCTIONAL INTERPRETATION

LOT NO.	Carr (1982)	Microwear Analysis	Agree/ Disagree
3907-5	whittle wood/bone	cut meat/fresh hide	disagree
3866-21	work wood/bone	cut meat/fresh hide	disagree
3862-5	lithic manufacturing	cut meat/fresh hide	disagree
4112-6	dehair hide	scrape dry hide	agree
3900-1	scrape plants/hide	scrape dry hide	(agree)
3907-11	lithic manufacturing	scrape dry hide	disagree
3883-1	cut meat/skin/sinew	scrape dry hide	disagree
4217-1	scrape (grain) hide	scrape wood	disagree
4100-2	smooth wooden shafts	engrave wood	disagree
4092-8	drill soft wood	drill bone/antler	disagree
3907-1	scrape plants/hide	scrape bone/antler	disagree
3910-1	work wood/bone	scrape bone/antler	(agree)
4274-1	smooth wooden shafts	unknown	N/A
4111-6	lithic manufacturing	unknown	N/A

Other Mississippian Features
ARTIFACT CLASSIFICATION

LOT NO.	CONTEXT	Phillips (1980)	Carr (1982)	"V" NO.
2652-1	Fea. 708	Retouched Flake	Unifacial Endscraper	V 39
840(a)	Fea. 20	Blade	Lamellar Blade	V 11a
2007(a)	Fea. 400	Unretouched Flake	Straight-edged Knife	V 84
881(a)	Fea. 20	Side Scraper	St/C'cave-edge Knife	83/89
1332(a)	Fea. 16	End Scraper	Straight-edged Knife	V 83
2719-1	Ex. Unit 19	Side Scraper	Drill	V 54
2672-1	Fea. 719	Primary Flake	Decortication Flake	V 14
546(a)	Fea. 25	Retouched Flake	Straight-edged Knife	V 83
3054-1	Fea. 784	Unretouched Flake	Spur/St-edge Knife	51/83
492(a)	Fea. 21	Perforator	Drill	V 54

LOT NO.	FUNCTIONAL INTERPRETATION Carr (1982)	Microwear Analysis	Agree/ Disagree
2652-1	deflesh hide	cut meat, scrape hide	(agree)
840(a)	whittle wood/bone	cut meat/fresh hide	disagree
2007(a)	whittle wood/bone/horn	cut meat/fresh hide	disagree
881(a)	scrape hide/wood/bone	scrape dry hide	(agree)
1332(a)	dehair hide	scrape dry hide	agree
2719-1	drill soft wood	scrape dry hide	disagree
2672-1	lithic manufacturing	scrape bone/antler	disagree
546(a)	dehair hide	scrape bone/antler	disagree
3054-1	work wood/bone/hide	scrape bone/antler	disagree
492(a)	drill soft wood	engrave bone/antler	disagree

(agree) = partial agreement

and around the wall-trench structures. Even though most of the chipped stone artifacts were recovered in the fill of the house basins and related features rather than from "living floors" or "activity areas," we can still use them to determine the kinds of activities that went on at each household cluster. This is possible because the Mississippian component at Labras Lake represents a single occupation, and there is no evidence that the house basins served as garbage pits that were used by later inhabitants of the site.

Instead, it appears that prior to the final abandonment of the site, the wall-trench houses were dismantled and the wall posts and roof-bearing posts were uprooted. Dismantling the house disturbed the tops of the wall trenches and postholes, and during the excavation of these structures the outlines of the internal features seemed irregular at the bottom of the house basins, but became clearer during the excavation and cleaning of the house "floors." This suggests that the house basins were deliberately filled in with the refuse that had accumulated around the house during the Mississippian occupation episode. Refit links and ceramic cross-mends show some mixing in the fill of the central three houses (figure 28), but long-distance refits are virtually absent, and the fill in the houses seems to have come from the immediate vicinity. Most likely, the activities that generated that lithic refuse occurred in close proximity to the place where the artifacts were ultimately deposited, and since the artifacts were recovered from sealed contexts, postdepositional disturbance has probably been minimal.

The functional information provided by microwear analysis must be considered in light of accumulation and deposition processes. Some tasks are harder on tools than others. Experiments have shown that chipped stone tools used to scrape wood hold their edge longer than hide- or bone-scraping tools. The proportions of different functional types in a microwear assemblage may not reflect the relative importance of different activities as much as the durability of the implements. Still, the microwear data allow the archeologist to determine what kinds of activities are associated with various tool assemblages.

For example, the three Mississippian houses in the central area of the Labras Lake site contained the only shell drills, wood saws, plant knives, and bone or antler saws in the entire Mississippian component, while hide scrapers, bone/antler scrapers, and meat knives were found in all of the Mississippian houses.

The used tools associated with Houses 1, 2, 3, and 6 suggest that a variety of domestic activities were performed in those households. All of these structures had internal hearths--with the possible exception of House 2, where several shallow depressions contained concentrations of charcoal and carbonized nutshell--but superimposed pit features made it difficult to determine if these features actually served as hearths.

There were no hearths within the walls of House 4 or House 5, and the tools in the microwear samples from these houses contained a more restricted variety of functional classes. While 43% of all of the used tools in the Mississippian microwear sample were hide-working tools, 58% of the tools from House 4 and 63% of the tools from House 5 were used on hide. Plant knives were absent from the microwear samples drawn from these houses, and it appears that these structures represent specialized hide-working facilities. But there are other lines of evidence that must be considered before the function of these wall trench structures without hearths can be understood.

The nature of the floral and faunal remains associated with these hearthless structures does not indicate that they were warm-weather dwellings. The wall-trench houses that had internal hearths contained similar floral and faunal remains. Although a hearth inside a structure has been interpreted as evidence for winter habitation in temperate climates, and the absence of a hearth has been one of the criteria used to identify summer houses (Fortier et al. 1984; Norris 1978), this dichotomy has not been corroborated by floral and faunal evidence from the Labras Lake site.

The number of potsherds recovered in the structures without hearths was less than the number found in the other houses, and this may suggest that fewer domestic activities went on there. Several of these structures contained some evidence of specialized activities.

For example, there were 187 bone fragments in House 4, while only 57 faunal elements were recovered in all of the other Mississippian structures. Microwear analysis showed that 10 out of the 11 used tools in House 4 were used on hide, meat, bone, or antler; and Feature 708, the pit linked to House 4 by a ceramic cross-mend, contained 143 bone fragments and a knife/scraper that was used on meat or fresh hide. Tools used to scrape bone or antler were also found in two other pits that were located near House 4. Butchering and hide-processing seem to have been the primary activities that went on in the House 4 area.

By contrast, House 5 contained only a single bone fragment, but there were thirty one hoe fragments and hoe chips in the fill of this structure, five times the average number of hoe flakes found in the other Mississippian houses at Labras Lake. A fair amount of carbonized maize, nuts, and charcoal was found inside House 5, even though the structure did not have an internal hearth. The reworked hoe and hoe-resharpening flakes found in House 5 suggest that tasks related to agriculture may have been the primary activities performed in that house. Although hide-working tools dominated the microwear sample, this may not have been the main activity that was performed. Bone- or antler-working and wood-working tools were also present in the House 5 microwear sample.

There was very little limestone in the fill of House 5, even though limestone was quite common in other Mississippian houses at Labras Lake (there were 212 grams of limestone inside of House 5, while the site average was 3,834 gram per house), but most of the ceramics found inside House 5 were limestone-tempered.

The lower level of House 3 also had very little limestone in its fill, but the ceramics associated with that house were usually tempered with shell. Very few floral or faunal remains were recovered inside the lower level of House 3, and the only evidence for specialized activities in that structure was the shell microdrill found on the lower floor.

Microdrills similar to the five that were distributed between the three central houses at Labras Lake have been found at other Mississippian sites in the Cahokia settlement system, and it has been assumed that they were used to produce shell disk beads (Mason and Perino 1961). Although microwear analysis of samples of microdrills from the Powell Mound and the Dunham Tract at Cahokia (Yerkes 1983) and from the Lohmann site (Yerkes in press) have shown that these tools were almost exclusively used to drill shell, this alone does not prove that they were used by craft specialists. Still, the distribution of the microdrills at Labras Lake and other Mississippi sites such as Lohmann, Turner, Mitchell, and BBB Motor is restricted, and this suggests that shell drilling may have been reserved for certain members of Mississippian society.

The central cluster at Labras Lake also contains the only sweat houses in the Mississippian component and the bulk of the storage facilities. It is possible that the configuration of the features and structures at the site reflects functional differences between the structures; but if a local leader did reside at Labras Lake during the Stirling phase, the concentration of storage pits near the central houses, the presence of sweat lodges, and the restricted distribution of shell drills may be a legacy of that kind of control. The evidence for this is rather weak, but the idea should not be completely discounted.

The functional information provided by the microwear analysis shows a fairly uniform distribution of task-specific artifacts throughout all of the houses at Labras Lake, with some functional variation that seems to correspond to the morphology of the structures and their spatial relationships. The numerous lithic refits between the three central houses show that material passed between these structures quite often; but very few of the refitted artifacts were used as tools, so the life histories of tools could not be reconstructed in any kind of detail.

A variety of domestic activities went on in and around each dwelling, with hunting and gathering tasks represented as well as agricultural activities. There is some evidence for specialization in the households, such as the shell-drilling activities which were restricted to the central three houses, the animal butchering and hide processing in House 4 and its associated features, and the hoe resharpening and other agricultural activities in House 5.

The picture that emerges is that the Mississippian settlement at Labras Lake was self-sufficient with a few specialized activities. Hunting as well as farming went on there, and wild plants and nuts were exploited along with maize and squash. Like the Early Bluff people who inhabited the site some 300 years earlier, the Mississippians exploited aquatic mammals, fish, turtles, and freshwater mussels. These species were probably obtained from the nearby abandoned meander scars that were occupied by oxbow lakes after the Mississippi River had moved to the western valley margin.

Microwear Analysis at Labras Lake: A Summary

In his morphological analysis of the lithic artifacts from the Labras Lake site, Phillips (1980, 1986) remarked that the only real differences between the Late Archaic, Late Woodland, and Mississippian lithics were the prevalence of bifaces and bifacial elements in the Late Archaic and the frequency of hoe fragments and hoe chips in the Mississippian. In nearly all of the other morphological categories the artifacts from the three components are similar.

Microwear analysis revealed the same sort of parallel pattern in the functional classification of the 308 utilized artifacts in the Labras Lake microwear sample. However, there were some differences. Plant knives were found in the Late Woodland and Mississippian samples, but they were absent in the Late Archaic microwear assemblage, and shell drills were only found in Mississippian contexts.

Hide-working tools were more common in the Mississippian assemblage, while there were more meat knives and wood-working tools in the Late Archaic microwear sample. Bone- or antler-working tools were very common in the Early Bluff sample, but wood working implements were rare. The ratio of bone- or antler-working tools to wood-working tools was 2.2:1 for the Mississippian collection, but only 1.3:1 for the Late Archaic microwear sample (table 24).

Several different morphological types were found in each functional class of artifacts, and there were some distinctive artifact forms that were found in several components, but evidently were used for quite different tasks. For example, the microgravers found in the Late Archaic assemblage from the north central portion of the Labras Lake site were used as hide reamers or borers. An artifact with a similar shape was found in the fill of House 2, a Mississippian wall-trench structure, and microwear analysis indicated that it had been used to scrape and cut wood.

The only relationships between form and function in the microwear assemblages from Labras Lake were that thin flakes and blades were often used to cut meat, while steep-edged implements (both retouched and unretouched) served as scrapers. The size of scrapers and the thickness of their bits were quite variable, and there was no direct correspondence between any of these variables and the specific material that had been scraped by the tools (figure 35).

When Carr's morphological system of classification was applied to the used artifacts in the Labras Lake microwear samples, there was little agreement between the functional interpretations based on formal attributes and those based on microwear evidence. In assemblages where tools were expediently selected from amorphous flakes and used for a variety of tasks, formal and functional relationships will show great latitude and defy any simple quantification based on edge-angle measurements and subjective assessments of artifact morphology. At Labras Lake, even the bifacial tools with more "standardized" shapes were used for a variety of tasks that were not often related to their form.

Bifacial tools in the microwear assemblages were used as bone, antler, or wood saws as often as they were used to cut meat, so the designation "bifacial knife" is something of a misnomer. In fact, the used tools from Labras Lake seem to have been chosen as needed from nonformalized blanks. These blanks were often retouched, but they were rarely chipped into standardized shapes (Phillips 1980: 364).

TABLE 24. Summary of tool functions in microwear samples from all of the components at the Labras Lake site.

TOOL FUNCTION	LATE ARCHAIC NO.	%	LATE WOODLAND NO.	%	MISSISSIPPIAN NO.	%	TOTAL NO.	%
Meat Knife	28	25%	2	9%	16	16%	46	20%
Hide Knife	4	4%	-	-	10	10%	14	6%
Hide Scraper	24	22%	6	28%	29	29%	59	26%
Hide Awl/Reamer	5	4%	-	-	1	1%	6	3%
Shell Drill	-	-	-	-	5	5%	5	2%
Wood Saw	3	3%	-	-	4	4%	7	3%
Wood Scraper	9	8%	1	5%	4	4%	14	6%
Wood Borer	1	1%	-	-	1	1%	2	1%
Wood Graver	2	2%	-	-	-	-	2	1%
Plant Knife	-	-	2	-	4	4%	6	3%
Bone/Antler Saw	3	3%	1	5%	4	4%	8	3%
B/A Scraper	13	12%	3	14%	11	11%	27	12%
B/A Graver	4	4%	1	5%	3	3%	8	1%
B/A Borer	-	-	-	-	2	2%	2	2%
Unknown Use	13	12%	5	24%	5	5%	23	10%
Total Tasks:	109	100%	21	100%	99	99%	229	100%
Total Tools:	101		19		82		202	

TOOL CATEGORY

	LATE ARCHAIC NO.	%	LATE WOODLAND NO.	%	MISSISSIPPIAN NO.	%	TOTAL NO.	%
BUTCHERY	28	25%	2	10%	16	16%	46	20%
HIDE-WORKING	33	30%	46	30%	40	40%	79	34%
SHELL-WORKING	-	-	-	-	5	5%	5	2%
WOOD-WORKING	15	13%	1	5%	9	9%	25	11%
PLANT PROCESSING	-	-	2	10%	4	4%	6	3%
BONE/ANTLER	20	18%	5	25%	20	20%	45	20%

Note: percentages may not sum to 100% due to rounding errors.

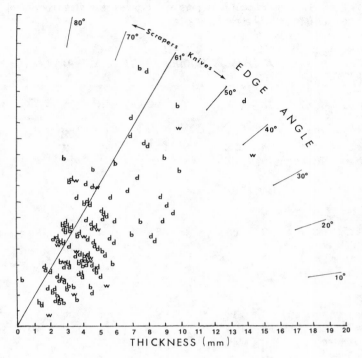

Figure 35. Polar coordinate plot of the thickness and
edge angles of scrapers from all of the components at
Labras Lake. Note the large number of scraping tools with
edge angles less than 61 degrees, the value that Carr (1982)
has used to separate knives and scrapers.

In all components, about 40% of the retouched implements (i.e., the
tools) that were microscopically examined had wear traces on their edges.
However, only 17:% of the unretouched blanks from the Late Archaic components
showed any evidence of use, while only 10% of the Mississippian blanks were
utilized. A paltry 5% of the blanks in the Early Bluff microwear sample had
use wear on their edges.

The larger percentage of used implements among the Late Archaic blanks confirms Phillip's (1980, 1986) interpretation that the Late Archaic knappers were more careful in their core preparation and flake removal techniques than the Early Bluff and Mississippian individuals. Cores with opposed platform are more common in the Late Archaic assemblage, while the Early Bluff and Mississippian cores are multiplatformed, suggesting that flakes were struck off at random.

Blades or prepared flakes were rare in all assemblages at Labras Lake. It seems that the utilized implements were selected from piles of detached flakes and were retouched as needed to complete the task at hand. With the exception of perforating tools and reamers, most of these artifacts showed a minimum of modification prior to use.

This lack of formalized tools in the lithic assemblage would make it difficult to derive site function from artifact typologies. Bifacial "knives," projectile points, end scrapers, and hoe flakes have been used as indices for hunting, domestic, and agricultural activities at sites on the American Bottom, but this microwear study has shown that these formal categories do not accurately reflect artifact function and site activities.

Concentrations of projectile points were associated with retooling sites, not "hunting camps," at Labras Lake (also see Keeley 1982), while there were relatively few end scrapers among the hide-working tools identified at the site. The bifacial artifacts served a variety of functions, and in the Late Archaic components they seem to have been primarily used as tool blanks or preforms that were roughed out, heated, and then chipped into their final shape.

A more accurate account of the past activities that went on at Labras Lake has been derived from the microwear analysis. However, one must not make too much of the proportions of different functional types in the lithic assemblages. The abundance of hide-working tools in the microwear samples could reflect the toll that hide scraping and cutting takes on stone implements as much as the importance of that activity in the prehistoric economy. Experiments have shown that a chipped stone wood saw can be used for a longer time than a bone or antler saw, and more wood can be cut with a single implement. Some microwear polishes form faster than others, so many tasks that were simple and did not take much time or effort may not be represented in the microwear samples.

The range of activities that went on at Labras Lake during each occupational episode is recorded here, not the relative importance of different activities in the domestic regimen. However, the degree of specialization during each occupational episode can be compared by evaluating the microwear data.

The earlier Late Archaic occupations at the site seemed to have been of shorter duration than the later Late Archaic occupations, and to have been more restricted in the scope of activities that were performed. One occupation in the south central area seems to have been primarily for hunting and butchering mammals such as deer and elk. Another early Labras Lake phase habitation was marked by tool manufacturing and repair. By contrast, the late Labras Lake phase settlements seem to have been occupied longer, and by larger groups. The functional analysis revealed a wider range of activities, and even though the floral and faunal remains were poorly preserved, it appears that terrestrial species of animals and slightly more mesic species of plants were the primary food sources (F. B. King 1980; Purdue and Styles 1980).

There is a 1,600-year gap in the occupational history of Labras Lake, and the Early Bluff people who inhabited the site around A. D. 900 established a base camp whose spatial configuration was similar to some of the earlier Late Archaic settlements. However, they subsisted on a wider range of foods, including aquatic plants and animals and starchy seeds. It is possible that the Early Bluff inhabitants were tending native domesticates such as maygrass and stumpweed, and may have used ground stone adzes to clear forested areas around the site.

The agricultural Mississippians who were the site's last prehistoric tenants erected a central cluster of three or four houses and several outlying wall-trench structures. While the evidence for farming at the site is compelling, there were also many stone tools present that were used to butcher animals, process hides, and modify antler, bone, wood, plant, and shell material. There were two sweat houses and numerous pits associated with the Mississippian houses, and there is some evidence to suggest the presence of specialists or local leaders at this site, but it is not overwhelming. The site's occupants seem to have been self-sufficient, with more autonomy than most would expect to find at fourth-line communities in the Mississippian settlement system.

7 Conclusion

A braided Mississippi River crossed the American Bottom at the close of the Pleistocene, and this flow regime probably persisted until around 5,000 years ago. At that time, the river began to meander across the middle of the floodplain and created many of the meander scars that can still be seen today. The earliest excavated archeological sites on the American Bottom were inhabited when this paleomeander belt was active.

The onset of meandering by the Mississippi River and the first Late Archaic habitations on the American Bottom correspond with the end of dry Hypsithermal conditions in the Middle Mississippi Valley and the beginning of wetter conditions around 5700-3200 B.P. (J.E. King 1980); however, it is not certain that this climatic amelioration caused the change in river configuration or led to the establishment of Late Archaic settlements on the bottom.

Most of the excavated Late Archaic sites on the American Bottom are located along the eastern margin of the floodplain, and data from six of these bluff base sites and three upland sites have been used to define four Late Archaic phases for the region (McElrath and Fortier 1983).

It has been argued that most of the known Late Archaic sites on the American Bottom are found on high terraces, talus slopes, or silty clay banks adjacent to meander scars because these bluff-base locations provided hunter-gatherer groups with stable surfaces that would not be threatened by Mississippi channel migrations. Some archeologists believe that these locations were surrounded by resource-rich wetlands and bluff-edge habitats that sustained a variety of wild plants and animals (Emerson 1984; McElrath and Fortier 1983).

McElrath and Fortier (1983: 220) suggest that most of the Late Archaic sites inhabited during the Falling Springs and Titterington phases were located in the uplands, while the intensive occupation of the bluff-base areas did not occur until the terminal Late Archaic Labras Lake and Prairie Lake phases. They believe this upland to lowland shift reflects the increased stability of the previously active Mississippi floodplain channels. In their scheme, the central meander belt would have been an inhospitable place that would not have been settled until the active channel had shifted westward leaving a series of oxbow lakes and backwaters scattered across the American

Bottom. McElrath and Fortier think the terminal Late Archaic populations that moved down onto the floodplain developed a subsistence pattern that was focused on the wetland flora and fauna.

It must be remembered that this upland to lowland shift in Late Archaic settlement patterns is based on information from three excavated sites in the uplands and six bottomland localities (figure 10). The three upland sites are the McLean site (11-S-640), the George Reeves site (11-S-650), and the Tep site (11-Mo-154). Two radiocarbon dates from the McLean site are listed as 2410 and 2650 b.c. (Porter 1983), and it may have been occupied during the Falling Springs or Titterington phases. No radiocarbon dates have been reported from the George Reeves site, but a few projectile points suggest a Titterington phase habitation. The southernmost bluff-top site is Tep, where a single radiocarbon date of 3200 B.C. has been reported (Porter 1983), but the major occupation is terminal Late Archaic or Early Woodland.

On the floodplain, the Go-Kart North site, which has been assigned to the Titterington phase (2300-1900 B.C.), and the early Labras Lake phase occupations at the Labras Lake site (1850-1400 B.C.), consist of several seasonal occupations that were short term but intensive. Hickory nut husks are relatively abundant at these sites, but other nut species such as hazelnut, black walnut, and acorns are also present. Seeds are rare, and it is assumed that nut collecting and processing were the primary gathering ivities at these sites, while seed harvesting was more casual (Johannessen 1981). The faunal remains from Late Archaic sites on the American Bottom are very poorly preserved, but deer and elk seem to have been the preferred game animals, although some fish and turtle were captured as well.

These earlier Late Archaic occupations do not have many deep pits, structures , or superimposed features. They have been interpreted   as short-term seasonal camps. At Labras Lake, there is evidence that hunting, butchering, and lithic manufacturing and repairing were the major tasks performed. However, a wider range of activities has been suggested for the Go-Kart North site (Fortier 1984: 188).

The Titterington phase settlement at the Go-Kart North site was located on the cut bank of the Hill Lake paleochannel, but it is not clear if that channel was active during the occupation of the site. The Hill Lake channel may have been a backwater lake or slough at that time. Labras Lake is located near a buried channel that may have been active during the earliest Late Archaic occupation episode, or that site may also have been bounded by a backwater area.

The late Labras Lake phase (1450-1000 B.C.) occupations at the Labras Lake site and the Prairie Lake phase (1000-600 B.C.) settlements at Labras Lake, Dyroff, Levin, Mopac #2, and Range all seem to be characterized by more "sedentary" base camps (Phillips and Gladfelter 1983; Yerkes and Phillips in press) or base locales (Emerson 1984) where a greater variety of activities were performed by the site's inhabitants. The Late Archaic settlements in the north central and southwestern areas of the Labras Lake site are marked by higher densities and greater varieties of floral remains, although hickory nuts still dominate the assemblages. Some members of the starchy seed complex that becomes established during later cultural phases are associated with these Late Archaic components (also see Griffin 1983: 251).

Most of these terminal Archaic sites seem to have been located next to abandoned channels and backwaters rather than active Mississippi River meanders. The exploitation of wetland plants and animals has been postulated as an economic focus of these Late Archaic groups. Unfortunately the poor preservation of faunal material from these sites makes it difficult to reconstruct their diet in any detail. It is possible that the existence of backwater areas and spring-fed streams near the Falling Springs locality contributed to the relatively high density of late Labras Lake and Prairie Lake phase settlements in the area, but it must be remembered that the floodplain surface in the Hill Lake-Prairie Lake area was more stable than the central meander belt, and the chances of finding intact Late Archaic sites are greater in this bluff-base zone (figure 5).

The high density of floral material and the diversity of plant and animal remains at the Cahokia Interpretive Center Tract indicates that Late Archaic populations were exploiting the aquatic resources of the central meander belt with an intensity that equaled or exceeded the subsistence system of the valley margin "base locales."

Lopinot (1983) has argued that the shifting channels in the meander belt could have kept the vegetation communities in a constant state of successional change. These disturbed habitats would have supported more species of plants with a greater biomass than the climax communities along the base of the bluff.

More excavations are needed before Late Archaic settlement patterns and subsistence strategies on the American Bottom can be fully understood. It is folly to reconstruct an upland to lowland shift in site location from nine excavated sites. The concentration of terminal Late Archaic sites along the eastern valley margin is probably the result of differential site preservation rather than cultural preference.

The Late Archaic sites excavated during the FAI-270 project provide a body of data that may result in some useful insights into the transition from food-collecting to food-producing economies and the associated changes in settlement patterns on the American Bottom. However, many of the recently published FAI-270 reports (Emerson 1984; Fortier 1984; McElrath and Fortier 1983) still rely on Winters's (1969) systemic index or Fowler's (1959) relative percentage of morphological tool classes to interpret the activities at these sites and to classify them within a site typology.

Despite Winters's (1969: 135) caution that his systemic index could not be applied to sites where bone artifacts were not preserved, the Dyroff, Levin, MoPac #2, and Go-Kart North sites have been categorized as "base camps" or "seasonal encampments" by comparing the percentage of stone artifacts classified as general utility tools, weapons, and fabricating, processing, or domestic tools in each of their assemblages.

Microwear analysis is a much more reliable method of obtaining functional information from stone tools. Use-wear data can be used to reconstruct the activities that went on at a prehistoric site with a greater degree of accuracy than functional techniques that are based on tool morphology and ethnographic analogy. Since no bone tools were recovered from any Late Archaic sites on the American Bottom, it is not appropriate to apply Winters's techniques in the first place; but even if bone artifacts were present, the assumed relationships between tool form and function that are the basis of Winters's systemic index have not been borne out by replication experiments and use-wear analysis. The results of functional studies of stone artifacts based on microwear traces and tool morphology that have been cited in this study show that the two methods produced the same functional interpretation in only one case out of ten (table 11).

The microwear analysis of the chipped stone artifacts from Labras Lake provided a more reliable index of site activities than do the older methods still used by the "new generation" of American Bottom archeologists. This is not meant as a criticism of Fowler and Winters or the techniques of functional analysis that they developed over thirty years ago. Rather, it is a call for the application of a new technique, microwear analysis, in studies of tool use, activity patterning, and site function.

Use-wear traces can reveal how chipped stone tools were used with a greater degree of accuracy and reliability than morphological techniques. Microwear analysis is not a panacea that will solve all of the problems associated with the investigations of settlement and subsistence practices in

prehistory, but it lets archeologists document some of the activities that
went on at sites with a degree of certainty that had been lacking. If Fowler
and Winters were beginning their careers today, I am sure their methods of
investigation would include use-wear analysis. Unfortunately, some of their
younger colleagues are unwilling to apply these new techniques.

The Later Prehistoric Occupations at Labras Lake

At Labras Lake, there is no evidence of habitation between the Late
Archaic (1850-850 B.C.) and the Early Bluff (A.D. 900) occupations. At the
other excavated sites in the vicinity of Prairie Lake and Falling Springs,
there are only Late Archaic and Late Woodland/Mississippian sites as well.
Early Woodland and Middle Woodland groups apparently did not settle in these
areas, although they did occupy the point bars and interchannel ridges of the
Goose Lake meander and the Hill Lake paleochannel.

The hiatus in the occupational history at Labras Lake corresponds with
the period when the Mississippi channel shifted from the central meander belt
to a straighter course along the western margin of the floodplain (450 B.C.
-A.D. 850). However, it is not clear how the shifting channel of the
Mississippi relates to the abandonment of the Labras Lake-Prairie Lake areas
during the Early and Middle Woodland periods.

The Early Bluff occupation at Labras Lake occurred after the Mississippi
channel had moved to the west and the site setting was between a spring-fed
stream and several oxbow lakes and sloughs that were now fed by
upland-draining water courses. The Early Bluff inhabitants seem to have
subsisted on cultivated and wild plants, including native domesticates. Maize
remains were only found in one Early Bluff feature at Labras Lake, and the
density of maize in the floral sample was only 0.02 grams per 10 liters of
flotation-processed soil. The density of maize in the Mississippian flotation
samples was fifty-six times greater, so maize does not seem to have been an
important part of the Early Bluff diet.

Both terrestrial and aquatic animals were being hunted and butchered at
the site, with aquatic species such as fish, turtle, mussels, and muskrat
occurring in greater quantities in the Early Bluff faunal sample than they had
in the Late Archaic assemblages. Cross (1982) has argued that fish and other
aquatic species are quite common in faunal assemblages from Early Bluff sites
located both in the uplands and on the floodplain, and it appears that there
was an expansion of populations into new areas of the American Bottom that
were not occupied previously. At Labras Lake, we see the resettlement of an
area that had been unoccupied since Late Archaic times.

This settlement pattern fits Hall's (1973) model of Late Woodland expansion into the uplands after the introduction of the bow and arrow and the beginnings of slash-and-burn cultivation. However, the bulk of the cultivated plants consisted of native starchy seed varieties, while maize was a minor component.

The Mississippian Occupation

The final occupation at Labras Lake involved a Mississippian population with Stirling phase affinities. This occupation was marked by a broad spectrum subsistence pattern that included maize cultivation, but also nut collecting, wild plant harvesting, the cultivation of native domesticates, and the hunting of a variety of terrestrial and aquatic animals. The Mississippian occupation does not seem to have been solely an agricultural settlement designed to produce food for the larger Mississippian towns, but rather seems to have functioned as a self-sufficient hamlet, where a variety of foods were exploited and some minor ceremonial activities may have gone on. There is also some evidence for shell drilling in the inner circle of three wall trench houses at Labras Lake that may relate to the production of trade items (Yerkes in press).

Changing Ecosystems

Environmental changes on the American Bottom seem to have been relatively minor, with the major developments relating to the emergence of wetlands and backwaters after the Mississippi River had moved west out of its central meander belt. However, an "aquatic mode" of subsistence seems to have its roots in the Late Archaic cultures that had begun to establish base camps near sloughs and oxbow lakes as early as 1400 B.C. At Labras Lake, the shift from a mobile to a semisedentary settlement pattern is documented in the four Late Archaic habitation areas at the site.

The Early Bluff occupation at the site was marked by a similar pattern of semisedentary settlement, but starchy seed and aquatic animals were more intensively exploited. This subsistence pattern was continued, by expanded, but the Mississippians, who cultivated more maize and added several other species of plants and animals to their diet. The evidence for the expansion of the Mississippian diet is significant, since it is often assumed that prehistoric societies who cultivated domesticated plants had less variety in their diets than groups who subsisted by hunting-gathering-fishing or wild plant tending.

The lithic assemblages from the Late Archaic, Late Woodland, and Mississippian components at Labras Lake show that new types of tools were being added as the subsistence base was expanded and certain resources were more intensively exploited. Plant knives were not found in the Late Archaic microwear samples, but they were present in the Late Woodland and Mississippian assemblages. This may correspond to the increased importance of starchy seed plants in the Early Bluff diet. Agricultural tools such as chipped stone hoes (and the hoe chips produced when these tools were resharpened), ground stone celts, and grinding stones are more common in the Mississippian assemblages than they were in the artifact collections from the older components at Labras Lake. These changes in stone tool function seem to match the changes in ceramic technology described by Braun (1983).

Even though the bone preservation at Labras Lake was poor, some comparisons are possible. Elk remains were only found in Late Archaic features, and the greatest number of large mammal bones were found in the Late Archaic flotation samples. Meat knives were more common in the Late Archaic microwear samples, and it is possible that the lower proportion of these butchering tools in Early Bluff and Mississippian assemblages and the lower density of faunal remains represents a decline in hunting and meat processing at the site. However, there is nothing to suggest that meat was imported from upland "hunting camps" or exchanged for maize or other plants that were grown at the Labras Lake "farmstead." Butchering tools still account for 10% of the tools in the Early Bluff microwear sample and 16% of the Mississippian tools, as compared to 25% in the Late Archaic microwear assemblage.

Hall (1973) believes that environmental stress due to both an increase and concentration of populations and the onset of drier climatic conditions led to an increase in centralized authority for the purposes of redistributing food during the rise of Mississippian culture on the American Bottom.

Outlying hamlets like Labras Lake appear to be self-sufficient and diversified in their subsistence strategy. While the finely made ceramics (Ramey Incised) and exotic goods (marine shell beads, galena, gypsum, quartz, Mill Creek hoes, and Ramey Knives) that are found at these communities suggest some interaction with larger Mississippian centers (Milner 1983), there is no evidence that these small moundless Mississippian sites were exporting surplus grain to the mound centers. Instead, dispersed settlements seem to have arisen on the American Bottom with local and regional interaction. The extent of centralized authority, redistribution, and the "divided risk" (Chmurney 1973) management of cultivated crops is uncertain.

Many believe the key to understanding the rise of Cahokia Mississippian Culture lies outside of the large temple towns. However, smaller Mississippian sites like Labras Lake do not contain the data needed to study the processes of urbanization and state formation. Excavations at these outlying sites have not produced evidence for large-scale food storage, full-time craft specialization, or social stratification. Perhaps these outlying sites were not in the mainstream of social and political developments and were free of much of the regimentation and authority that was in place at the larger sites.

This study shows that the inhabitants of the Labras Lake site developed subsistence systems that allowed them to adjust to the dynamic conditions of life on the American Bottom floodplain. A trend toward more sedentary settlement patterns can be documented by the Late Archaic, Late Woodland, and Mississippian occupations at Labras Lake; but it remains to be seen if population pressure or climatic change set this trend in motion.

The variety of plant and animal species exploited at Labras Lake increased over time, and specialized food production is not recognized in the functional and bioarcheological data. New techniques of cultivation, hunting (with the bow and arrow), and food processing (pottery vessels) may have allowed the prehistoric populations to add new food items to their diets, but they retained most of their old staples. Food complexes do not seem to have been displaced at American Bottom sites. Nuts were not "replaced" by starchy seeds, and seeds were not superseded by maize (Rindos and Johannessen 1983). Instead, we have evidence from the Cahokia Interpretive Center Tract (Lopinot 1983) that shows that Late Archaic groups were exploiting a variety of seeds, nuts and other wild plant foods by at least 1200 B.C. At Labras Lake, wild nuts, were harvested in quantity by agricultural Mississippians around A.D. 1230, and many species of starchy seeds were also present in the floral sample.

Starchy seeds, native domesticates, and tropical cultigens seem to have been more intensively exploited by the later prehistoric groups on the American Bottom, but the new evidence from the Cahokia Museum Tract and FAI-270 sites suggests that a broad spectrum of plants had been utilized since Late Archaic times.

It has been suggested that the human ecosystem concept is a more productive framework for the study of prehistoric cultural change, since questions pertaining to **why** cultures changed can be addressed as well as queries about **what** changes occurred in prehistory and **when** they occurred

(Stoltman and Baerreis 1983). However, the ecosystem approach must consider the biases inherent in the data used to reconstruct the subsistence and the settlement systems that are compared when cultural change is investigated.

Ford (1977) and Stoltman and Baerreis (1983) have described several successive ecosystem types that existed in eastern North America between 10,000 and 500 years ago. They used published bioarcheological data which recorded the relative amounts of different types of preserved food residues recovered at sites that were assigned to different cultural periods (and geographical areas) when they constructed their models. The relative abundance of different identified faunal elements or floral remains may not reflect the importance of different species of animals and plants in the aboriginal diet. Preservation biases must be considered, and the methods of food processing and disposal must be understood before bioarcheological assemblages can be used to reconstruct dietary habits and subsistence strategies (Butzer 1982; Gilbert and Singer 1982).

These ecosystem reconstructions also use data on site size and location to study prehistoric cultural change in the midlands. But one must consider if all sites in these ecosystem areas have an equal chance at being preserved and if the settlement patterns reflect preservation bias rather than cultural preference. The different ecosystem types have been related to certain modes of community patterning (Beardsley 1956) and social organization (Service 1962), but one wonders if these organizational analogs are really that useful. Winters (1981: 32) suspects that the familiar quartet of bands, tribes, chiefdoms, and states are about as useful to anthropologists as earth, air, fire, and water are to biochemists.

In a sense, these general frameworks are necessary to archaeologists who wish to outline the major trends in cultural development in large geographic areas and over long spans of time. However, when the issue of cultural change is addressed, the scale used in these general models may be too large to identify exactly what aspects of prehistoric cultures were changing and why these changes were occurring (Bee 1974).

On the American Bottom, geomorphic changes make it difficult, if not impossible, to reconstruct the settlement patterns of the Late Archaic (and older) groups that inhabited the region. However, the data from the few Late Archaic sites that have been excavated show that the terminal Late Archaic occupations were more sedentary than the earlier Late Archaic habitations, and that a wide range of floral and faunal resources were being exploited within a dynamic floodplain environment associated with an actively meandering Mississippi River that traversed the central portion of the bottom.

The microwear analysis of four Late Archaic components at the Labras Lake site shows an increase in the number of activities performed at the later habitation areas that corresponds to an increase in the number, size, and density of features associated with these younger settlements. Domestic areas (or structures) are much more common in the terminal Late Archaic components, and a new type of feature, the roasting pit, is associated with these settlements. Late Archaic structures may have been present at the MoPac #2 site as well (McElrath and Fortier 1983), and the density and variety of features at that site argue for a more intensive utilization of the Prairie Lake meander scar during the later portion of the Late Archaic period.

The degree of social complexity within these terminal Late Archaic cultures is more difficult to ascertain. Generally, they are characterized as "band-level" hunter-gatherer societies that were basically egalitarian. However, the Late Archaic domestic areas in the southwestern and north central areas of the Labras Lake site consist of one large structure with a number of internal pits, hearths, and activity areas, surrounded by several small domestic areas that contain no other features (figures 13, 17).

It is possible that the morphological differences in these domestic areas reflect status differences among the inhabitants of the settlements. Burials associated with these groups have not yet been discovered, so evidence for status differentiation based on grave lots comparable to what is available for the Shell Mound Archaic groups (Marquardt and Watson 1983; Rothschild 1979; Winters 1968) is lacking. The absence of Late Archaic burials also makes it difficult to estimate the size of the Late Archaic groups who inhabited the American Bottom and the density of human population.

McElrath and Fortier (1983) have suggested that Late Archaic groups moved from the uplands to the periphery of the floodplain during the terminal Late Archaic Prairie Lake phase (1000-600 B.C.). These authors also suggest that the Woodland and Mississippian populations migrated further out onto the central portion of the American Bottom after the floodplain had "stabilized" as the Mississippi River abandoned the central meander belt and flowed along the western valley margin. This-upland-to-lowland-to-central-floodplain shift in settlement patterns is more apparent than real. Fluvial activity has erased much of the early archaeological record on the American Bottom, and the likelihood of finding late prehistoric sites near the paleochannels inscribed on the floodplain is much greater than the chances of finding Archaic sites that were occupied when the channels were active. It may appear that settlement patterns were changing during this period, but what is really being recorded is a change in river configuration that allowed more sites in the central meander belt to be preserved. The evidence from the Cahokia Interpretive Center Tract shows that Late Archaic groups were intensively exploiting a broad spectrum of floodplain resources by at least 1200 B.C., and the base locales or base camps along the valley margin may have been the peripheral sites, not the nuclear centers of this subsistence system (Binford 1980).

Even though the Late Archaic settlement and subsistence system on the American Bottom cannot be completely reconstructed at this time, it seems clear that more substantial communities were being established on the floodplain during the terminal Archaic period, and these groups had adjusted to life on the floodplain of a centrally located meandering river.

When the Mississippi River shifted its course westward during the Early and Middle Woodland periods, the core of settlements on the American Bottom may have moved with it. Woodland groups seem to have developed technologies that enabled them to process the floodplain resources more efficiently and to store more of the foods they had collected and captured. Their broad-spectrum subsistence system seems to have allowed them to adjust to the new habitats on the bottom where backwater lakes and marshes replaced the active river channels.

Middle and Late Woodland groups were cultivating native and exotic plants, but maize was not a major component of this complex. Technological advances enabled them to open up forested areas and move out from the alluvial valley, but much of their subsistence base remained the same, and the faunal and floral remains found at upland Late Woodland sites and bottomland localities are similar (Cross 1982; Johannessen 1982).

The Mississippian occupants of outlying sites on the American Bottom continued to expand their subsistence base even after maize horticulture became widespread. Rather than simplifying their ecosystem (Ford 1977: 179-80) and concentrating on a few crops that were grown in large cleared fields, the Mississippians at Labras Lake and similar farmsteads seem to have added some new varieties of wild plants to their diet and continued to hunt game and catch fish like their Late Woodland counterparts. While the large Mississippian centers contain evidence for a degree of social stratification and specialization never before seen on the American Bottom, the outlying Mississippian sites continued the subsistence systems of earlier cultural groups with the addition of maize horticulture (Muller 1983: 410).

Griffin (1983: 278) has argued that the shift from Late Woodland to the more complex Cahokia Mississippian Culture was contemporary with similar shifts elsewhere in the South and Southeast. There is little evidence for the rapid appearance of significant amounts of cultural material from the Lower Mississippi Valley or the Caddoan area (Kelly 1980; Porter 1974, 1980) on the American Bottom prior to the emergence of Cahokia Mississippian Culture.

It cannot be shown that environmental change was the cause of cultural change on the American Bottom. However, the environmental dynamics of this floodplain setting must be appreciated if settlement and subsistence shifts are to be investigated. In fact, the dynamic hydrology may have influenced the local biota and led to the development of a broad-spectrum subsistence system.

Geoarchaeological investigations were combined with a functional analysis of chipped stone tools at one site on the American Bottom in this study. The results showed that the changes in site utilization and subsistence were gradual and subtle, with later technologies and economies expanding the base established by the earlier cultural groups. The methods used in this study provided some new insights into site activities and settlement patterns and fostered some criticism of earlier interpretations of American Bottom prehistory. It is hoped that future research will lead to the revision and correction of the conclusions presented here.

Appendix A
Photomicrographs of Microwear Traces on Experimental Chert Tools and Selected Implements from Labras Lake

Magnifications are given in the plate captions. Approximate lengths of the photomicrographs are as follows:

MAGNIFICATION	LENGTH IN MICRONS
50x	1300
100x	654
200x	332
250x	253
300x	218

Photomicrographs were taken with an Olympus PM-10-M photomicrographic system through a model BHM metalurgical microscope in the Laboratory of Archeology, Department of Anthropology, University of Wisconsin-Madison. Ilford XP1 black-and-white print film was used in the camera, and the prints were made on Ilfospeed multigrade MG1M glossy paper.

Plate 1

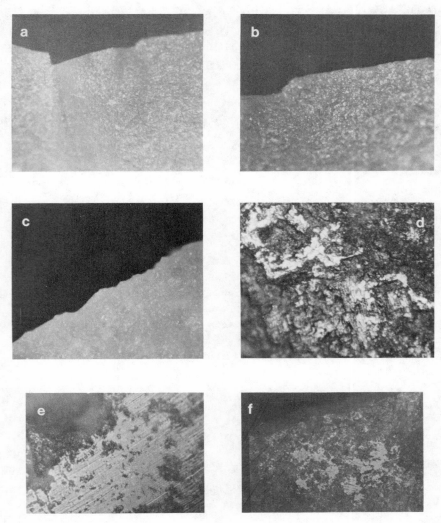

Plate 1

Unmodified Artifacts, Retouched Flakes, and Stone-on-Stone Polish

a. Unmodified flake of Burlington chert (50x).
b. same as a (100x).
c. Unused retouched flake, Burlington chert (thermally altered) (100x).
d. Stone-on-stone polish on surface of ground stone celt (100x).
e. Experimental Burlington chert drill used to bore holes in stone (200x).
f. Denticulate flake from Feature 170 in the Late Woodland component showing stone-on-stone polish (Lot #1491a). The implement was also used to scrape dry hide. See figure B-14(b).

Plate 2

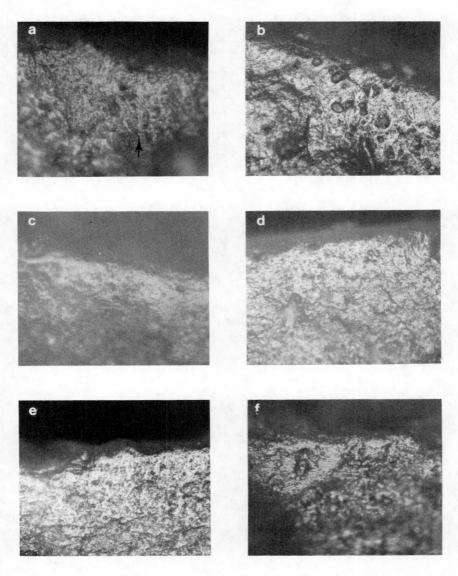

Plate 2

Dry Hide Polish

a. Experimental Burlington chert scraper used on dry deer hide (200x). Note striation.
b. End scraper from the Ogden-Fettie site (Fv196 2/23) in the Illinois valley with well-developed dry-hide polish (200x).
c. Side scraper from Feature 559 (inside the Feature 171 domestic area) in the north central Late Archaic component (Lot #2030a). Used to scrape dry hide (250x). See figure B-6(f).
d. Side scraper from Feature 169 in the Late Woodland component (Lot #1359a). Used to scrape dry hide (200x). See figure B-13(c).
e. Side scraper from Feature 169 (Lot #1359b). Used to scrape dry hide (200x). See Figure B-13(d).
f. Denticulate/retouched flake from the fill of House 2 in the Mississippian component (Lot #1281a). Used to scrape dry hide (300x). See figure B-19(e).

Plate 4

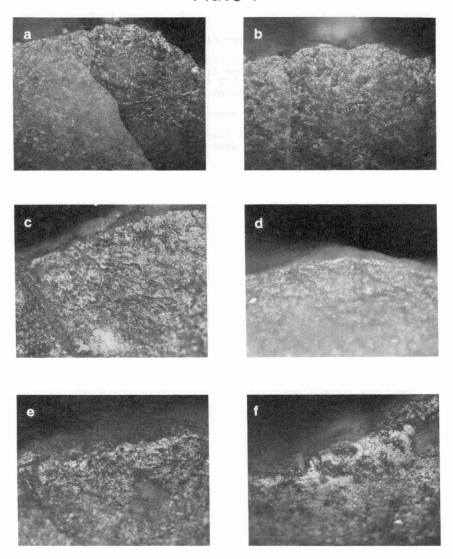

Plate 4

Meat Polish

a. Experimental Burlington chert meat knife (thermally altered) (100x).
b. Same as a (200x).
c. Experimental grey chert meat knife (200x).
d. Side scraper from Feature 22 in House 1, Mississippian component (Lot #520a). Used to cut meat (100x). See figure B-15(a).
e. Same as d (300x).
f. Large retouched flake from Feature 22 (Lot #572-2). Used to cut meat (300x). See figure B-15(f).

Plate 5

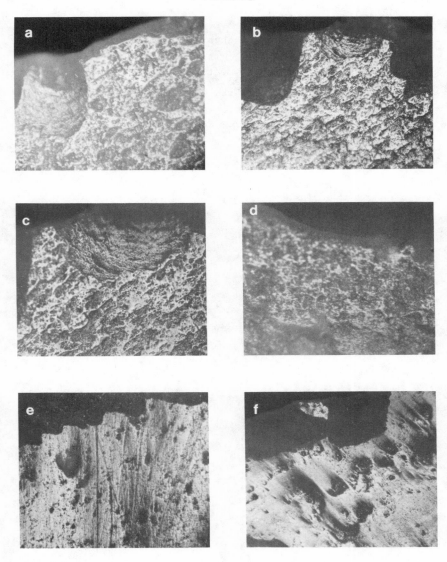

Plate 5

Plant Polish

a. Experimental Burlington chert knife (thermally altered)
   used to cut grass (100x).
b. Plant knife from the floor of House 2, Mississippian
   component (Lot #1229-3). Probably used to cut some type
   of grass (100x). See figure B-21(c).
c. Same as b (200x).
d. Side scraper from Feature 22 in House 1, Mississippian
   component (Lot #572-1). Distal left lateral edge used
   to cut plant material (200x). See figure B-16(a).
e. Broken biface from Feature 8, Late Woodland component
   (Lot #431a) with "corn gloss" or "hoe polish" on distal
   edge (50x). See figure B-14(e).
f. Corn gloss on a hoe chip from the lower fill of House 3,
   Mississippian component (50x).

Plate 6

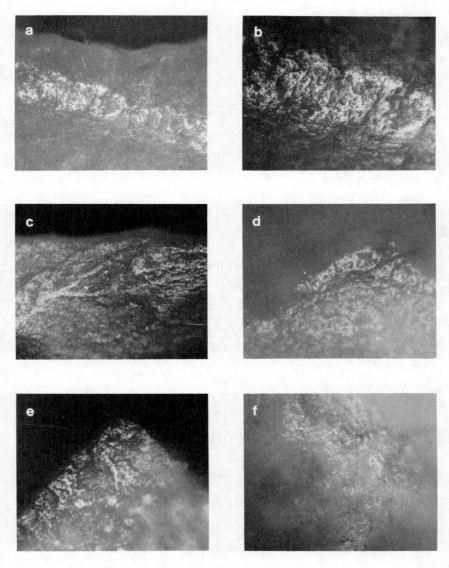

Plate 6

Wood Polish

a. Experimental flake, grey chert, used to "girdle" a soft wood branch (50x).
b. Same as a (100x).
c. Experimental Burlington chert flake used to saw wood (100x).
d. Experimental Burlington chert drill used to bore holes in soft wood (200x).
e. Experimental wood drill (200x).
f. Wood borer from the fill of House 2, Mississippian component (Lot #1627-4). Burlington chert (200x). See figure b-21(a).

Plate 7

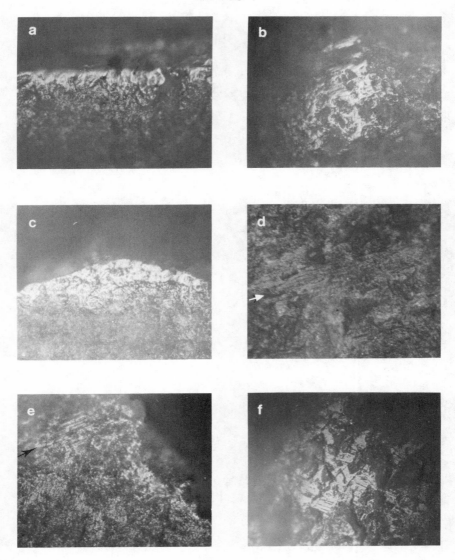

Plate 7

Bone or Antler Polish

a. Experimental Burlington chert scraper used on dry bone (300x).
b. Experimental Burlington chert drill used to bore holes in soaked antler (200x).
c. Broken biface from Feature 778, southwestern Late Archaic component (Lot #3025-1). Used to saw bone or antler (200x). See figure B-4(d).
d. Striations and polish on graver/denticulate from Feature 785, Late Woodland component (Lot #3515-3). Used to saw and engrave bone or antler (200x). See figure B-14(f).
e. Striations and ploish on flake from the fill of House 2, Mississippian component (Lot #1535-4). Used to saw bone or antler (300x). See figure B-21(d).
f. Perforator from the fill of House 2 (Lot #1463a). Used to bore antler or stone? (200x). See figure B-21(e).

Plate 8

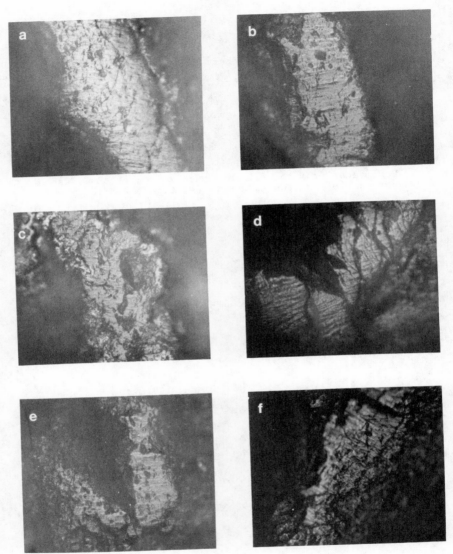

Plate 8

Shell Polish

a. Experimental Burlington chert microdrill. Used on shell (200x).

b. Grey chert microdrill from the fill of House 1 in the Mississippian component (Lot #376a). Used to drill shell (200x). See figure B-16(i).

c. Burlington chert microdrill from the upper-level floor of House 3, Mississippian component (Lot #893a). Used to drill shell (200x). See figure B-22(i).

d. Grey chert microdrill from the lower-level floor of House 3 (Lot #1256a). Used to drill shell (200x). See figure B-23(f).

e. Burlington chert microdrill found beneath the Powell Mound (11-Ms-46/546d) at the Cahokia site. Used to drill shell (200x). See Yerkes (1983, figure 5d).

f. Burlington chert microdrill found beneath the Powell Mound (11-Ms-46/556h). Used to drill shell (200x). See Yerkes (1983, figure 5c).

Appendix B
Location of Microwear Traces on Utilized
Implements from Labras Lake

KEY TO FIGURES

 extent of microwear polish and use-damage scars

 evidence for cutting or sawing

 evidence for scraping or whittling

 evidence for graving (incising)

 burin blow

 cortex

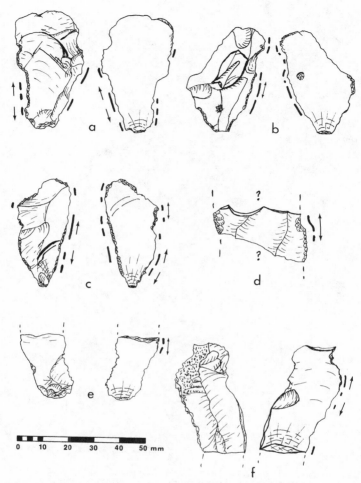

Figure B-1. Southwestern Late Archaic component. Tools used to cut meat or fresh hide: a. retouched flake, Feature 910 (Lot #3718-1); b. retouched flake, Feature 896 (Lot #3726-9/3726-25); c. retouched flake, Feature 900 (#3730-20); d. retouched flake, Feature 900 (#3730-21); e. broken blade, Feature 901 (#3724-1); f. blade, Feature 910 (#3727-3). All artifacts are thermally altered.

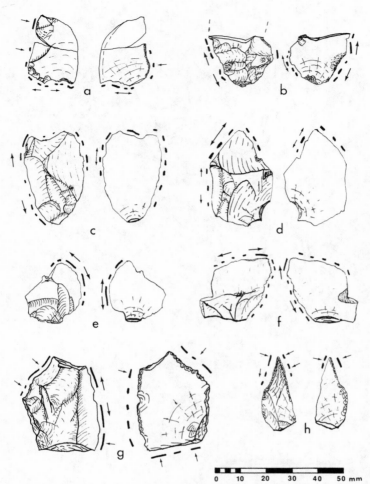

Figure B-2. Southwestern Late Archaic component. Tools used to cut meat or fresh hide: a. denticulate/retouched flake, Feature 778 (Lot #3034-2/3025-4), the left lateral edge was also used to scrape bone; b. retouched flake, Feature 779 (Lot #3031-1); c. unretouched flake, Feature 767 (#2835-2); d. notched flake, Feature 272 (#1523a). Tools used to cut fresh or dry hide: e. unretouched flake, Feature 941 (#3700-1); f. unretouched flake, Feature 779 (#3032-3); g. biface/notch, Feature 277 (#1515a), the left distal edge was also used to scrape dry hide. Hide awl or reaming tool: f. perforator, Excavation Unit 6 (#862a). All artifacts are thermally altered.

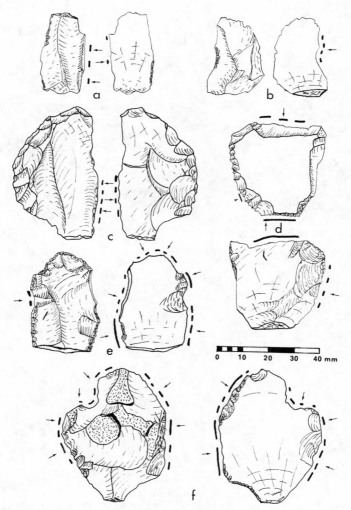

Figure B-3. Southwestern Late Archaic component. Tools used to scrape dry hide: a. retouched flake, Feature 1172 (Lot #3993-1); b. notched flake, Feature 779 (Lot # 3032-2); c. broken biface, Feature 778 (#3025-2); d. biface/scraper, Feature 778 (#3025-3); e. end scraper, Excavation Unit 21 (#2786-2); f. notch/primary flake, Feature 72 (#1512a); b and e were thermally altered.

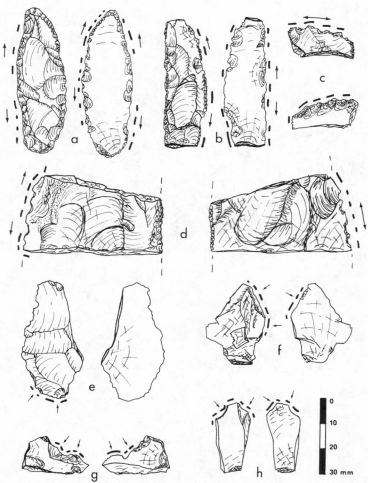

Figure B-4. Southwestern Late Archaic component. Tools used to saw wood: a. retouched blade, Feature 944 (Lot #4145-1), also used to saw bone; b. retouched blade, Excavation Unit 21 (Lot #2942), also used to saw bone; c. retouched flake, Features 941/946 (#4045-3). Tool used to saw bone or antler: d. broken biface, Feature 778 (#3025-1). Tools used to whittle or scrape wood: e. un-retouched flake, Feature 271 (#1509a); f. unretouched flake, Feature 901 (#3724-2); g. unretouched flake, Feature 1172 (#3730-50). Tool used to chisel or engrave wood: h. unretouched flake, Feature 777 (#2950-3); a and b were thermally altered.

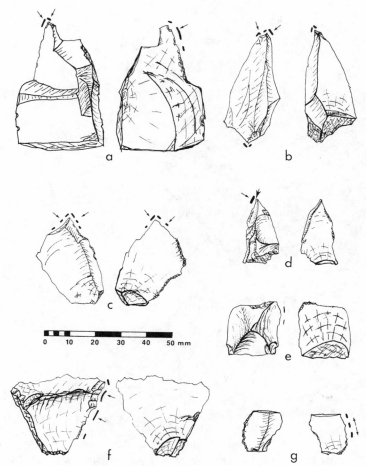

Figure B-5. Southwestern Late Archaic component. Tools used to engrave bone or antler: a. unretouched flake, Feature 899 (Lot #3726-14); b. unretouched flake, Feature 1172 (Lot #3730-38); c. retouched flake, Feature 779 (#3032-1); d. burin, Feature 778 (#3027-4). Tool used to whittle or scrape bone or antler: f. unretouched flake, Feature 946 (#4048-1). Implements with unidentifiable wear traces: e. unretouched flake, Feature 910 (#4049-2); g. truncation, Feature 1172 (#3730-6); a,c,e and g were thermally altered.

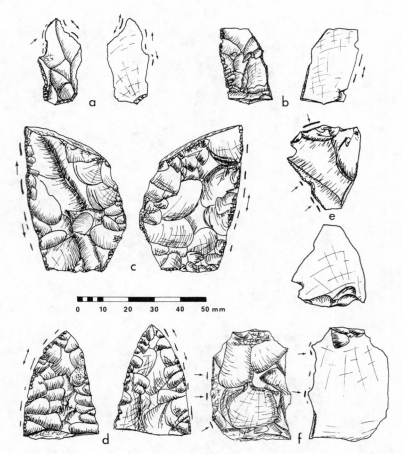

Figure B-6. North Central Late Archaic component. Tools used to cut meat or fresh hide: a. retouched flake, Feature 857 (Lot #3478-3); b. retouched flake, Feature 831 (Lot #3229-1); c. biface, Feature 841 (#3313-7); d. broken biface, Feature 885 (#3679-1). Tools used to scrape dry hide: e. retouched flake, Feature 557 (#1984b); f. side scraper, Feature 559 (#2030a); a,b,c and d were thermally altered.

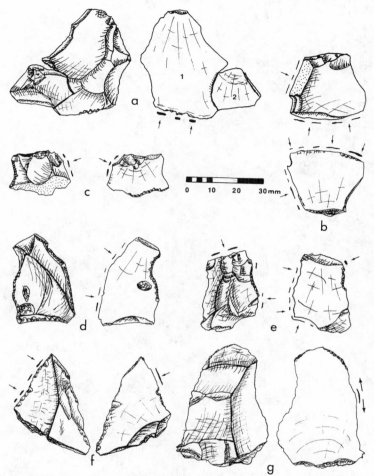

Figure B-7. North Central Late Archaic component. Tools
used to scrape dry hide: a. end scraper, Feature 559 (Lot
#2030b); b. unretouched flake, Feature 173 (Lot #1272b);
c. retouched flake, Feature 857 (#3477-1);   d. side scraper
notch, Feature 831 (#3085-1);   e. side scraper/notch, Feature 821 (#3050-1) proximal edge (ventral) also used to
scrape bone; f. broken biface, Feature 174 (#1859a). Tool
used to cut fresh or dry hide: g. unretouched flake, Feature 887 (#3670-1); d and g are thermally altered.

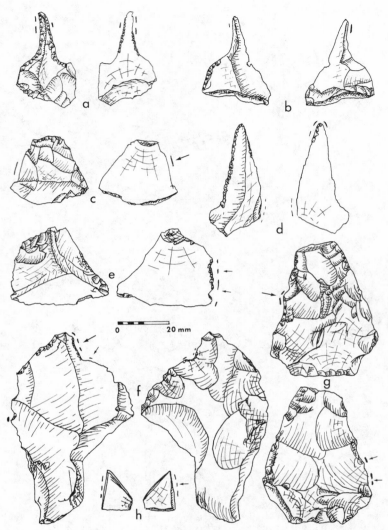

Figure B-8. North Central Late Archaic component. Tools used to bore or ream dry hide (awls): a. perforator, Feature 172 (Lot #1269a); b. perforator, Feature 559 (Lot #2030a). Tool used to whittle or scrape wood: c. core trimming flake, Feature 831 (#3085-3). Wood boring tool: d. perforator, Feature 555 (#1826). Tools used to scrape bone or antler: e. retouched flake, Feature 171 (#1268); f. broken biface, Feature 171 (#1872b); g. biface, Feature 841 (#3312-1); h. unretouched flake, Feature 173 (#1272f); a,c and g are thermally altered.

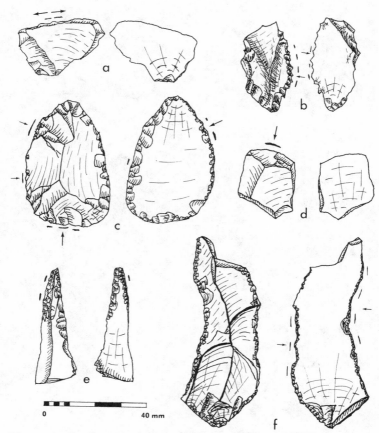

Figure B-9. Northwestern Late Archaic component. Tool used to cut meat or fresh hide: a. unretouched flake, Feature 57 (Lot #768b). Tools used to scrape dry hide: b. denticulate, Excavation Unit 14 (Lot #1816a); c. biface, Feature 45 (#651a); d. unretouched flake, Feature 52 (#1157q). Tool used to bore or ream dry hide (awl): e. perforator, Excavation Unit 7 (#566a). Tool used to whittle or scrape wood: f. side scraper, Excavation Unit 7 (#687a); a,e and f are thermally altered.

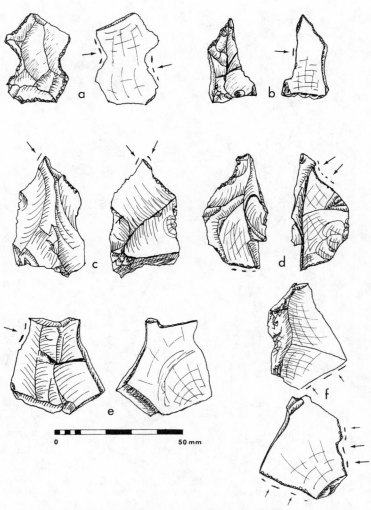

Figure B-10. Northwestern Late Archaic component. Tools used to whittle or scrape wood: a. notched flake, Excavation Unit 7 (Lot #556-7); b. perforator, Excavation Unit 7 (Lot #687-1); Tool used to engrave wood: c. retouched flake, Excavation Unit 7 (#566-2). Tools used to scrape bone or antler: d. biface (fragment), Feature 52 (#905b); e. unretouched flake, Feature 52 (#648c); f. unretouched flake, Feature 57 (#767); a,b,c and d were thermally altered.

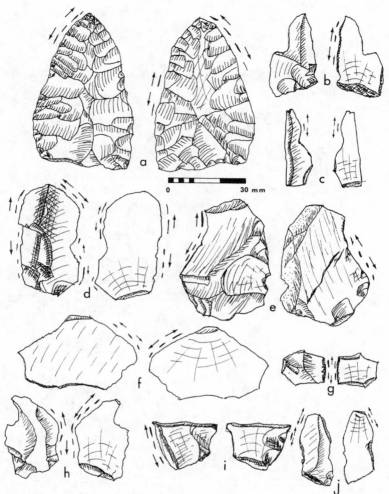

Figure B-11. South Central Late Archaic component. Tools used to cut meat or fresh hide: a. biface, Feature 700 (Lot #2506-1); b. unretouched flake, Feature 700 (Lot # 2638-6); c. blade, Feature 746 (#2789-7); d. notched flake, Feature 700 (#2505-1); e. retouched flake, Feature 700 (#2528-1) proximal right lateral edge also used to scrape hide; f. unretouched flake, Feature 700 (#2638-4); g. retouched flake, Feature 145 (#1182); h. unretouched flake, Feature 746 (#2807-8); i. unretouched flake, Feature 27 (#393a); j. retouched flake, Feature 298 (#1197a); c,h,i and j are thermally altered.

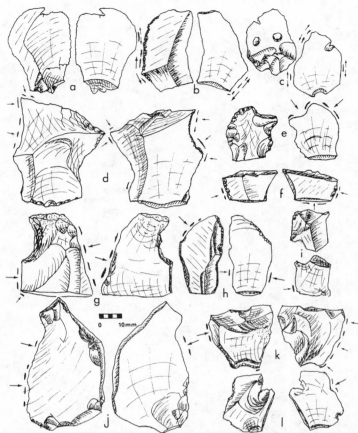

Figure B-12. South Central Late Archaic component. Tools
used to cut meat or fresh hide: a. retouched flake, Feature 746 (Lot #2809-4); b. retouched flake, Feature 835
(Lot #3274-1); c. unretouched flake, Feature 746 (#2809-9)
Tools used to scrape fresh or dry hide: d. unretouched
flake, Feature 700 (#2638-2) distal left lateral edge used
to ream dry hide, proximal right lateral edge (ventral)
used to scrape bone; e. notched flake, Feature 746
(#2807-11); f. retouched flake, Feature 746 (#2907-9);
g. unretouched flake, Feature 712 (#2720-1); h. side
scraper, Excavation Unit 26 (#3348-1); k. retouched flake
Feature 750 (#2628-1). Tool used to whittle or scrape
wood: j. unretouched flake, Feature 702 (#2507-4). Tools
used to scrape bone or antler: i. unretouched flake, Feature 700 (#2698-4); l. notch/retouched flake, Feature 702
(#25-7-5); a,b,c,e,i,k and l are thermally altered.

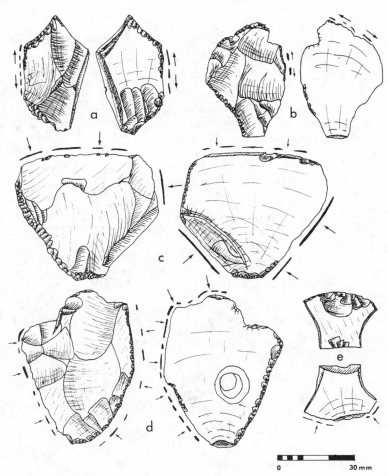

Figure B-13. Late Woodland component. Tools used to cut meat or fresh hide: a. retouched flake, Feature 169 (Lot #1278); b. retouched flake, Feature 8 (Lot #408a). Tools used to scrape dry hide: c. side scraper, Feature 169 (#1359a); d. side scraper, Feature 169 (#1359b); e. retouched flake, Feature 7 (#389); all artifacts are thermally altered.

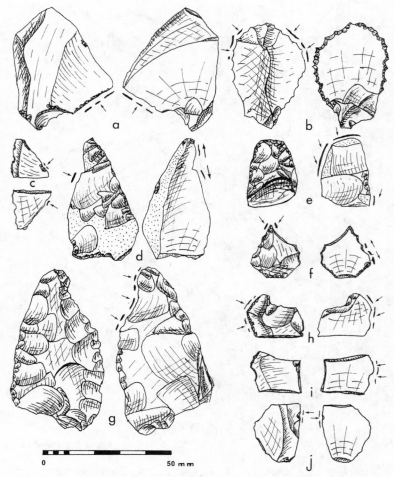

Figure B-14.   Late Woodland component. Tools used to scrape
dry hide: a. unretouched flake, Feature 170 (Lot #1491b);
b. denticulate, Feature 170 (Lot #1491a);   c. denticulate,
Feature 785 (#3209-1).   Tools used to cut or cultivate
plants: d. core trimming flake, Feature 170 (#1491-12);
e. broken biface, Feature 8 (#431a).   Tool used to saw
and engrave bone or antler: f. graver/denticulate, Feature
785 (#3515-3).   Tool used to scrape wood: g. Biface, Feature 169 (#1360c).   Tools used to whittle or scrape bone or
antler: h. retouched flake, Feature 8 (#408g) also used to
saw bone or antler;   i. unretouched flake, Feature 8 (#690c)
j. unretocuhed flake, Feature 745 (#2817-1);   a,c,d and g
are thermally altered.

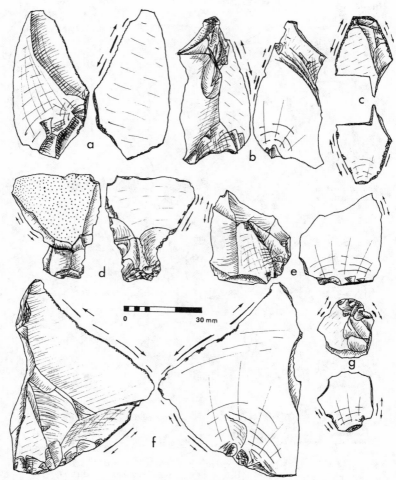

Figure B-15. Mississippian component (House 1). Tools used to cut meat or fresh hide: a. side scraper, Feature 22 (Lot #520a); b. unretouched flake, Feature 77 (Lot #896a); c. retouched flake, Feature 22 (#551a); d. core trimming flake, Feature 22 (#615b) proximal right lateral edge (ventral) used to scrape bone; e. unretouched flake, Feature 76 (#846a); f. retouched flake, Feature 22 (#572-2). Tool used to cut dry hide: g. unretouched flake, Feature 22 (#474-24).

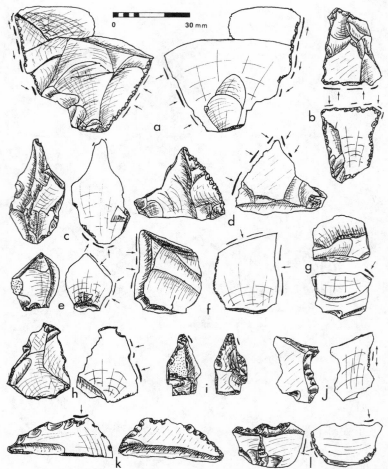

Figure B-16. Mississippian component (House 1). Tools used to scrape dry hide: a. side scraper, Feature 22 (Lot #572-1) distal left lateral edge used to cut plant material and hide; b. end scraper, House 1 Floor (Lot #432b); c. end scraper, House 1 Floor (#432c) distal edge also used to ream hide; d. end scraper, House 1 Floor (#645a); e. unretouched flake, Feature 22 (#474-9); f. retouched flake, House 1 Fill (#331a); g. unretouched flake, Feature 22 (#474-21); h. retouched flake, House 1 Fill (#382b). Shell drill: i. microdrill, House 1 Fill (#376a). Wood saw: j. unretouched flake, House 1 Fill (#376a). Tools used to whittle or scrape wood: k. end scraper, Feature 22 (#474-4/474-8); l. retouched flake, House 1 Fill (#772a); f is thermally altered.

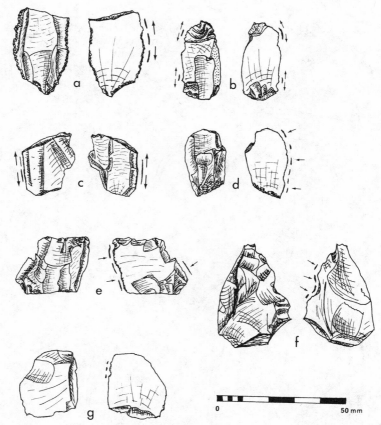

Figure B-17. Mississippian component (House 1). Tools used to saw bone or antler: a. retouched flake, Feature 22 (Lot #615c); b. core trimming flake, Feature 22 (Lot #474-6); c. unretouched flake, Feature 22 (#474-25). Tools used to scrape bone or antler: d. core trimming flake, Feature 22 (#474-10); e. unretouched flake, Feature 22 (#474-11); f. notched flake, Feature 22 (#474-14). Unknown use: g. unretouched flake, Feature 22 (#474-15); b is thermally altered.

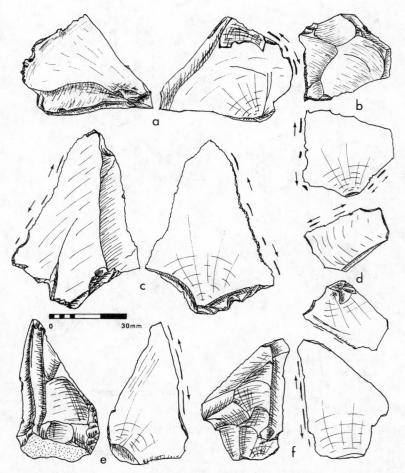

Figure B-18. Mississippian component (House 2). Tools
used to cut meat or fresh hide: a. notched flake, House
2 Fill (Lot #1697-14); b. retouched flake, House 2 Fill
(Lot #1415-14); c. primary flake, House 2 Fill (#1303a);
d. unretouched flake, House 2 Fill (#997b); e.unretouched
flake, House 2 Fill (#1013a). Tool used to cut dry hide:
f. unretouched flake, House 2 Floor (#1431-1).

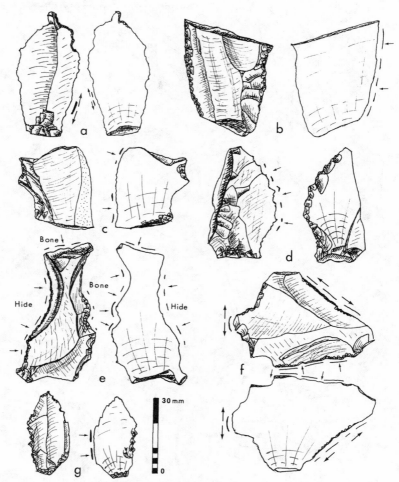

Figure B-19. Mississippian component (House 2). Tool used to cut dry hide: a. retouched blade, Feature 591 (Lot #2154a). Tools used to scrape dry hide: b. side scraper, House 2 Fill (Lot #1096a); c. notched flake, Feature 425 (#2049a); d. denticulate, Feature 404 (#2009a); e. denticulate/retouched flake, House 2 Fill (#1281a), distal and right lateral edges used to scrape bone; f. retouched flake, House 2 Fill (#1015a), left lateral edge also used to cut dry hide; g. retouched flake, House 2 Fill (#1031a).

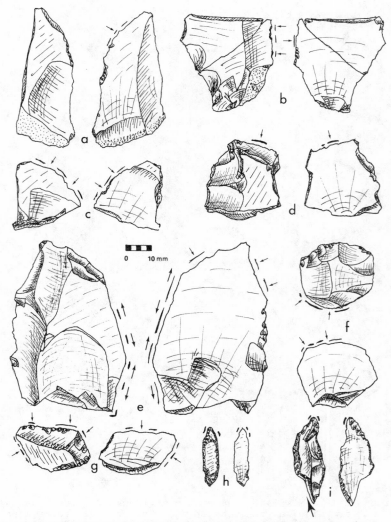

Figure B-20. Mississippian component (House 2). Tools used
to scrape dry hide: a. primary flake, House 2 Fill (Lot #290a);
b. unretouched flake, Feature 591 (#2155a), also used to cut
dry hide; c. unretouched flake, House 2 Fill (#891b), also
used to cut dry hide; d. unretouched flake, House 2 Fill
(#1634-14); e. unretouched flake, Feature 410 (#2033a), also
used to cut dry hide; f. unretouched flake, Feature 445
(#2259-2); g. unretouched flake, House 2 Fill (#1471a). Shell
drills: h. microdrill, House 2 Fill (#2003-12); i. microdrill,
House 2 Fill (#995a); g and h are thermally altered.

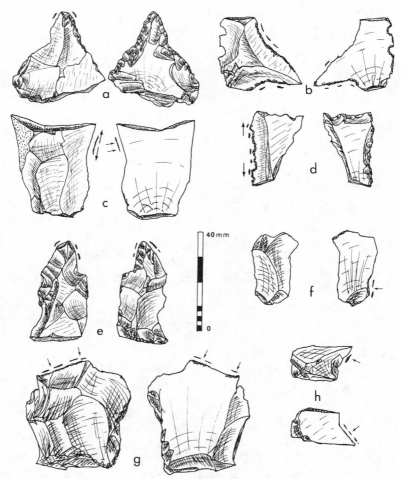

Figure B-21. Mississippian component (House 2). Wood
borer: a. perforator, House 2 Fill (LOt #1627-4). Wood
saw: b. denticulate/perforator, House 2 Fill (#804a).
Plant Knife: c. primary flake, House 2 Floor (#1229-3).
Bone or antler saw: d. unretouched flake, House 2 Fill
(#1535-4). Antler drill: e. perforator, House 2 Fill
(#1463a). Tools used to scrape bone or antler: f. retouched flake, House 2 Fill (#2129a); g. core trimming
flake, House 2 Fill (#1229-1); h. unretouched flake,
House 2 Fill (#3381d); e and f are thermally altered.

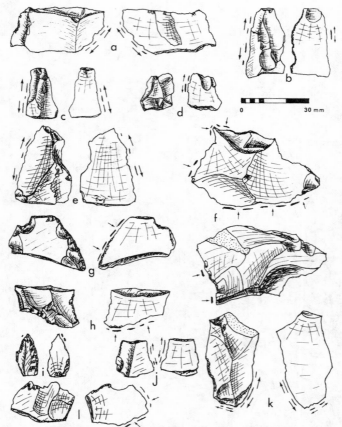

Figure B-22. Mississippian component (House 3 Upper Level).
Tools used to cut meat or fresh hide: a. retouched flake,
House 3 Upper Fill (Lot #887a); b. broken blade, House 3
Upper Fill (Lot #1003a); c. unretouched flake, House 3 Upper
Fill (#859a); d. unretouched flake, Feature 239 (#1405a)
Tool used to cut dry hide: e. notched flake, Feature 600
(#1461a). Tools used to scrape dry hide: f. notched flake,
House 3 Upper Floor (#833a), proximal edge used to scrape
and engrave bone or antler; g. end scraper, House 3 Upper
Fill (#812a); h. end scraper, House 3 Upper Fill (#728a);
Shell drill: i. microdrill, House 3 Upper Floor (#893a).
Tools used to cut plant material: j. unretouched flake,
House 3 Upper Fill (#599a), also used to cut wood; k. re-
touched flake, House 3 Upper Fill (#692a), may be a reworked
hoe fragment. Bone or antler scraper: l. retouched flake,
House 3 Upper Floor (#839a): b,e,f,h and i are thermally
altered.

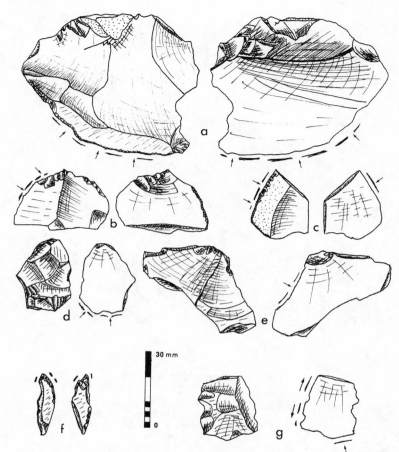

Figure B-23.   Mississippian component (House 3 Lower Level)
Tools used to scrape dry hide: a. notch/retouched flake,
House 3 Lower Floor (Lot #1256b);   b. retouched flake, Fea-
ture 290 (#1607b);   c. retouched flake, House 3 Lower Fill
(#1073a);   d. core trimming flake, House 3 Lower Fill
(#1124a) also used to cut dry hide;   e. unretouched flake,
House 3 Lower Fill (#1231a) also used to cut dry hide.
Shell drill: f. microdrill, House 3 Lower Floor (#1256a).
Wood saw: g. denticulate, Feature 290 (#1650) distal edge
used to scrape wood.

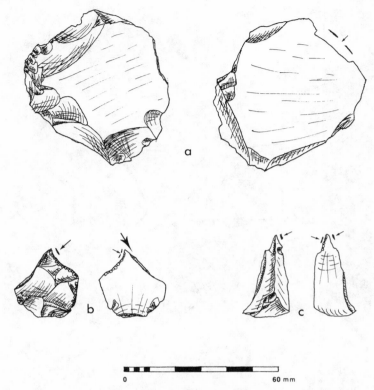

Figure B-24. Mississippian component (House 3 Lower Level).
Wood scraper: a. retouched flake, House 3 Lower Fill (Lot
#1073c), also used to scrape bone. Tools used to engrave
bone or antler: b. perforator, Feature 290 (Lot #1607a); c.
unretouched flake, Feature 366 (#1832a); b is thermally
altered

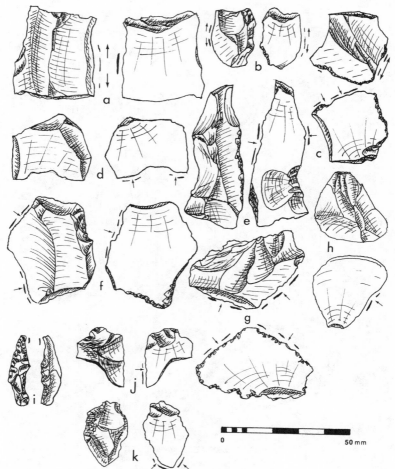

0

50 mm

Figure B-25. Mississippian component (House 4). Tools used to cut meat or fresh hide: a. unretouched flake, House 4 Fill (Lot #2749-1); b. unretouched flake, Feature 703 (Lot #2588-5). Tools used to scrape dry hide: c. notched flake, Feature 703 (#2620-5), right lateral edge used to cut dry hide; d. notched flake, House 4 Fill (#2692-1); e. retouched flake, Feature 728 (#3058-2); f. retouched flake, Feature 721 (#2682-1); g. retouched flake, House 4 Fill (#2749-2); h. retouched flake, Feature 728 (#2890-3). Wood drill: i. perforator, Feature 703 (#2547-3). Tools used to scrape bone or antler: j. retouched flake, Feature 703 (#2588-1); k. retouched flake, Feature 730 (#2998-3); c,d,e,h,i and j were thermally altered.

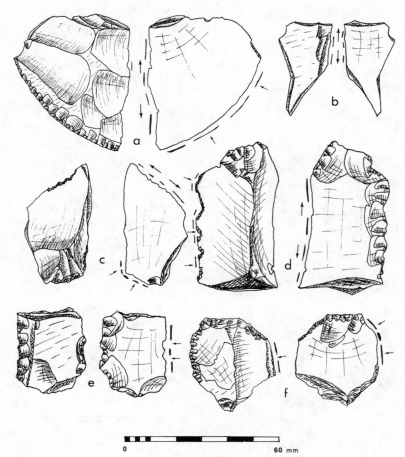

Figure B-26. Mississippian component (House 5). Tools used to cut meat or fresh hide: a. end scraper, Feature 1024 (Lot #035-1) distal edge used to scrape hide; b. unretouched flake, Feature 958 (#3892-4). Tools used to scrape dry hide: c. denticulate/retouched flake, House 5 Fill (#3758-1) distal edge used to cut dry hide; d. denticulate/retouched flake, House 5 Fill (#3846-1), right lateral edge used to cut dry hide; e. side scraper, Feature 911 (#3961-1); f. retouched flake, Features 912/916 (#4015-6).

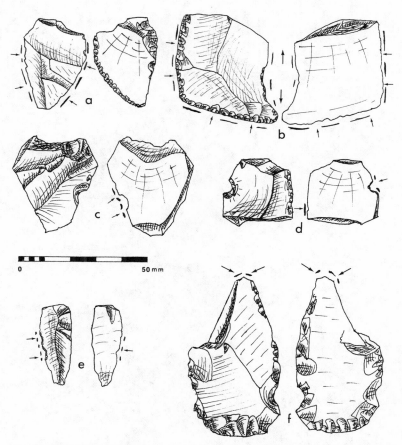

Figure B-27. Mississippian component (House 5). Tools used to scrape dry hide: a. side scraper, Feature 926 (Lot # 4005-1); b. side and end scraper, House 5 Fill (#3815-2) right lateral edge used to cut dry hide. Wood-whittling tool: c. notched flake, Feature 1024 (#4035-2). Tools used to scrape bone or antler: d. notch/side scraper, Feature 917 (#3847-1); e. blade, Feature 926 (#4005-3). Tool used to engrave bone or antler: f. broken biface, Features 912/916 (#4015-1).

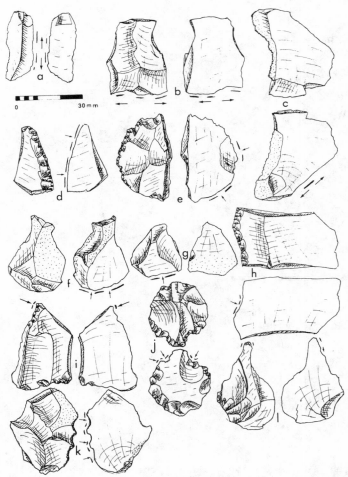

Figure B-28. Mississippian component (House 6). Tools used
to cut meat or fresh hide: a. blade, House 6 Fill (Lot #
3907-5); b. unretouched flake, House 6 Fill (#3866-21);
c. unretouched flake, House 6 Fill (#3862-5). Tools used
to scrape dry hide: d. side scraper, Feature 982 (#4112-6)
e. retouched flake, House 6 Fill (#3900-1); f. primary
flake, House 6 Fill (#3907-11); g. unretouched flake,
House 6 Fill (#3883-1). Tool used to scrape wood:
h. side scraper, Feature 1102 (#4217-1) also used to scrap
dry hide. Tool used to engrave wood: i. retouched flake
Feature 981 (#4100-2). Tools used to scrape bone or antler
j. notch/end scraper, House 6 Floor (#3910-1); k. denticulate, House 6 Fill (#3907-1). Bone or antler drill:
l. perforator, House 6 Fill (#4092-8); a,b and c are thermally altered.

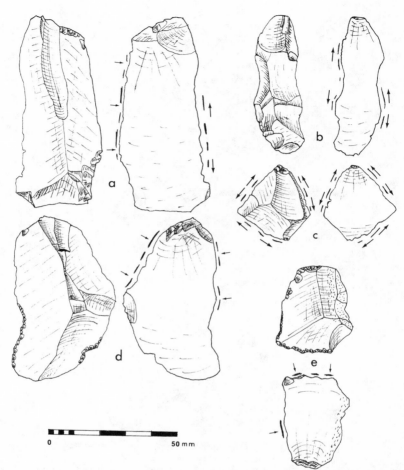

Figure B-29. Mississippian component (other features). Tools used to cut meat or fresh hide: a. retouched flake, Feature 708 (Lot #2652-1), left lateral edge used to scrape hide; b. blade, Feature 20 (Lot #840a); c. unretouched flake, Feature 400 (#2007a). Tools used to scrape dry hide: d. side scraper, Feature 20 (#881a); e. end scraper, Feature 16 (#1332a); e is thermally altered.

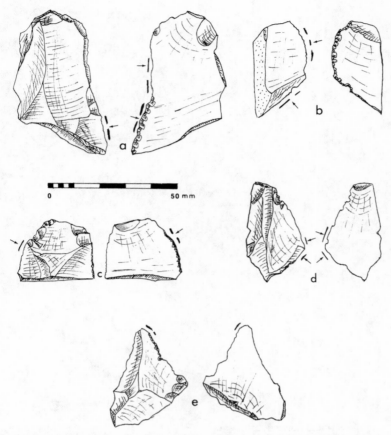

Figure B-30. Mississippian component (other features). Tool used to scrape dry hide: a. side scraper, Excavation Unit 19 (Lot #2719-1). Tools used to scrape bone or antler: b. primary flake, Feature 719 (Lot #2672-1); c. retouched flake, Feature 25 (#546a); d. unretouched flake, Feature 784 (#3054-1). Tool used to engrave bone or antler: e. perforator, Feature 21 (#492a); c is thermally altered.

Bibliography

Ahler, S. 1971. Projectile Point Form and Function at Rodgers Shelter, Missouri. Research Series 8. Missouri Archaeological Society, Columbia, Missouri.

———. 1982. Review of Experimental Determination of Stone Tool Uses: a Microwear Analysis, by L.H. Keeley. American Antiquity 47:688-90.

Akoshima, K. 1979. An Experimental Study of Microwear Traces on Shale Artifacts. Master's Thesis, Department of Archaeology, Tohoku University, Japan.

Alland, A., Jr. 1975. Adaptation. Annual Review of Anthropology 4:59-73.

Anderson, P.C. 1980. A Testimony of Prehistoric Tasks: Diagnostic Residues on Stone Tool Working Edges. World Archaeology 12:181-94.

Asch, D.L., and N.B. Asch. 1978. The Economic Potential of Iva annua and its Prehistoric Importance in the Lower Illinois Valley. In The Nature and Status of Ethnobotany, edited by R.I. Ford, pp. 300-41, Anthropological Papers 67, Museum of Anthropology, University of Michigan, Ann Arbor.

Asch, D.L., K.B. Farnsworth, and N.B. Asch. 1978. Woodland Subsistence and Settlement in West Central Illinois. In Hopewell Archaeology: The Chillicothe Conference, edited by D.S. Brose and N. Greber, pp. 80-85, Kent State University Press, Kent, Ohio.

Asch, N.B., R.I. Ford, and D.L. Asch. 1972. Paleoethnobotany of the Koster Site: The Archaic Horizons. Reports of Investigations 24, Illinois State Museum, Springfield.

Audouze, F., D. Cahen, L.H. Keeley and B. Schmider. 1981. Le Site Magdalenien du Buisson Campin A Verberie (Oise). Galla Prehistorie 24(1):97-143.

Baerreis, D.A. 1971. Environmental Reconstruction through Molluscan Remains: A Preliminary Report on the A.C. Banks site. In Prehistoric Investigations, edited by A. Anderson, pp. 95-108 Report 3, Office of the State Archaeologist, Iowa City, Iowa.

Baerreis, D.A., and R.A. Bryson. 1965. Climatic Episodes and the Dating of the Mississippian Cultures. The Wisconsin Archaeologist 46:203-20.

Baerreis, D.A., R.A. Bryson, and J.E. Kutzbach. 1976. Climate and Culture in the Western Great Lakes Region. Mid-Continental Journal of Archaeology 1:39-57.

Bamforth, D.R. 1985. The technological organization of Paleo-indian Small-group Bison Hunting on the Llano Estacado. Plains Anthropologist 30:243-58.

Bardwell, J. 1980. Palynology. In Annual Report of 1979 Investigations by the University of Illinois-Urbana FAI-270 Archaeological Mitigation Project, edited by J.W. Porter, pp. 169-82, Department of Anthropology, University of Illinois at Urbana.

Bareis, C.J. 1964. Meander Loops and the Cahokia Site. American Antiquity
    30:89-91.

_____. 1976. The Knobel Site, St. Clair County, Illinois. Circular 1.
    Illinois Archaeological Survey, Urbana.

_____. 1979. Annual Report of 1978 Investigations by the University of
    Illinois-Urbana FAI-270 Archaeological Mitigation Project, University
    of Illinois-Urbana Archaeological Field Laboratory, Columbia, Illinois.

Bareis, C.J., and P.J. Munson. 1973. The Linkeman Site (Ms-108), Madison
    County, Illinois. In Late Woodland Site Archaeology in Illinois 1:
    Investigations in South-central Illinois, edited by J.A. Brown, pp.
    23-33, Bulletin 9. Illinois Archaeological Survey, Urbana.

Bartlein, P.J., and T. Webb III. 1982. Holocene Climatic Changes Estimated
    from Pollen Data from the Northern Midwest. In Quaternary History of
    the Driftless Area, pp. 67-82. Wisconsin Geological and Natural History
    Survey Field Trip Guidebook 5. Madison.

Beardsley, R. 1956. Functional and Evolutionary Implications of
    Community Patterning. In Seminars in Archaeology: 1955, edited by R.
    Wauchope. Memoir 11. Society for American Archaeology, Salt Lake
    City.

Bee, R.L. 1974. Patterns and Processes. Free Press, New York.

Benchley, E.D. 1974. Mississippian Secondary Mound Loci: A Comparative
    Functional Analysis in a Time-Space Perspective. Ph.D. dissertation,
    Department of Anthropology, University of Wisconsin-Milwaukee.

_____. 1975. An Overview of the Archaeological Resources of the St.
    Louis Area. Illinois State Museum, Springfield.

Benchley, E.D., and P.J. DePuydt. 1982. Final Report of 1980 Test
    Excavations at the Interpretive Center Tract, Cahokia Mounds
    Historic Site. Report of Investigations 61. University of Wisconsin-
    Milwaukee Archaeological Research Laboratory.

Bender, M.M., D.A. Baerreis, and R.L. Steventon. 1981. Further Light on
    Carbon Isotopes and Hopewell Agriculture. American Antiquity 46
    346-53.

Bergstrom, R.E., and T. R. Walker. 1956. Groundwater geology of the East St.
    Louis area, Illinois. Illinois State Geological Survey Report of
    Investigations 191, Urbana.

Binford, L.R. 1973. Interassemblage Variability: The Mousterian and the
    "Functional" Argument. In The Explanation of Culture Change, edited by
    C. Renfrew, pp. 227-54. Duckworth, London.

_____. 1980. Willow Smoke and Dog's Trails: Hunter-Gatherer Settlement
    Systems and Archaeological Site Formation. American Antiquity 45
    1-17.

Binford, L.R., and S.R. Binford. 1966. A Preliminary Analysis of Functional Variability in the Mousterian of Levallois Facies. American Anthropologist 68:238-95.

Binford, L.R., S.R. Binford, R. Whallon, and M.A. Hardin. 1970. Archaeology at Hatchery West. Memoir 24. Society for American Archaeology, Washington.

Binneman, J. 1981. Experimental Determination of Adze and Scraper Use-wear from Boomplaas Cave, Southern Cape: A Microwear Analysis. Paper presented at the Seventh Meeting of the South Africa Association of Archaeologists, Pretoria.

Boserup, E. 1965. The Conditions of Agricultural Growth. Aldine Press Chicago.

Brakenridge, H.M. 1814. Views of Louisiana Together with a Journal of a Voyage up the Missouri River in 1811. Pittsburgh (reprinted by Quadrangle Books, Chicago, 1962).

Brandt, K. 1972. American Bottom Settlements: University of Wisconsin-Milwaukee Cahokia Archaeology Project. Paper presented at the 37th Annual Meeting of the Society for American Archaeology, Bal Harbour, Florida.

Braun, D.P. 1983. Pots as Tools. In Archaeological Hammers and Theories, edited by J.A. Moore and A.S. Keene, pp. 107-34, Academic Press, New York.

Braun, D.P., and S. Plog. 1982. Evolution of "Tribal" Social Networks: Theory and Prehistoric North American Evidence. American Antiquity 47:504-25.

Brown, J.A., and R.K. Vierra. 1983. What Happened in the Middle Archaic? Introduction to an Ecological Approach to Koster Site Archaeology. In Archaic Hunters and Gatherers in the American Midwest, edited by J.L. Phillips and J.A. Brown, pp. 165-96. Academic Press, New York.

Bryson, R.A., and W.M. Wendland. 1967. Tentative Climatic Patterns for some Late Glacial and Post-glacial Episodes in Central North America. In Life, Land, and Water, edited by W.J. Mayer-Oakes, pp. 271-98. University of Manitoba Press, Winnipeg.

Butler, B.M. 1977. Mississippian Settlement in the Black Bottom, Pope and Massac Counties, Illinois. Ph.D. dissertation, Department of Anthropology, Southern Illinois University, Carbondale.

Butzer, K.W. 1977. Geomorphology of the Lower Illinois Valley as a Spatial-Temporal Context for the Koster Archaic Site. Reports of Investigations 34. Illinois State Museum, Springfield.

_____. 1980. Context in Archaeology: An Alternative Perspective. Journal of Field Archaeology 7:417-22.

_____. 1982. Archaeology as Human Ecology: Method and Theory for a Contextual Approach. Cambridge University Press, Cambridge.

Cahen, D., L.H. Keeley, and F.L. VanNoten. 1979. Stone Tools, Toolkits, and Human Behavior in Prehistory. Current Anthropology 20:661-83.

Caldwell, J.R. 1958. Trend and Tradition in the Prehistory of the Eastern United States. Scientific Papers 10. Illinois State Museum, Springfield.

Cantwell, A.M. 1979. The Functional Analysis of Scrapers: Problems, New Techniques, and Cautions. Lithic Technology 8(1):5-11.

_____. 1980. Dickson Camp and Pond: Two Early Havana Tradition Sites in the Central Illinois Valley. Reports of Investigations 36. Illinois State Museum, Springfield.

Carr, C. 1982. A Functional and Distributional Study of Surface Artifacts from the Crane Site. In Handbook of Soil Resistivity Surveying, by C. Carr, pp. 183-351. Center for American Archaeology Press, Evanston, Illinois.

Chapman, C.H. 1975. The Archaeology of Missouri 1. University of Missouri Press, Columbia.

Chapman, J.C., and A.B. Shea. 1977. Paleoecological and Cultural Interpretation of Plant Remains recovered from Archaic Period Sites in the Lower Little Tennessee River Valley. Paper presented at the 34th Southeastern Archaeological Conference, Lafayette, Louisiana.

Chmurney, W.W. 1973. The Ecology of the Middle Mississippian Occupation of the American Bottom. Ph.D. dissertation, Department of Anthropology, University of Illinois-Urbana.

Chomko, S.A., and G.W. Crawford. 1978. Plant Husbandry in Prehistoric North America: New Evidence for its Development. American Antiquity 43:405-8.

Christenson, A.L. 1980. Change in the Human Niche in Response to Population Growth. In Modeling Change in Prehistoric Subsistence Economies, edited by T.K. Earle and A.L. Christenson, pp. 31-72. Academic Press, New York.

Cleland, Charles E. 1976. The Focal-Diffuse Model: An Evolutionary Perspective on the Prehistoric Cultural Adaptations of the Eastern United States. Mid-Continental Journal of Archaeology 1:59-76.

Collins, M.B., ed. 1979. Excavations at Four Archaic Sites in the Lower Ohio Valley, Jefferson County, Kentucky (2 volumes). Occasional Papers in Anthropology 1. Department of Anthropology, University of Kentucky, Lexington.

Cook, T.G. 1976. Koster: An Artifact Analysis of Two Archaic Phases in West-Central Illinois. Prehistoric Records 1, Koster Research Reports 3. Northwestern University Archaeological Research Program, Evanston, Illinois.

Cowan, C.W., and R.I. Ford. 1979. Early Agricultural Evidence from
    Cloudsplitter Rockshelter, Kentucky. Paper presented at the 44th
    Annual Meeting of the Society for American Archaeology, Vancouver,
    B.C.

Crabtree, D.E. 1972. An Introduction to Flintworking. Occasional Papers
    28. Idaho State Museum, Pocatello, Idaho.

Cross, P.G. 1982. Faunal Exploitation Patterns of Late Woodland Inhabitants
    of the American Bottom. Paper presented at the 1982 Midwest
    Archaeological Conference, Cleveland.

Cutler, H.C., and L.W. Blake. 1979. Plant Remains from the Upper Nodena
    Site (3Ms4). The Arkansas Archaeologist 20:53-58.

Del Bene, T.A. 1979. Once Upon a Striation: Current Models of Striation
    and Polish Formation. In Lithic Use-Wear Analysis, edited by B. Hayden,
    pp, 167-77. Academic Press, New York.

Dickens, C. 1972. American Notes for General Circulation. Penguin Books,
    Baltimore (originally published in 1842).

Dunnell, R.C.   1975. Archaeological Potential of Anthropological and
    Scientific Models of Function. In Archaeological Essays in Honor
    of Irving B. Rouse, edited by R.C. Dunnell and E.S. Hall,
    pp. 41-73. Mouton, The Hague.

Earle, T.K. 1980. A Model of Subsistence Change. In Modeling Change in
    Prehistoric Subsistence Economies, edited by T.K. Earle and A.L.
    Christenson, pp. 1-29. Academic Press, New York.

Earle, T.K., and A.L. Christenson, eds. 1980. Modeling Change in Prehistoric
    Subsistence Economies. Academic Press, New York.

Emerson, T.E. 1984. The Dyroff and Levin Sites. American Bottom
    Archaeology FAI-270 Site Reports 9 (Part 2), University of Illinois
    Press, Urbana and Chicago.

Emerson, T.E., and D.L. McElrath. 1983. A Settlement-subsistence Model of the
    Terminal Late Archaic Adaptation in the American Bottom, Illinois. In
    Archaic Hunters and Gatherers in the American Midwest, edited by J.L.
    Phillips and J.A. Brown, pp. 219-42, Academic Press, New York.

Emerson, T.E., and G.R. Milner. 1982. Community Organization and
    Settlement Patterns of Peripheral Mississippian Sites in the American
    Bottom, Illinois. Paper presented at the 47th Annual Meeting of the
    Society for American Archaeology, Minneapolis.

Emerson, T.E., G.R. Milner, and D.K. Jackson. 1983. The Florence Street
    Site. American Bottom Archaeology FAI-270 Site Reports 2. University
    of Illinois Press, Urbana and Chicago.

Esarey, D., with T.W. Good. 1981. Final Report on FAI-270 and Illinois
    Route 460 Related Excavations at the Logmann Site (11-S-49), St.
    Clair County, Illinois. Reports of Investigations 3. Western Illinois
    University Archaeological Research Laboratory, Macomb.

Esarey, D., and C. Moffat. 1981. Final Report on the Investigation of Three Archaeological sites in Luhr Brother's Borrow Pit #4, Monroe County, Illinois. University of Illinois-Urbana FAI-270 Archaeological Mitigation Project Final Report 35. Urbana.

Evenson, E.B., W.R. Farrand, D.F. Eschman, D.M. Mickelson, and L.J. Maher 1976. Greatlakean Substage: A Replacement for Valderan Substage in the Late Michigan Basin. Quaternary Research 6:411-24.

Farnsworth, K.B. 1973. An Archaeological Survey of the Macoupin Valley. Reports of Investigations 26. Illinois State Museum, Springfield.

Fedje, D. 1979. Scanning Electron Microscopy Analysis of Sub-striae. In Lithic Use-Wear Analysis, edited by B. Hayden, pp. 179-87. Academic Press, New York.

Fenneman, N.M. 1909. Physiography of the St. Louis Area. Bulletin 12. Illinois State Geological Survey, Urbana.

Finney, F.A. 1985. The Carbon Dioxide Site. American Bottom Archaeology FAI-270 Site Reports 11 (Part 1). University of Illinois Press, Urbana and Chicago.

Fisk, H.N. 1944. Geological Investigations of the Alluvial Valley of the Lower Mississippi River. U.S. Army Corps of Engineers, Mississippi River Commission. Vicksburg, Mississippi.

Flannery, K.V. 1973. The Origins of Agriculture. Annual Review of Anthropology 2:271-310.

_____. 1976. The Early Mesoamerican Village. Academic Press, New York.

_____. 1982. The Tierras Largas Phase and Analytical Units of the Early Oaxacan Village. In The Cloud People, edited by K.V. Flannery and J. Marcus, pp. 44-45. Academic Press, New York.

Flint, T. 1828. A Condensed Geography and History of the Western States or the Mississippi Valley (2 volumes). E.H. Flint, Cincinnati (reprinted by Scholars Facsimilies and Reprints, Gainesville, Florida, 1970).

Ford, R.I. 1977. Evolutionary Ecology and the Evolution of Human Ecosystems: A Case Study from the Midwestern U.S.A. In Explanations of Prehistoric Change, edited by J.N. Hill, pp. 153-84, University of New Mexico Press, Albuquerque.

_____. 1981. Gardening and Farming before A.D. 1000: Patterns of Prehistoric Cultivation North of Mexico. Journal of Ethnobiology 1: 6-27.

Fortier, A.C. 1984. The Go-Kart North Site. American Bottom Archaeology FAI-270 Site Reports 9 (Part 1). University of Illinois Press, Urbana and Chicago.

Fortier, A.C., R.B. Lacampagne, and F.A. Finney. 1984. The Fish Lake Site. American Bottom Archaeology FAI-270 Site Reports 8. University of Illinois Press, Urbana and Chicago.

Fowler, M.L. 1959. Modoc Rock Shelter: A Summary and Analysis of Four Seasons of Excavations. Reports of Investigations 8. Illinois State Museum, Springfield.

_____. 1962. First Annual Report: American Bottoms Archaeology, July 1, 1961-June 30, 1962. Illinois Archaeological Survey, Urbana.

_____. 1963. Second Annual Report: American Bottoms Archaeology, July 1, 1962-June 30, 1963. Illinois Archaeological Survey, Urbana.

_____. 1964. Third Annual Report: American Bottoms Archaeology, July 1, 1963-June 30, 1964. Illinois Archaeological Survey, Urbana.

_____. 1974. Cahokia: Ancient Capital of the Midwest. Addison-Wesley Module in Anthropology 48. Reading, Massachusetts.

_____. 1978. Cahokia and the American Bottom: Settlement Archaeology. In Mississippian Settlement Patterns, edited by B.D. Smith, pp. 455-78, Academic Press, New York.

Fowler, M.L., and R.L. Hall. 1975. Archaeological Phases at Cahokia. In Perspectives in Cahokia Archaeology, edited by M.L. Fowler and R.L. Hall, pp. 1-14, Bulletin 10. Illinois Archaeological Survey, Urbana.

_____. 1978. Late Prehistory in the Illinois Area. In Handbook of North American Indians, Volume 15: Northeast, edited by B.G. Trigger, pp. 560-68, The Smithsonian Institution, Washington, D.C.

Frison, G.C. 1968. A Functional Analysis of Certain Chipped Stone Tools. American Antiquity 33:144-55.

Frison, G.C., and B.A. Bradley. 1980. Folsom Tools and Technology at the Hanson Site, Wyoming. University of New Mexico Press, Albuquerque.

Gendel, P.A. 1982. Functional Analysis of Scrapers (from Neerharen-DeKip). Studia Praehistorica Belgica , (Tervuren, Belgium) 1:49-51.

Gendel, P.A., and L. Pirnay. 1982. Microwear Analysis of Experimental Stone Tools: Further Test Results. Studia Praehistorica Belgica (Terveuren, Belgium) 2:251-65.

Gerwitz, L.R. 1980. A Microwear Analysis of Labras Lake Artifacts. In Investigations at the Labras Lake Site, Volume 1, Archaeology, edited by J.L. Phillips, R.L. Hall, and R.W. Yerkes, pp. 265-317, Department of Anthropology, University of Illinois at Chicago.

Gifford, D.P. 1981. Taphonomy and Paleoecology: A Critical Review of Archaeology's Sister Disciplines. In Advances in Archeological Method and Theory 4, edited by M.B. Schiffer, pp. 365-438, Academic Press, New York.

Gilbert, A.S., and B.H. Singer. 1982. Reassessing Zoolarchaeological Quantification. World Archaeology 14:21-40.

Gilmore, M.R. 1931. Vegetable Remains of the Ozark Bluff Dweller Culture. Papers of the Michigan Academy of Sciences, Arts, and Letters 14:83-102.

Gladfelter, B.G. 1979a. Geomorphic Change in the Mississippi Floodplain near St. Louis. Revision of a paper presented at the 75th Annual Meeting of the Association of American Geographers. Philadelphia.

_____. 1979b. Geomorphic Contributions to Archaeological Interpretations in a Floodplain Setting. Revision of a paper presented at the 44th Annual Meeting of the Society for American Archaeology, Vancouver, B.C.

_____. 1980a. Investigations at the Labras Lake Site, Volume 2: Geomorphology. Department of Geography, University of Illinois at Chicago.

_____. 1980b. Paleogeomorphic Settings and Prehistoric Settlement in the American Bottom (Middle Mississippi River). Paper presented at the Annual Meeting of the Geological Society of America, Atlanta.

_____. 1981. Investigations at the Labras Lake Site, Volume 3: Geomorphological Observations in the Vicinity of the Site. Department of Geography, University of Illinois at Chicago.

_____. 1985. On the Interpretation of Archaeological Sites in Alluvial Settings. In Archaeological Sediments in Context, edited by J.K. Stein and W.R. Farrand, pp. 41-52. Peopling of the Americas Series 1, Center for the Study of Early Man, Orono, Maine.

Gladfelter, B.G., B.R. Weston, and J.L. Phillips. 1977. Report of Investigations at the East St. Louis Stone Quarry (11-S-468) and Labras Lake (11-S-299) Sites, St. Clair County, Illinois. Report submitted to the Illinois Department of Transportation by the Departments of Anthropology and Geography, University of Illinois at Chicago.

Gould, R.A. 1980. Living Archaeology. Cambridge University Press, Cambridge.

Gould, R.A., D.A. Koster, and A.H.L. Sontz. 1971. The Lithic Assemblage of the Western Desert Aboriginies of Australia. American Antiquity 36:144-69.

Green, S.W. 1980a. Broadening Least-cost Models for Expanding Agricultural Systems. In Modeling Change in Prehistoric Subsistence Economies, edited by T.K. Earle and A.L. Christenson, pp. 209-41. Academic Press, New York.

_____. 1980b. Towards a General Model of Agricultural Systems. In Advances in Archaeological Method and Theory 3, edited by M.B. Schiffer, pp. 311-55, Academic Press, New York.

Gregg, M.L. 1975. Settlement Morphology and Production Specialization: The Horseshoe Lake Site, a Case Study. Ph.D. dissertation, Department of Anthropology, University of Wisconsin-Milwaukee.

Griffin, J.B. 1983. The Midlands. In Ancient North Americans, edited by J.D. Jennings, pp. 243-301, W.H. Freeman, San Francisco.

Griffin, J.B., and V.H. Jones. 1977. The University of Michigan Excavations
at the Pulcher Site in 1950. American Antiquity 42:462-90.

Griffin, J.B., and A.C. Spaulding. 1951. The Central Mississippi Valley
Archaeological Survey, Season 1950, A Preliminary Report. Journal of
the Illinois Archaeological Survey (new series) 1(3):74-81.

Hajic, E.R., and T.R. Styles. 1982. Dynamic Surficial Geology of the Lower
Illinois Valley Region and the Impact on the Archaeological Record.
Paper presented at the 47th Annual Meeting of the Society for
American Archaeology, Minneapolis.

Hall, R.L. 1973. An Interpretation of the Two-climax Model of Illinois
Prehistory. Revision of a paper presented at the Ninth International
Congress of Anthropological and Ethnological Sciences, Chicago
(reprinted in Early Native Americans: Prehistoric Demography,
Economy, and Technology, edited by D.L. Browman, pp. 401-61,
Mouton, The Hague, 1980).

_____. 1975. Some Problems of Identity and Process in Cahokia
Archaeology. Revision of a paper prepared for discussion November,
1974, at an advanced seminar on Mississippian Cultural Development
at the School of American Research, Santa Fe, New Mexico.

_____. 1980. Ceramics. In Investigations at the Labras Lake Site, Volume
I:Archaeology, edited by J.L. Phillips, R.L. Hall, and R.W. Yerkes,
pp. 366-406. Department of Anthropology, University of Illinois at Chicago.

_____. 1986. Radiocarbon Chronology for the Labras Lake Site. In Labras
Lake: Investigations into the Prehistoric Occupations of a Floodplain
Locality in St. Clair County, Illinois, edited by J.L. Phillips and R.L.
Hall, University of Illinois Press, Urbana and Chicago, in press.

Hall, R.L., and J.O. Vogel. 1963. Illinois State Museum Projects. In
Second Annual Report: American Bottoms Archaeology, July 1, 1962-June 30,
1963, edited by M.L. Fowler, pp. 24-30, Illinois Archaeological Survey,
Urbana.

Hally, D.J. 1981. Plant Preservation and the Content of Paleobotanical
Samples A Case Study. American Antiquity 46:723-42.

Harn, A.D. 1971. Archaeological Survey of the American Bottoms in
Madison and St. Clair Counties, Illinois. Reports of Investigations 21
(Part 2). Illinois State Museum, Springfield.

_____. 1973. Comments on the Spatial Distribution of Late Woodland and
Mississippian Ceramics in the General Cahokia Sphere. Revision of a
paper presented at the Cahokia Ceramics Conference, July 1971,
Collinsville, Illinois (reprinted in Rediscovery 1980:17-26).

Harris, D.R. 1972. The Origins of Agriculture in the Tropics. American
Scientist 60:180-93.

Hayden, B. 1977. Stone Tool Functions in the Western Desert. In Stone
    Tools as Cultural Markers: Change, Evolution, and Complexity, edited by
    R.V.S. Wright, pp. 178-88. Australian Institute of Aboriginal Studies,
    Canberra.

Hayden, B., and A. Cannon. 1983. Where the Garbage Goes: Refuse Disposal
    in the Maya Highlands. Journal of Anthropological Archaeology 2:
    117-63.

Hilliard, J.E. 1980. Prehistoric Ozark Settlement-subsistence and Nut
    Resource Utilization. Master's thesis, Department of Anthropology,
    University of Arkansas, Fayetteville.

Hus, H. 1908. An Ecological Cross-section of the Mississippi River in the
    Region of St. Louis, Missouri. Missouri Botanical Garden 19th Annual
    Report: 127-258.

Jeffries, R.W., and B.M. Butler. 1982. The Carrier Mills Archaeological
    Project: Human Adaptation in the Saline Valley, Illinois. Research Paper
    33. Center for Archaeological Investigations, Southern Illinois
    University at Carbondale.

Jelinek, A.J. 1976. Form, Function, and Style in Lithic Analysis. In Culture
    Change and Continuity, edited by C.E. Cleland, pp. 19-34, Academic
    Press, New York.

Johannessen, S. 1981. The Effect of Aboriginal Populations on the
    Vegetation of the American Bottom of Illinois. Paper presented at the
    Fourth Ethnobiology Conference, Columbia, Missouri.

_____. 1982. Paleoethnobotany. In Annual Report of Investigations 1981
    by the University of Illinois-Urbana FAI-270 Archaeological Mitigation
    Project, edited by J.W. Porter, pp. 36-38, Department of Anthropology,
    University of Illinois, Urbana.

_____. 1983. Paleoethnobotany. In Annual Report of Investigations 1982
    by the University of Illinois-Urbana FAI-270 Archaeological Mitigation
    Project, edited by J.W. Porter, pp. 24-25. Department of Anthropology,
    University of Illinois, Urbana.

Jones, V.H. 1936. The Vegetable Remains of Newt Kash Hollow Shelter. In
    Rockshelters in Menifee County, Kentucky, by W.S. Webb and W.D.
    Funkhouser, pp. 147-65, Reports in Archaeology and Anthropology 3.
    University of Kentucky, Lexington.

Jordan, P.R. 1965. Fluvial Sediment of the Mississippi River at St. Louis,
    Missouri. Water Supply Paper 1802. United States Geological Survey,
    Washington, D.C.

Katz, S.H., M.L. Hediger, and L.A. Valleroy. 1974. Traditional Maize
    Processing Techniques in the New World. Science 184:765-73.

Kay, M., F.B. King, and C.K. Robinson. 1980. Cucurbits from Phillips Spring:
    New Evidence and Interpretations. American Antiquity 45:806-22.

Keeley, L.H. 1974. Technique and Methodology in Microwear Studies: A
    Critical Review. World Archaeology 5:323-36.

_____. 1977. The Functions of Paleolithic Flint Tools. _Scientific American_ 237:108-26.

_____. 1980. _Experimental Determination of Stone Tool Uses: A Microwear Analysis._ University of Chicago Press, Chicago.

_____. 1981. Reply to Holley and Del Bene. _Journal of Archaeological Science_ 8:348-52.

_____. 1982. Hafting and Retooling: Effects on the Archaeological Record. _American Antiquity_ 47:798-809.

Keeley, L.H., and M.L. Newcomer. 1977. Microwear Analysis of Experimental Flint Tools: a Test Case. _Journal of Archaeological Science_ 4:798-809.

Keeley, L.H., and N. Toth. 1981. Microwear Polishes on Early Stone Tools from Koobi Fora, Kenya. _Nature_ 293:464-65.

Keene, A.S. 1979. Economic Optimization Models and the Study of Hunter-gatherer Subsistence Settlement Systems. In _Transformations: Mathematical Approaches to Culture Change_, edited by C. Renfrew and K. Cooke, pp. 369-404. Academic Press, New York.

Kelly, J.E. 1980. _Formative Developments at Cahokia and the Adjacent American Bottom: a Merrell Tract Perspective._ Ph.D. dissertation, Department of Anthropology, University of Wisconsin-Madison (reprinted by the Archaeological Research Laboratory, Western Illinois University, Macomb, 1982).

_____. 1982. Annual Report of Investigations at the Range Site 1981. In _Annual Report of Investigations 1981 by the University of Illinois-Urbana FAI-270 Archaeological Mitigation Project_, edited by J.W. Porter, pp. 6-19. Department of Anthropology, University of Illinois, Urbana.

Kelly, J.E., J.R. Linder, and T.J. Cartmell 1979. _The Archaeological Intensive Survey of the Proposed FAI-270 Alignment in the American Bottom Region of Southern Illinois._Illinois Transportation of Archaeology Scientific Reports 1. Illoinois Department of Transportation, Springfield.

Kelly, L.S. 1981. Annual Report of the Faunal Analysis Laboratory. In _Annual Report of Investigations 1980 by the University of Illinois-Urbana FAI-270 Archaeological Mitigation Project_, edited by J.W. Porter, pp. 96-104, Department of Anthropology, University of Illinois, Urbana.

King, F.B. 1978. Additional Cautions on the Use of the GLO Survey Records in Vegetational Reconstructions in the Midwest. _American Antiquity_ 43:99-102.

_____. 1980. Plant Remains from Labras Lake. In _Investigations at the Labras Lake Site, Volume 1, Archaeology_, edited by J.L. Phillips, R.L. Hall, and R.W. Yerkes, pp. 325-37, Department of Anthropology, University of Illinois at Chicago.

King, F.B., and R.W. Graham. 1981. Effects of Ecological and
    Paleoecological Patterns on Subsistence and Paleoenvironmental
    Reconstructions. American Antiquity 46:128-52.

King, F.B., and D.C. Roper. 1976. Floral Remains from two Middle to Early
    Woodland Sites in Central Illinois and their Implications. The Wisconsin
    Archaeologist 57:142-51.

King, J.E. 1980. Post-Pleistocene Vegetational Changes in the Midwestern
    United States. In Archaic Prehistory on the Prairie-Plains Border,
    edited by A.E. Johnson, pp. 3-11. Publications in Anthropology 12.
    University of Kansas, Lawrence.

_____. 1981. Late Quaternary Vegetation History of Illinois. Ecological
    Monographs 51:43-62.

King, J.E., and W.H. Allen, Jr. 1977. A Holocene Vegetation Record from the
    Mississippi River Valley, Southeast Missouri. Quaternary Research
    8:307-23.

Kirch, P.V. 1980. The Archaeological Study of Adaptation. In Advances
    in Archaeological Method and Theory 3, edited by M.B. Schiffer, pp. 101
    -56. Academic Press, New York.

Langbein, W.B., and S.A. Schumm. 1958. Yield of Sediment in Relation
    to Mean Annual Precipitation. American Geophysical Union Transactions
    39:1076-84.

Leopold, L.B., and M.G. Wolman. 1957. River Channel Patterns: Braided,
    Meandering, and Straight. Professional Paper 282-B. United States
    Geological Survey, Washington, D.C.

Lewotin, R.C. 1970. The Units of Selection. Annual Review of Ecology and
    Systematics 1:1-18.

_____. 1978. Adaptation. Scientific American 239:212-30.

Lopinot, N.H. 1982. Plant Macroremains and Paleoethnobotanical
    Implications. In The Carrier Mills Archaeological Project: Human
    Adaptation in the Saline Valley, Illinois, edited by R.W. Jefferies and
    B.M. Butler, pp. 671-860, Research Paper 33. Center for Archaeological
    Investigations, Southern Illinois University at Carbondale.

_____. 1983. Analysis of Flotation Sample Materials from the Late
    Archaic Horizon. In The 1982 Excavations at the Cahokia Interpretive
    Center Tract, St. Clair County, Illinois, by M.S. Nassaney, N.H. Lopinot,
    B.H. Butler, and R.W. Jefferies, pp. 77-108. Research Paper 37. Center
    for Archaeological Investigations, Southern Illinois University at
    Carbondale.

Lopinot, N.H., and D.E. Brussell. 1982. Assessing Uncarbonized Seeds from
    Open-air Sites in Mesic Environments: an Example from Southern
    Illinois. Journal of Archaeological Science 9:95-108.

McAdams, W. 1887. Records of Ancient Races in the Mississippi Valley.
    C.R. Barns, St. Louis.

McCollough, M.C.R., and C.R. Faulkner. 1976. Third Report of the Normandy Reservoir Salvage Project. Report of Investigation 16. Department of Anthropology, University of Tennessee, Knoxville.

McDowell, P.F. 1983. Evidence of Stream Response to Holocene Climatic Change in a Small Wisconsin Watershed. Quaternary Research 19: 100-116.

McElrath, D.L. 1981. The Material Assemblage. In The Missouri Pacific #2 Site: A Late Archaic Occupation in the American Bottom, by D.L. McElrath and A.C. Fortier, pp. 91-196. FAI-270 Archaeological Mitigation Profect Report 34. Department of Anthropology, University of Illinois-Urbana.

McElrath, D.L., and C. Bentz. 1981 McLean Site: Borrow Pit #6 In Annual Report of Investigations 1980 by the University of Illinois-Urbana FAI-270 Archaeological Mitigation Project, edited by J.W. Porter, pp. 63-65. Department of Anthropology, University of Illinois, Urbana.

McElrath, D.L., and A.C. Fortier. 1983. The Missouri Pacific #2 Site American Bottom Archaeology FAI-270 Site Reports 3, University of Illinois Press, Urbana and Chicago.

McElrath, D.L., A. Stahl, and C. Bentz. 1980. Annual Report of 1979 Excavations at FAI-270 Related Borrow Pit Sites. In Annual Report of 1979 Investigations by the University of Illinois-Urbana FAI-270 Archaeological Mitigation Project, edited by J.W. Porter, pp. 109-37. Department of Anthropology, University of Illinois, Urbana.

Mansur, M.E. 1982. Microwear Analysis of Natural and Use Striations: New Clues to the Mechanisms of Striation Formation. Studia Praehistorica Belgica (Tervuren, Belgium) 2:213-33

Marquadt, W.H., and P.J. Watson. 1977. Current State Research: Kentucky Shell Mound Archaeological Project. Southeastern Archaeological Conference Newsletter 19(2):4.

_____. 1983. The Shell Mound Archaic of Western Kentucky. In Archaic Hunters and Gatherers in the American Midwest, edited by J.L. Phillips and J.A. Brown, pp. 323-39, Academic Press, New York.

Mason, R.J., and G.R. Perino. 1961. Microblades at Cahokia, Illinois. American Antiquity 26:553-57.

Meltzer, D.J. 1981. A Study of Style and Function in a Class of Tools. Journal of Field Archaeology 8:313-326.

Milner, G.R. 1980. Annual Report of 1979 Excavations at the Robinson's Lake, Turner, and Demange Sites in the Selected Archaeological Sites Package. In Annual Report of 1979 Investigations by the University of Illinois-Urbana FAI-270 Archaeological Mitigation Project, edited by J.W. Porter, pp. 65-74, Department of Anthropology, University of Illinois, Urbana.

_____. 1983. The Turner and DeMange Sites. American Bottom Archaeology FAI-270 Site Reports 4, University of Illinois Press, Urbana and Chicago.

Milner, G.R., T.E. Emerson, M.W. Mehrer, J.A. Williams, and D. Esarey. 1984. Mississippian and Oneota. In American Bottom Archaeology: FAI-270 Site Reports Summary Volume, edited by C.A. Bareis and J.W. Porter, pp. 158-86. University of Illinois Press, Urbana and Chicago.

Minnis, P.E. 1981. Seeds in Archaeological Sites: Sources and Some Interpretive Problems. American Antiquity 46:143-51.

Monks, G.G. 1981. Seasonality Studies. In Advances in Archaeological Method and Theory 4, edited by M.B. Schiffer, pp. 177-240. Academic Press, New York.

Montet-White, A. 1968. The Lithic Industries of the Illinois Valley in the Early and Middle Woodland Periods. Anthropological Papers 35. Museum of Anthropology, University of Michigan, Ann Arbor.

Moss, E.H. 1983. The Functional Analysis of Flint Implements: Pincevent and Pont d'Ambon: Two Case Studies from the French Final Paleolithic. BAR International Series 177, Oxford.

Muller, J. 1978. The Kincaid System: Mississippian Settlement in the Environs of a Large Site. In Mississippian Settlement Patterns, edited by B.D. Smith, pp. 269-92. Academic Press, New York.

———. 1983. The Southeast. In Ancient North Americans, edited by J.D. Jennings, pp. 373-419. W.H. Freeman, San Francisco.

Munson, P.J. 1971. An Archaeological Survey of the American Bottom and Wood River Terrace. Reports of Investigations 21 (Part 1). Illinois State Museum, Springfield.

———. 1974. Terraces, Meander Loops, and Archaeology in the American Bottoms, Illinois. Transactions of the Illinois State Academy of Science 67:384-92.

Nassaney, M.S., N.H. Lopinot, B.H. Butler, and R.W. Jeffries. 1983. The 1982 Excavations at the Cahokia Interpretive Center Tract, St. Clair County, Illinois. Research Paper 37. Center for Archaeological Investigations, Southern Illinois University at Carbondale.

Nero, R. W. 1957. A "Graver" Site in Wisconsin. American Antiquity 22:300-4.

Norris, T. 1978. Excavations at the Lily Lake Site: 1975 Season. Reports in Contract Archaeology 4. Southern Illinois University at Edwardsville.

Odell, G.H. 1975. Microwear in Perspective: A Sympathetic Response to Lawrence H. Keeley. World Archaeology 7:226-40.

———. 1980. Toward a More Behavioral Approach to Archaeological Lithic Concentrations. American Antiquity 45:404-31.

———. 1981. The Morphological Express at Function Junction: Searching for Meaning in Lithic Tool Types. Journal of Anthropological Research 37:319-42.

———. 1982. Emerging Directions in the Analysis of Prehistoric Tool Use. Reviews in Anthropology 9:17-33.

Odell, G.H., and F. Odell-Vereeken. 1980. Verifying the Reliability of Lithic Use-wear Assessments by "Blind Tests": the Low-power Approach. Journal of Field Archaeology 7:87-120.

Odum, E.P. 1969. The Strategy of Ecosystem Development. Science 164 262-70.

Pace, R.E., and G.A. Apfelstadt. 1978. Allison-LaMotte Culture of the Daughtery-Monroe Site, Sullivan County, Indiana. Indiana State University Anthropological Laboratory, Terre Haute.

Parkington, J. 1980. Time and Space: Some Observations on Spatial and Temporal Patterning in the Late Stone Age Sequence in Southern Africa. South Africa Archaeological Bulletin 35:73-112.

Parmalee, P.W. 1968. Cave and Archaeological Faunal Deposits as Indicators of Post-Pleistocene Animal Populations in Illinois. In The Quaternary of Illinois, edited by R.E. Bergstrom, pp. 104-13. Special Publication 14. College of Agriculture, University of Illinois, Urbana.

_____. 1975. A General Summary of the Vertebrate Fauna from Cahokia. In Perspectives in Cahokia Archaeology, edited by M.L. Fowler and R.L. Hall, pp. 137-55. Bulletin 10. Illinois Archaeological Survey, Urbana.

Perino, G. 1973. The Late Woodland Component at the Pete Klunk Site, Calhoun County, Illinois. In Late Woodland Site Archaeology in Illinois 1: Investigations in South-central Illinois, edited by J.A. Brown, pp. 58-89. Bulletin 9. Illinois Archaeological Survey, Urbana.

Phillips, J.L. 1980. The Archaic Component. In Investigations at the Labras Lake Site, Volume 1, Archaeology, edited by J.L. Phillips, R.L. Hall, and R.W. Yerkes, pp. 41-114. Department of Anthropology, University of Illinois at Chicago.

_____. 1986. The Archaic Period Occupation at Labras Lake. In Labras Lake: Investigations into the Prehistoric Occupations of a Floodplain Locality in St. Clair County, Illinois, edited by J.L. Phillips and R.L. Hall. University of Illinois Press, Urbana and Chicago.

Phillips, J.L., and B.G. Gladfelter. 1983. The Labras Lake Site and the Paleogeographic Setting of the Late Archaic on the American Bottom. In Archaic Hunters and Gatherers in the American Midwest, edited by J.L. Phillips and J.A. Brown, pp. 197-218. Academic Press, New York.

Phillips, J.L., R.L. Hall, and R.W. Yerkes. 1980. Investigations at the Labras Lake Site, Volume 1, Archaeology, Department of Anthropology, University of Illinois at Chicago.

Phillips, J.L., and R.L. Hall, eds. 1986. Labras Lake: Investigations into the Prehistoric Occupations of a Floodplain Locality in St. Clair County, Illinois. University of Illinois Press, Urbana and Chicago.

Plisson, H. 1982. Analyse Fonctionnelle de 95 Micrograttoirs "Tourassiens". Studia Praehistorica Belgica (Tervuren, Belgium) 2:279-87.

Porter, J.W. 1969. The Mitchell Site and Prehistoric Exchange Systems at
    Cahokia: A.D. 1000+/-300. In Explorations into Cahokia Archaeology,
    edited by M.L. Fowler, pp. 137-64, Bulletin 7. Illinois Archaeological
    Survey, Urbana.

_____. 1974. Cahokia Archaeology as Viewed from the Mitchell Site: a
    Satellite Community at A.D. 1150-1200. Ph.D. dissertation, Department
    of Anthropology, University of Wisconsin-Madison.

_____. 1980. Introduction. In Annual Report of 1979 Investigations by
    the University Illinois-Urbana FAI-270 Archaeological Mitigation
    Project, edited by J.W. Porter, pp. 1-17. Department of Anthropology,
    University of Illinois, Urbana.

_____. 1982. Introduction. In Annual Report of Investigations 1981 by
    the University of Illinois-Urbana FAI-270 Archaeological Mitigation
    Project, edited by J.W. Porter, pp. 1-5. Department of Anthropology,
    University of Illinois, Urbana.

_____. 1983. Introduction. In Annual Report of Investigations 1982
    by the University of Illinois-Urbana FAI-270 Archaeological Mitigation
    Project, edited by J.W. Porter, pp. 1-9, Department of Anthropology,
    University of Illinois, Urbana.

Porter, J.W., and C.R. Szuter. 1978. Thin Section Analysis of Schlemmer
    Site Ceramics. Mid-Continental Journal of Archaeology 3:3-14.

Price, T.D., S. Chappell, and D.J. Ives. 1982. Thermal Alteration
    in Mesolithic Assemblages. Proceedings of the Prehistoric Society
    48:467-85.

Purdue, J.R., and B.W. Styles. 1980. Analysis of the Faunal Remains from
    the Labras Lake Site (11-S-299), St. Clair County, Illinois. In
    Investigations at the Labras Lake Site, Volume 1, Archaeology,
    edited by J.L. Phillips, R.L. Hall, and R.W. Yerkes, pp. 338-52.
    Department of Anthropology, University of Illinois at Chicago.

Ralph, E.K., H.N. Michael, and M.C. Han. 1973. Radiocarbon Dates and Reality.
    M.A.S.C.A. Newsletter 9(1) (reprinted in Archaeology of Eastern North
    America 2, [1974]): 1-20.

Reidhead, V.A. 1979. Linear Programming Models in Archaeology. Annual
    Review of Anthropology 8:543-78.

Rindos, D., and S. Johannessen 1983. Uniformity and Diversity in
    Mississippian Plant Use. Paper presented at the 48th Annual Meeting of
    the Society for American Archaeology, Pittsburgh.

Riordan, R. 1975. Ceramics and Chronology: Mississippian Settlement in
    the Black Bottom, Southern Illinois. Ph.D. dissertation, Department of
    Anthropology, Southern Illinois University, Carbondale.

Robertson, P. 1983. Some Problems of the Middle Mississippi River Region
    During Pleistocene Time. Transactions of the Academy of Science, St.
    Louis 29:169-240.

Rothschild, N.A. 1979. Mortuary Behavior and Social Organization at Indian Knoll and Dickson Mounds. _American Antiquity_ **44**:658-75.

Rubey, W.W. 1952. _Geology and Mineral Resources of the Hardin and Brussels Quadrangles in Illinois._ Professional Paper **218**. United States Geological Survey, Washington, D.C.

Rubin, M., and C. Alexander. 1958. U.S. Geological Survey Radiocarbon Dates 4. _Science_ **127**:1476-87.

Sabo, D.R. 1982. Preliminary Use-wear Analysis of a Michigan chert. _The Michigan Archaeologist_ **28**:55-72.

Salzer, R.J. 1975. Excavations at the Merrell Tract of the Cahokia Site: Summary Field Report 1973. In _Cahokia Archaeology: Field Reports,_ edited by M.L. Fowler, pp. 1-18. Research Series, Papers in Anthrpology **3**. Illinois State Museum, Springfield.

Saucier, R.T. 1974. _Quaternary Geology of the Lower Mississippi Valley._ Publications in Archaeology, Research Series **6**. Akansas Archaeological Survey, Fayetteville.

_____. 1981. Current Thinking on Riverine Processes and Geologic History as Related to Human Settlement in the Southeast. _Geoscience and Man_ **22**:7-18.

Schicht, R.J., and E.C. Jones. 1962. _Groundwater Levels and Pumpage in the St. Louis Area, Illinois._ Report of Investigations **44**. Illinois State Water Survey, Urbana.

Schoenwetter, J. 1962. A Late Post-glacial Pollen Chronology from the Central Mississippi Valley. In _First Annual Report: American Bottoms Archaeology, July 1, 1961-June 30, 1962,_ edited by M.L. Fowler, pp. 39-48. Illinois Archaeological Survey, Urbana.

_____. 1963. Survey of Palynological Results. In _Second Annual Report: American Bottoms Archaeology, July 1, 1962-June 30, 1963,_ edited by M.L.Fowler, pp. 42-45. Illinois Archaeological Survey, Urbana.

Schumm, S.A. 1963. _The Disparity Between Present Rates of Denudation and Orogeny._ Professional Paper **454-H**. United States Geological Survey, Washington D.C.

_____. 1977. _The Fluvial System._ Wiley and Sons, New York.

Seitzer, D.J. 1977-78. Form vs. Function: Microwear Analysis and its Application to Upper Paleolithic Burins. _Meddelanden Fran Lunds Universitete Historiska Museum_(n.s.) **2**:5-20.

Semenov, S.A. 1964. _Prehistoric Technology._ Cory, Adams, and McKay, London (translated by M.W. Thompson).

Service, E.R. 1962. _Primitive Social Organization: An Evolutionary Perspective._ Random House, New York.

Simons, D.B., S.A. Schumm, and M.A. Stevens. 1974. Geomorphology of the
    Middle Mississippi River. Contract Report Y-74-2. U.S. Army Corps of
    Engineers, St. Louis District.

Slobodkin, L.D., and A. Rapoport. 1974. An Optimal Strategy of Evolution.
    Quarterly Review of Biology 49:181-200.

Smith, B.D. 1978. Prehistoric Patterns of Human Behavior: a Case Study in
    the Mississippi Valley. Academic Press, New York.

Smith, I.F. III. 1976. A Functional Interpretation of Keyhole Structures in
    the Northeast. Pennsylvania Archaeologist 46:1-12.

Sonnefield, J. 1962. Interpreting the Functions of Primitive Implements.
    American Antiquity 28:56-65.

Stevens, M.A., D.B. Simons, and S.A. Schumm. 1975. Man-induced Changes of
    Middle Mississippi River. Journal of the Waterways, Harbors, and
    Coastal Engineering Division, Proceedings of the A.S.C.E. 101, (WW2)
    119-33.

Steyermark, J.A. 1963. Flora of Missouri. Iowa State University Press,
    Ames, Iowa.

Stoltman, James B. 1978. Temporal Models in Prehistory: An Example from
    Eastern North America. Current Anthropology 19:703-46.

Stoltman, J.B., and D.A. Baerreis. 1983. The Evolution of Human
    Ecosystems in the Eastern United States. In Late Quaternary
    Environments of the United States, Volume 2, The Holocene, edited by
    H.E. Wright, Jr., pp. 252-68. University of Minnesota Press, Minneapolis.

Struvever, S. 1969. Archaeology and the Study of Cultural Process: Some
    Comments on Data Requirements and Research Strategy. Revision of a
    paper prepared for an advanced seminar on Cultural Process and the
    Evolution of Civilization, School of American Research, Santa Fe.

Styles, B.W. 1981. Faunal Exploitation and Resource Selection: Early Late
    Woodland Subsistence in the Lower Illinois Valley, Scientific Papers
    3. Northwestern University Archaeological Program, Evanston, Illinois.

Symens, N. 1982. Gebruikssporenanalyse op Artefacten van de
    Magdaleniaannederzetting te Verberie. Licentiaat, Katholieke
    Universiteit, Leuven, Belgium (thesis, Catholic University, Leuven,
    Belgium [with English synposis]).

Szuter, C.R. 1978. The Schlemmer Site: A Late Woodland-Mississippian
    Site in the American Bottom. Master's thesis, Department of
    Anthropology, Loyola University of Chicago.

Tixier, J. 1974. Glossary for the Description of Stone Tools With Special
    Reference to the Epipaleolithic of the Maghreb. Special Publication I
    Newsletter of Lithic Technology, San Antonio (translated by M.H.
    Newcomber).

Tringham, R.G., G. Cooper, G.H. Odell, B. Voytek, and A. Whitman. 1974.
Experimentation in the Formation of Edge Damage: A New Approach to
Lithic Analysis. Journal of Field Archaeology 1:171-96.

Van Zant, K.L. 1979. Late- and Post-glaciual Pollen and Plant Macrofossils
from Late West Okoboji, Northwestern Iowa. Quaternary Research
12:358-80.

Vaughan, P. 1985. Use-wear Analysis of Flaked Stone Tools. University of
Arizona Press, Tucson.

Vickery, K.D., J.L. Theler, and O.C. Shane III. 1981. Climatic Significance
of Rice Rat (Oryzomys palustris) Remains in the Midwest. Paper
presented at the 1981 Midwest Archaeological Conference, Madison,
Wisconsin.

Watson, P.J. ed. 1974. Archaeology of the Mammoth Cave Area. Academic
Press, New York.

Watson, P.J., et al. 1969. The Prehistory of Salts Cave, Kentucky.
Reports of Investigations 16. Illinois State Museum, Springfield.

Webb,T., and R.A. Bryson. 1972. Late and Postglacial Climatic Change in
the Northern Midwest, U.S.A: Quatitative Estimates Derived from Fossil
Pollen Spectra by Multivariate Statistical Analysis. Quaternary
Research 2:70-115.

Welch, D.J. 1975. Wood Utilization at Cahokia: Identification of Wood
Charcoal from the Merrell Tract. Master's thesis, Department of
Anthropology, University of Wisconsin-Madison.

Wetterstrom, W. 1978. Plant Foods from the Gypsy Joint Site. In
Prehistoric Patterns of Human Behavior: A Case Study in the
Mississippi Valley, by B.D. Smith, pp. 101-15. Academic Press,
New York.

White, J.P. 1967. Ethno-archaeology in New Guinea: Two Examples. Mankind
6:409-14.

White, J.P., and D.H. Thomas 1972. What Mean These Stones?
Ethnotaxonomic Models and Archaeological Interpretations in the New
Guinea Highlands. In Models in Archaeology, edited by D.L. Clarke,
pp. 275-308. Methuen, London.

White, W.P. 1981. Geomorphic Investigations at the Julien (11-S-63),
Byron (11-S-432), and Florence Street (11-S-458) Sites. FAI-270
Archaeological Mitigation Project Geomorphological Report 8.
University of Illinois, Urbana.

_____. 1982. Spatial and Temporal Variations in Geomorphic Floodplain
Phenomena and Their Effects on Prehistoric Cultural Patterns in the
American Bottom. Paper presented at the 47th Annual Meeting of the
Society for American Archaeology, Minneapolis.

White, W.P., and L.M. Bonnell. 1981. Geomorphic Investigations at the
    Missouri Pacific #2 Site. FAI-270 Archaeological Mitigation Project
    Geomorphological Report 7. University of Illinois, Urbana.

Wiant, M.D., E.R. Hajic, and T.R. Styles. 1983. Napoleon Hollow and Koster
    Site Stratigraphy: Implications for Holocene Landscape Evolution and
    Studies of Archaic Period Settlement Patterns in the Lower Illinois
    Valley. In Archaic Hunters and Gatherers in the American Midwest,
    edited by J.L. Phillips and J.A. Brown, pp. 147-64. Academic Press,
    New York.

Wild, J.C. 1841. The Valley of the Mississippi Illustrated in a Series of
    Views. J.C. Wild, St. Louis (reprinted by Hawthorne Publishing, St.
    Louis 1978).

Williams, K.R. 1979. The Jarrot/Fairmount Phase Problem: A Local Origin
    Model for the Cahokia Phenomenon and a Test Case for the Concept of
    Nucleation of Population in the American Bottom. Ph.D. dissertation,
    Department of Anthropology, University of Wisconsin-Milwaukee.

Willman, H.B., and J.C. Frye. 1970. Pleistocene Stratigraphy of Illinois.
    Bulletin 94. Illinois State Geological Survey.

Wilmsen, E.N. 1970. Lithic Analysis and Cultural Inference: A Paleo-Indian
    Case. Anthropological Papers 16. University of Arizona, Tuscon.

Winter, M.C. 1976. The Archaeological Household Cluster in the Valley of
    Oaxaca. In The Early Mesoamerican Village, edited by K.V. Flannery,
    pp. 25-31. Academic Press, New York.

Winterhalder, B. 1980. Environmental Analysis in Human Evolution and
    Adaptation Research. Human Ecology 8:135-70.

Winterhalder, B., and E.A. Smith eds. 1981. Hunter-Gatherer Foraging
    Strategies. University of Chicago Press, Chicago.

Winters, H.D. 1968. Value Systems and Trade Cycles of the Late Archaic in
    the Midwest. In New Perspectives in Archaeology, edited by S.R.
    Binford and L.R. Binford, pp. 175-222. Aldine, Chicago.

_____. 1969. The Riverton Culture. Reports of Investigation 13. Illinois
    State Museum, Springfield.

_____. 1981. Excavating in Museums: Notes on Mississippian Hoes and
    Middle Woodland Copper Gouges and Celts. In The Research Potential of
    Anthropological Museum Collections, edited by A.M. Cantwell, J.B.
    Griffin, and N.A. Rothschild, pp. 17-34. Annals of the New York Academy
    of Sciences 376.

Witthoff, J. 1967. Glazed Polish on Flint Tools. American Antiquity 32:
    383-88.

Wittry, W.L. 1959. The Raddatz Rockshelter, Sk5, Wisconsin. Wisconsin
    Archaeologist 40:33-69.

Wood, W.R. 1976. Vegetational Reconstruction and Climatic Episodes.
   American Antiquity 41:206-7.

Wood, W.R., and D.L. Johnson 1978. A Survey of Disturbance Processes in
   Archaeological Site Formation. In Advances in Archaeological Method
   and Theory 1, edited by M.B. Schiffer, pp. 315-81. Academic Press,
   New York.

Wright, H.E., Jr. 1976. Pleistocene Ecology-Some Current Problems.
   Geoscience and Man 13:1-12.

Yarbrough, R.E. 1974. The Physiography of Metro East. Bulletin of the
   Illinois Geographical Society 16:12-27.

Yarnell, R.A. 1972. Iva annua var. macrocarpa: Extinct American Cultigen?
   American Anthropologist 74:335-41.

_____. 1976. Early Plant Husbandry in Eastern North America. In Cultural
   Change and Continuity, edited by C.L. Cleland, pp. 265-74. Academic
   Press, New York.

_____. 1977. Native Plant Husbandry North of Mexico. In Origins of
   Agriculture, edited by C.A. Reed, pp. 861-75. Mouton, The Hague.

_____. 1978. Domestication of Sunflower and Sumpweed in Eastern North
   America. In The Nature and Status of Ethnobotany, edited by R.I. Ford,
   pp. 289-99. Anthropological Papers 67. Museum of Anthropology,
   University of Michigan, Ann Arbor.

Yerkes, R.W. 1977. An Analysis of Fish Bone and Scale Remains from the
   Larson Site (11-S-1109): A Spoon River Variant Mississippian Town
   in the Central Illinois Valley. Masters thesis, Department of
   Anthropology, University of Wisconsin-Madison.

_____. 1980. A Microblade from the Mississippian Component of the
   Labras Lake Site (11-S-299). In Investigations at the Labras Lake Site,
   Volume 1, Archaeology, edited by J.L. Phillips, R.L. Hall, and R.W.
   Yerkes, pp. 318-24, Department of Anthropology, University of Illinois at
   Chicago.

_____. 1981a. The Potential of Fish Utilization in Riverine Environments.
   Mid-Continental Journal of Archaeology 6:207-18.

_____. 1981b. Fish Scale Analysis at the Pipe Site (47-Fd-10), Fond du
   Lac County, Wisconsin: An Investigation of Seasonal Patterns in Oneota
   Fishing Practices. The Wisconsin Archaeologist 62:533-56.

_____. 1982. Flotation, Fish Scales, and Seasonal Patterns in the
   Abundance of Charcoal, Maize, and Nuts at the Site of Aztalan,
   Jefferson County, Wisconsin. Manuscript on file at the Department of
   Anthropology, Ohio State University, Columbus.

_____. 1983. Microwear, microdrills, and Mississippian craft
   specialization. American Antiquity 48:499-518.

_____. in press. Mississippian Craft Specialization on the American Bottom. In Cahokia and its Neighbors: Mississippian Cultural Variation in the American Midwest, edited by T.E. Emerson and R.B. Lewis, Kent State University Press .

Yerkes, R.W., and J.L. Phillips. In press. Functional and Morphological Analyses of Chipped Stone Artifacts from Late Archaic Base Camps at the Labras Lake Site (11-S-299), a Foodplain Locality in St. Clair County, Illinois. American Antiquity.

Zawaki, A.A., and G. Hausfater. 1969. Early Vegetation of the Lower Illinois Valley. Reports of Investigations 17. Illinois State Museum, Springfield.

Index

Adaptation, 2
Adzes. *See* Celts
Agriculture, 1, 8, 80, 92, 112, 156, 185, 190,
  196, 201
Ahler, S., 114, 152
Akoshima, K., 116
Alexander, C., 25
Alland, A., Jr., 2
Allen, W. H., 26-27
Alorton chute, 34, 36-37
Altithermal. *See* Hypsithermal
American Bottom, 2, 3, 9, 13, **14**, 15, 18, 20,
  22, **23**, 24, 28-31, 191, 201
Anderson, P., 114
Animals. *See* Faunal remains
Antler tools, 137
Antler-working, 4, 126, 134, 136-37, 140, 147,
  153, 156-57, 160, 166, 172, 182-84, 190
Apfelstadt, G. A., 81
Archaic, 30; chronology, 54, 191; Early Archaic,
  1; Middle Archaic, 1, 100; Late Archaic, 2, 6,
  10, 31; components at Labras Lake site, 3-5,
  18, 40, 49, 58-75; central area at Labras Lake,
  68, **69**; north central area at Labras Lake, 4-5,
  49, 68-71, **70**; northwestern area at Labras
  Lake, 3-4, 49, 71-73, **72**; south central area at
  Labras Lake, 3-4, 49, 73-75, **74**; southwestern
  area at Labras Lake, 4-5, 49, 58-68, **59**; Late
  Archaic sites on the American Bottom, 45, 50,
  52-58, **53**
Artifact concentrations, 3, 11, 58, 64, 66, 68, 71,
  73, 75, 80, 84
Asch, D. L., and N.B. Asch, 1, 16, 24, 100-101, 107
Audouze, F., 126
Aztalan site, 10-11, 98-99

Backwater lakes, 3, 6, 91, 192-93, 195-96
Baerreis, D. A., 1, 16, 29, 198-99
Bamforth, D. R., 116
Bardwell, J., 40-41
Bareis, C. J., 15, 31-33, 81
Bartlein, P. J., 25
Base Camps: Late Archaic, 5, 58, 66, 68, 71,
  99, 112, 148-49, 193-94, 201; Late
  Woodland, 190; summer base camps, 52;
  winter base camps, 147

BBB Motor site, 184
Beardsley, R., 199
Bee, R. L., 199
Benchley, E. D., 15, 20, 34, 44, 54
Bender, M. M., 16
Bentz, C., 51, 56, 92
Binford, L. R., 81, 130, 147, 149, 151
Binford, S. R., 81, 151
Binneman, J., 116
Bioarcheological data, 8, 10, 198-99
Biotic communities, 2-3, 51
Bison, 17
Blake, L. W., 16-17
Blind test, 115
Bone tools, 137, 195
Bone-working. *See* antler-working
Bonnell, L. M., 41-43
Bordes, F., 129
Boserup, E., 100
Bow and arrow, 8, 16, 195, 198
Bradley, B. A., 114, 129
Braided Streams: on American Bottom, 24-25;
  in Illinois Valley, 25; in St. Francis basin,
  24
Brakenridge, H. M., 20, 28
Brandt, K., 15
Braun, D. P., 6, 101, 104, 197
Brown, J. A., 58, 107
Brussell, D. E., 108
Bryson, R. A., xvii, **xviii**, 29
Bullfrog Station site, 32
Burned areas. *See* Hearths
Butchering, 4, 7, 75, 99, 116, 126, 134, 137,
  140, 142, 145, 148, 153-54, 156-57,
  160, 166, 172, 182-83, 185, 190, 197
Butler, B. M., 34, 54, 56, 61, 63-64, 92, 146
Butzer, K. W., 2, 9, 25, 199

Caddoan ceramics, 84
Cahokia Alluvium, 21
Cahokia Creek, 32
Cahokia Interpretive Center Tract, 5-6, 34, 52,
  56, 58, 68, 108, 146-47, 193, 198, 201
Cahokia Lake, 37
Cahokia microdrills, 166, 184
Cahokia settlement system, 89, 198, 202

273

	DATE DUE